RING

OF SPIES

T0322401

RING OF SPIES

HOW MI5 AND THE FBI BROUGHT DOWN THE NAZIS IN AMERICA

RHODRI JEFFREYS-JONES

The History Press

For Alex and Ava,
and in memory of Lily Pincus

First published 2020
This edition first published 2022

The History Press
97 St George's Place, Cheltenham,
Gloucestershire, GL50 3QB
www.thehistorypress.co.uk

British Library Cataloguing in Publication Data.
A catalogue record for this book is available from the British Library.

ISBN 978 1 80399 036 1

Typesetting and origination by The History Press
Printed and bound in Great Britain by TJ Books Limited, Padstow, Cornwall.

Trees for LYfe

Contents

List of Illustrations

Following page 172

Preface

Reacting to the carnage of the First World War and to the rise of Hitler, the United States Congress passed Neutrality Acts in the years 1935–37. The nation vowed never again to take sides in a European war. Yet in the year immediately following the final and most draconian of those acts, opinion changed on the subject of neutrality. Americans began to favour Britain and turned against Germany. One reason for the transformation was the exposure, following an MI5 tip-off in 1938, of a Nazi spy ring operating within the United States. Leon Turrou, a special agent with the Federal Bureau of Investigation (FBI), was instrumental in securing that exposure and launched a campaign to warn the American people about the Nazi menace.

The exposure resulted in increased powers and funds for the FBI. Yet the Bureau's director, J. Edgar Hoover, turned against the ace detective who had once been his darling and undertook a decades-long campaign to blacklist Turrou and ensure that he would never become a household name. That is one reason why the story unravelled in this book is unfamiliar and has not been heeded by historians writing about American foreign relations.

The ensuing pages are an attempt to restore the balance and to tell in full the story of German espionage directed against the United States. They identify the masterspy with a duelling scar who directed operations against US targets. They unravel some of the case's mysteries: Who was behind the 'Mata Hari' plot to seduce young Army officers in Washington, DC? Was anybody innocent in the McAlpin Hotel murder plot? Why did our chief protagonist, Leon Turrou, deny he was Jewish?

The story tells of fast cars and louche liaisons. At the same time, it carries a serious message about spies from a totalitarian country who tried to subvert American democracy and in the end inflamed public opinion to the detriment of the fascist cause.

In January 2013, I applied under the terms of the Freedom of Information Act to be allowed access to FBI documents relating to the case. It was a big ask – the name of one of the spies discussed in the ensuing pages, Scotland's Jessie Jordan, appeared on no fewer than 14,500 pages. Jon Russo of the FBI information management division laboured over a two-year period to supply me, in a manageable format, with digital copies of the documents I needed. Richard Bareford, with great generosity, helped me obtain and wade through the FBI's file on Leon Turrou. Still more archival help came from Rod Bailey and Andrew Jeffrey, who shared with me their expertise on MI5 files.

Individuals who encouraged, criticised or otherwise helped me were Robert Anderson, Doug Charles, Owen Dudley Edwards, John Fox, Fabian Hilfrich, Dolores Janiewski, Knud Krakaw, Andrew Johnstone, Kevin Kenny, Marianne Mooijweer, Kathryn Olmsted, David Silkenat, Jill Stephenson and Bertrand Villain.

My research assistant Leonie Werle, a graduate student at the Free University of Berlin and worker at the Resistance Memorial Centre in the same city, was diligent and showed initiative. Andrew Lownie demonstrated why he is a top boutique literary agent. At The History Press, Mark Beynon gave encouragement and support. My wife Mary keeps me on an even keel by never reading my books and is a source of joy and support beyond compare.

To all the foregoing, my deepest gratitude.

This book is for my latest grandchildren, toddlers Alex and Ava. May they never witness crimes like those of the 1930s. And it is in memory of my godmother, the late Lily Pincus, who escaped Berlin just in time. After my mother welcomed her as a refugee in Wales, she moved to London to work at the Tavistock Institute, where she remained a source of wisdom and strength.

1

Lonkowski's Legacy

The time was mid-evening, 27 September 1935, the place Pier 86, on the Hudson River in New York City. The man wearing Customs Guard badge No. 572 was Morris Josephs. His gaze fell upon a familiar scene. Passengers, relatives and friends milled around in an excited throng anticipating the departure of the North German Lloyd steamship *Europa*.

Just after 8.30 p.m., Josephs, a keen musician, spied a smooth-faced man in a dark hat carrying on board what appeared to be a violin case. Citizens of that mobster-ridden era knew how Thompson submachine guns fitted snugly into such receptacles, and the customs guard stayed alert. After a short while, the smooth-faced man left the ship and walked back down the pier, having failed to deposit the object still tucked under his arm. At 8.50 p.m., Josephs arrested him. Upon closer inspection, the parcel contained neither a gun nor a Stradivarius, and was not even a violin case. It did, however, contain copies of military plans.[1]

The man in the dark hat was Wilhelm 'Willy' Lonkowski, code name Sex. When the American press belatedly found out about him, one journalist declared that he was 'the cream' among spies. Lonkowski certainly had one useful attribute, a

talent for obscurity. After months of intensive if belated investigation, an FBI special agent finally lamented, 'little is known
concerning the personal history of Lonkowski'.[2]

No FBI agent ever knowingly encountered Agent Sex. Yet
over the years a partial picture emerged of this most secretive
of secret agents. Lonkowski was slender and tall, with brown
hair and blue eyes. He had a long nose and floppy ears. He
suffered from stomach ulcers exacerbated by the anxieties of
years of espionage. His heavy drinking did not help his medical condition, though it was an operational advantage that
he was a cold soak – he could remain sober while plying the
keepers of secrets with drink that loosened their tongues.[3]

Like several spies in our story, Lonkowski came from con-
tested territory. He was born in 1896 in Worliny (in German,
Worleinen), a village Prussia claimed following the eighteenth-century partition of Poland, and which then passed to
the unified state of Germany in 1871. In the First World War he
served as an airman in the German Army and suffered griev-
ous injuries when a French pilot shot him down. Just before
the end of hostilities, the recovering aviator married Auguste
'Gunny' Krüger, the daughter of a barber from Obernik, also
in East Prussia.

After the war, Lonkowski tried to carve out a career as an
aircraft designer. He never explained why he became a spy.
The embittered patriotism of a wounded and defeated soldier
no doubt played its part. The patriotism had a special twist for
a man who came from the German–Polish borderland with
its threatened identities. Adolf Hitler would promise a greater
Germany under Teutonic control, an aspiration that appealed
to ethnic partisans. Like other German spies, Lonkowski may
have felt aggrieved with America for its role in helping to
defeat his country, as well as in the subsequent peace settlement that punished Germany on the ground of war guilt.

Lonkowski operated within a German tradition. Prussia had
a history of espionage – Frederick the Great (1712–86) once

dismissed a military foe with the words, 'Marshal de Soubise is always followed by a hundred cooks, [whereas] I am always preceded by a hundred spies.' Defeat in the First World War threatened to end that tradition. According to the Versailles peace settlement, German military activity was supposed to be confined to specified units and that excluded spying. But old ways returned. In 1921 Friedrich Gempp, who had been deputy to the wartime intelligence chief Walter Nicolai, took charge of a group of ten officers together with support personnel in the newly formed Abwehr, which literally meant 'defence' but soon expanded its mission. By 1935 staff numbers had reached 150 and three years later 1,000.[4]

The Abwehr sought technical data to enable Germany to rebuild its military. In September 1926, Gempp singled out Lonkowski for a mission to the technologically advanced United States. For while Germany was hitherto renowned for the quality of its technical education, such education was stagnating for want of money and because of resistance from the nation's traditional elite.[5] By comparison, America had by the mid-1920s demonstrated it had the prowess and the means to outstrip its European rivals. On 27 March 1927 the secret agent arrived at Hoboken, New Jersey, carrying a passport in the name of Wilhelm Schneider. This was one of a string of aliases that included 'William Sexton', the mundane origin, through abbreviation, of his mid-1930s operational code name 'Sex'.

Lonkowski and his wife were gifted individuals. Gunny knew about hats and, once they had both settled in Long Island in 1929, managed a millinery shop and then a dress emporium in Queens Village. Willy could repair and tune practically any musical instrument. He worked at this trade for the Temple of Music store in Hempstead, Long Island. More significantly for his mission as a spy, he worked between 1929 and 1931 as a mechanic at the Ireland Aircraft Corporation at nearby Roosevelt Field, and then at Fairchild Aviation Corporation in Farmingdale, New York.[6]

According to Willy's cover story, the childless Lonkowskis accumulated enough capital in the United States to permit him to return to Germany in February 1934 and engage in wire manufacturing in Berlin. His cover story held that he then sold up and arrived back in America on 18 January 1935 with considerable funds. That would have been a remarkable feat, given the brevity of his stay in Germany. The truth is that the money came from the German foreign intelligence service. The time had come to reinvigorate Abwehr spying operations in America.

Lonkowski built up a formidable spy network. He was able to recruit German–Americans working in the defence industry. Managers in that industry had been glad to hire well-trained workers and, perhaps reassured by the supposed demilitarisation of Germany, did so with scant regard to security checks. While working at the Ireland Aircraft Corporation, Lonkowski secured work there for the future secret agent Otto Hermann Voss. A native of Hamburg who had trained as a machinist and served with the German Army's Company of Engineers in the First World War, Voss was an aeroplane mechanic and keen yachtsman who worked for a succession of American defence industry businesses after his arrival in the United States in October 1928. He and his wife Anna, whom he married in 1934, socialised with their neighbours, the Lonkowskis.[7]

On one such occasion, Willy introduced Voss to Karl Eitel, a German agent who worked as a steward on the steamship SS *Bremen*. Built for North German Lloyd and launched in 1929, the *Bremen* achieved a cruising speed of 27 knots and until 1932 held the Blue Riband for the fastest transatlantic crossing. It was the pride of a resurgent German maritime industry. However, the *Bremen* and its sibling ship the SS *Europa* served as vehicles for propaganda, censorship and espionage. When the Nazis gained power, they installed 'stormtroopers', or political bosses, to enforce totalitarian discipline on these and other German ships. There was a ban on magazines such as *Harper's* and *Life* that expressed free American opinions and the atmosphere became so poisoned that passengers began to shun the shipping line.

In July 1935, just two months prior to Lonkowski's arrest, the *Bremen* took centre stage in the international fight against fascism. Communist-led members of the International Seamen's Union in New York wanted to protest against the imprisonment of Lawrence Simpson, an American sailor whom the German authorities had arrested for distributing anti-Nazi literature in Hamburg. The protesters looked for a target and found one close at hand. Activist Bill Bailey described the great German ship that dominated the waterfront: 'Her bow jutted up, looming over the street. Large, powerful floodlights in various parts of the ship directed their beams at one spot: the jackstaff that held the Nazi swastika.'

Demonstrators boarded the ship and Bailey was one of those who tore down the swastika, casting it into the cold, black wetness of the Hudson River.

The New York seamen's protest sparked imitation anti-swastika demonstrations across the world. What had started as a communist-inspired movement soon won wider sympathy. When the case against the flag vandals went to court in September, a New York Jewish magistrate, Louis B. Brodsky, dismissed the charges and condemned the swastika as a piratical emblem. Hitler reacted. At the annual Nuremburg Party rally that month, he declared that the swastika would replace the imperial tricolour as Germany's official national standard.[8]

Ships such as the *Bremen* supported not just the Nazi apparatus, but also Abwehr operations. The commanding officers of German passenger ships knowingly facilitated the transport of spy couriers with their letters, as well as bulky documents. The British Royal Navy had intercepted Berlin's messages and broken its codes in the First World War and transatlantic cables remained an unreliable means of sending secret data.

Sea transport in Party-disciplined ocean liners was slower, but more secure.

Karl Eitel agreed to courier for Lonkowski, for example by delivering a letter asking Berlin for more money. By way of reverse traffic, Eitel relayed to Voss the German authorities' desire for specified US military technical secrets. In the course of six subsequent meetings, Voss supplied Eitel with design details and photographs of Army training planes under construction at the Seversky Aircraft Corporation, covering the wings, fuselage, engines and landing gear – Voss had himself re-engineered the landing gear to make it stronger.[9]

Germany paid Lonkowski generously. He received $500 a month, with bonuses for particularly useful intelligence. With his expenses paid, Willy was able to reward his informants handsomely. He claimed to have dispensed to a single group of spies as much as $30,000 in one year – perhaps an exaggeration, but the material benefits of the advanced technology that his agents purloined were of great value to his employers. Neither industry nor government in America was prepared for such an espionage onslaught and Lonkowski had a sharp eye for opportunities. From Johannes Karl Steuer, an inspector at the Sperry Gyroscope Company, Brooklyn, he solicited information on bombsights. Johann Koechel, a foreman at the Kollmorgan Optical Corporation in Brooklyn, supplied him with data on periscopes.[10]

Another of Lonkowski's recruits at the Ireland Aircraft Corporation was Werner Georg Gudenberg. A native of Hamburg and a trained coppersmith, Gudenberg first stepped ashore in the United States on 22 October 1928, having arrived in New York on the SS *Deutschland*. By the end of the year, he was foreman of the fuselage and fitting department at Ireland Aircraft. Under Lonkowski's tutelage, he would obtain secrets from a contact in the Boston Navy Yard and scheme to lure German-born technicians to return to the Fatherland, where they would be induced to divulge the secrets of American military technology. In still another venture, Lonkowski set up an agent in Montreal, first as a means of forwarding rolls of film to Germany and then to spy on the Canadian aviation industry.[11]

Lonkowski was the Abwehr's main man in America, yet he was not in overall control of German espionage operations in the United States. The Abwehr abided by what was a valued principle of good security, compartmentalisation. The left hand was not allowed to know about the right hand, lest the right hand had fallen under the control of a rival agency making it liable to betray the secrets of both hands. For such security reasons, Willy was not directly in control of Abwehr operations in California.[12]

For the same reason, he may not have known about the Abwehr's effort to get hold of a code-deciphering machine developed for the US Navy Department by the gifted American code-breaker, Agnes Meyer Driscoll, née Meyer. Together with Poland and Germany, America was in the early stages of progress towards computer-driven encryption and decryption. Driscoll – a later FBI report noted drily that she was 'of German ancestry' – obtained a secret appropriation of $6,250 from the US government in recompense for her contribution. But that was less than she had claimed. Furthermore, she suffered a car accident at this time that temporarily incapacitated her and she may have felt aggrieved when the Navy Department stopped her salary during the period of her recuperation. According to FBI sources, the woman who is today remembered as a pioneer of US cryptography sold the device for $7,000 to the Abwehr, prompting jubilation in Berlin.[13]

The Driscoll mission was never directly traced to the Lonkowski network. The same was only partially true of another high-technology venture. Wilhelm Canaris, head of the Abwehr between 1935 and 1945, commissioned this operation. He entrusted its execution to Nikolaus Adolf Fritz Ritter.

A native of Rheydt in the Rhineland and the son of a university president, Ritter had been twice wounded fighting as an infantry officer in the First World War. In the course of that conflict, he spent some time in America on the staff of Franz von Papen, who, as military attaché in Washington 1914–16, ran sabotage operations against British and Canadian installations – von Papen later became Chancellor of Germany and facilitated the rise of Hitler.[14]

In 1924, Ritter arrived in America on an immigration visa. Tall, blond and blue-eyed, he stirred feelings in an Alabama girl, Mary Aurora 'Lady May' Evans. Two years after his arrival in the United States they married. They had a boy and a girl and seemed a happy family, but, in the Crash and Depression era, Ritter's business ventures enjoyed indifferent success. An official at the German embassy suggested a resumption of military duties. Ritter returned to Germany and, on 1 September 1936, became an agent of the Abwehr, attached to its Hamburg office. Under the tutelage of an experienced intelligence officer, Hilmar Gustav Johannes Dierks, he won the confidence of his superiors and would receive the Iron Cross for his intelligence work against the UK.[15]

If Ritter conformed to one facet of the typical Abwehr profile in having served in the First World War, he subscribed to another by engaging in extra-marital activities. Soon after he joined the Abwehr, the man described by an associate as 'a very brutal, ambitious individual' developed an interest in his secretary. Aurora frowned on his secret service work and his marital infidelity was the last straw. In 1938 she divorced Nikolaus and the following year he remarried. Nikolaus had custody of the children each summer and he banned his ex-wife from returning to the United States. Aurora was bitter about her former husband's behaviour. When she obtained a job at the American Consulate in Hamburg, it would be only a matter of time before she told what she knew.[16]

For in July 1937, Canaris had ordered Ritter to spy on Aurora's native land. According to Ritter's later account of the mission, he was not keen on the assignation. He claimed that this was because he was fond of the United States – even if he had reservations about what he termed Americans' tendency to treat women like royalty (evidently he had not treated Aurora that way). But an order was an order and he obeyed it. At first, things did not go well. He was violently seasick on the Atlantic voyage and then a German–American journalist recognised him as he passed through immigration, which might have blown the whole operation. Perhaps he had not quite got over his queasiness when he reacted by changing his name to 'Mr Landing'.[17]

Initially, Ritter's aim was to establish contact with Frederick (Fritz) Joubert Duquesne, someone Canaris identified as having been involved in secret service work in the First World War. Duquesne had been the intelligence officer for the Order of '76, a whites-only, anti-New Deal, pro-Nazi organisation founded in March 1934. Aurora recalled that, after meeting Duquesne, her husband broadened his activities and 'visited all the important aeroplane factories' in the United States. She said that 'his sole reason for going to the United States was to visit the agents planted in such factories'.[18]

In what Ritter later described as a 'cold' letter of instruction, Canaris gave him a mission that was more specific than this. He was to secure the details of the Norden bombsight. Carl Norden was a Dutch immigrant who had worked for the Sperry Gyroscope Company and then launched his own Norden Company. Sperry and Norden had competed to produce an improved bombsight. Norden won the race to produce a marketable device equipped with a gyroscopic stabilisation mechanism that promised to deliver bombs to their targets with unprecedented accuracy.

Ritter operated through the German–American network. His prior list of contacts included not only Duquesne, but also Gudenberg, who by this time had inherited Lonkowski's responsibilities.[19] Exploiting such contacts, Ritter met a man who was in a position to help him.

Hermann W. Lang had long-standing fascist sympathies and in 1923 participated in the Munich Putsch, an early Hitler-led attempt to overthrow the democratically elected government of Germany. He had emigrated to the United States in 1927. Taking out US citizenship two years later, he worked at the Manhattan factory that produced the sought-after bombsight. Ritter arranged to meet Lang, whom he described as tall, blond and trustworthy (Ritter habitually praised men with 'Aryan' characteristics). Lang was so dedicated to the Nazi cause that he refused payment for his services. After a trial run of the transmission chain, the engineer gave Ritter a partial blueprint for the Norden bombsight.[20]

The blueprint was rather large and could not fit into a normal briefcase or small package, so Ritter arranged for it to be rolled up inside a customised umbrella that he had brought with him into America. On 30 November 1937 a spy courier with a fake limp boarded the SS *Reliance* of the Hamburg America line, his hobble giving him the appearance of someone who needed to lean on the (loaded) umbrella for support. It was the first of several Norden consignments.

By 1941, the Luftwaffe had its own gyroscopic device. Ernst Heinkel, the German aeroplane designer, said that the Norden acquisition had been pivotal in the development of its German equivalent. However, German bombsight engineers denied this. Whether or not the German version was a copy of the American prototype, knowledge of American capability was of interest to Berlin, whose armed forces might one day have to face more accurate bombing. The Norden theft impressed Germany's spymasters and helped Ritter further his career.[21]

The Ritter–Lang story shows how Willy Lonkowski's network was not all-embracing. Lonkowski's was nevertheless the principal German intelligence operation in the United States.

Berlin valued Lonkowski's services and had plans to reward him with a sinecure in its Air Force Ministry. However, he did not stay on in America long enough to witness the full fruits of his clandestine labours. For this, he blamed a woman.

It had all begun with a sortie by his wife. Gunny drank heavily. One day in March 1935, she ventured out into the Hempstead community to buy wine and gin. She fell into conversation with Senta de Wanger, the proprietor of Clinton Wine Shop. In the course of subsequent purchasing trips and chats, she supplied Senta with the false news that her husband William Lonkowski was terminally ill. Knowing that Senta had a large house and lived alone, Gunny suggested it would be mutually advantageous if she and Willy were to move in.

This came about for a rental of $20 a month. The benefits included the use of an additional space that served as a photographer's dark room. The Lonkowskis installed a telephone in Senta de Wanger's name. They operated a 1929 Nash sedan automobile under someone else's name. Willy told Senta he was a piano tuner, but the Lonkowskis' lavish expenditure pattern suggested otherwise. The three inhabitants of 83 Lincoln Boulevard threw wild parties with US Navy and Army personnel among the guests. Her tongue loosened by alcohol, Gunny eventually confided to Senta that Willy was in receipt of money from the German government.[22]

The woman in whom Gunny confided had been born in 1907 in the southern German city of Ulm and her parents Paul and Dina Dirlewanger lived in nearby Stuttgart, where Paul was a banker. She was a slender 5ft 9in with dark brown hair, blue eyes and the slight remains of a German accent. To her friends, she was *Die wilde Senta*, a reference to her willful personality. Bored by the tedium of being a banker's daughter in provincial Stuttgart, Senta Dirlewanger had immigrated to New York, where, to mark her new start in life, she chose a new name. Now Senta de Wanger, she worked as a secretary and then set up an interior-decorating store at 7 Park Avenue in Manhattan with undisclosed but possibly parental funds before moving out to run her liquor store on Long Island. In September 1935, she became a US citizen.[23]

Meantime, according to a statement Senta later signed for the FBI, the Lonkowskis had turned nasty. They told her that, if she did not cooperate with them, financial measures would be taken against her parents, who were already in dire straits because of the Depression. So it came to pass that, in late August 1935, Senta delivered a package. It had arrived from Buffalo, where Lonkowski was spending a few days, and contained materials supplied by Gudenberg, who at the time worked at Buffalo's Curtiss-Wright aircraft manufacturing plant. The item for delivery had been wrapped inside a larger package with a note telling Wanger what to do. The note stipulated that the interior missive was to be given to a courier aboard the SS *Europa*, berthed on the Hudson River. However, the courier was nowhere to be found when she arrived at Pier 86. She gave the package to the ship's purser instead.[24]

The combustible Willy was furious that Senta had trusted the purser, shouting that he would kill her if the package went astray. He calmed down only when a receipt arrived confirming that the package had reached its intended destination. Thereafter, operations continued smoothly until the night of 27 September. On that evening, Willy left the house on Lincoln Boulevard to deliver a package in person to his contact on the steamship *Europa*.

He did not return. When the new day broke, Gunny feared the worst and expected the Feds to appear any minute, so she fled to her sister's place nearby. In an attempt to raise immediate funds, she tried to sell her the Nash sedan.

Gunny's fears were well founded. Lonkowski had fallen victim to his own tradecraft. For when he failed to locate his courier, he would not trust any other recipient. Instead, he came back on shore with his spy bundle. The package that Customs Officer Josephs found on Gunny's husband was rather obviously marked 'Für Berlin' (for Berlin). Josephs saw at a glance that it contained rolls of film and materials relating to aviation. He handed it over to his superiors, who called in Major Stanley Grogan of US Military Intelligence. Grogan found a diagram of Navy aeroplane machine gunsights. There were notes on the Army's Langley Field, Virginia. There was a memorandum, signed 'Sex', about tenders for a new 'flying fortress' bomber being submitted to the Army by Boeing and by Douglas aircraft of Santa Monica, California. There was a note indicating that von Papen was commissioning military intelligence from Lonkowski.

In spite of all this, Lonkowski half-convinced his interrogators that he was a journalist writing an article for the German aviation magazine, *Die Luftreisen*. Perhaps because military intelligence was at a low point at the time – sixty-nine headquarters personnel compared with 1,441 in 1918 – the package received only perfunctory and local analysis. The interrogation team provisionally concluded that none of 'this material was considered Confidential'. The authorities remained suspicious of Lonkowski, but decided to release him the following morning, with the warning that they would want to question him again in three days' time.[25]

Scarcely able to believe his luck, Lonkowski planned an immediate evacuation. He sped out to Hempstead, where he destroyed documents and gathered up personal belongings. After that, he returned to New York and, in the dead of night, drove out to a summer residence in the Peekskill area. An Abwehr colleague lent him $100 to assist his escape and, after two days, a German First World War pilot, Ulrich Hausmann, appeared. He drove Lonkowski to Canada at speeds of 85–90mph. There were no problems at the border. The German consul in Montreal arranged for Lonkowski and Gunny to be smuggled onto the *Hagen*, a small, homebound freighter.

From onboard ship he wrote to his sister-in-law saying all was well except for a shortage of underwear and he expected to reach the Fatherland on 22 October. He asked for articles he had left behind to be dispatched to an address in Berlin and made a special plea. On no account was the 'booze hound' Senta de Wanger to be allowed to take possession of his car. It was worth at least $100 and she wanted it for her lover who was driving around in an automobile that was 'only a wreck'.[26]

'Sex' had had to flee America before enjoying the full fruits of his spying activities, even if he left behind agents such as Voss and Gudenberg who continued to operate effectively. Back in Germany, he joined a Party organisation as an affirmation of loyalty and was duly rewarded with a job as technical adviser with the Luftwaffe.[27] His road would not be smooth. He declined to accept the rigours of further military training. After creating a stir by dismissing two of his colleagues on charges of incompetence, he was transferred to the engineering corps at a lower salary. His reputation for partying continued and, in 1940, the Gestapo investigated him because on one festive occasion he and Gunny supplied their guests with a feast that defied his means and the rationing regulations by then in force in wartime Germany. Rumours about his American connections did not help – his spying escapade was such a well-kept secret that his US connections were open to misinterpretation until the Abwehr had a discreet word with the Gestapo.[28]

A prickly individual, Lonkowski remained bitter about the circumstances that led to his departure from the United States. He accused Senta de Wanger of betraying him and from his German base sent her threatening letters. She lived in fear of the Gestapo. Senta declared herself baffled by what her former tenant meant by betrayal and was at a loss to explain his anger. According to FBI speculation, Lonkowski's spite may have stemmed from amatory rebuttal – and Eitel recalled there had been jealousy between Gunny and Senta.[29]

In the event, Wanger resisted Lonkowski's bullying just as she had his putative seduction. In a statement to the FBI, she declared:

> I have no connection whatsoever with any organisation of the German government and I am not a member of any political party in Germany and consider myself nothing other than a good American citizen. My sole interest in Germany are my parents and sister who reside there.

Perhaps her betrayal was that although she did Lonkowski's bidding under duress, she never became a willing member of his team and failed to develop enthusiasm for his enterprise. *Die wilde Senta.* Her independence of mind was dangerous to the German spy ring.[30]

When Lonkowski faced his questioners after his arrest on Pier 86, they did not include an agent from the FBI. At the time the Bureau had neither responsibilities nor a track record in the area of counter-espionage. In 1935, it was gathering strength as a crime-fighting agency, but neither it nor any other agency had the remit of combatting foreign spies in peacetime.[31] There was no follow-up on the Pier 86 incident that, for the time being, joined history's list of forgotten events. Lonkowski remained an unknown entity. The Bureau did not even begin to figure him out and had no inkling of his legacy, a web of spies who were out to steal America's secrets.

All this stood ready to change when the curtain rose on a further act in the drama and revealed Jessie Jordan, a minor spy with major consequences.

A Spy from Scotland

Her mother was Scottish, but her parents decreed that Marga should be a patriotic German. In a nod to Kaiser Wilhelm II, they christened her 'Margaretha Frieda Wilhelmina'. The First World War broke out two months later and Marga's parents were proud of their acquaintanceship with one of its military heroes. Referring to Field Marshal Paul von Hindenburg, who had at the outset of the war crushed a Russian army at the Battle of Tannenberg, a British newspaper recorded how 'Little Marga Jordan sat on the knee of the victor of Tannenberg and pulled his long moustache. Von Hindenburg laughed and murmured "Liebchen" (darling).'[1]

The years passed. Von Hindenburg became President of Germany and Marga started a career as a teenage actress and singer. In 1931, she married Hermann Wobrock, a Hamburg merchant, and three years later gave birth to little Jessie.

The enchantment in Marga's life now began to fade. Marga's mother, also called Jessie, was a Scottish immigrant of humble birth and fluctuating fortunes who had invested in Wobrock's business. In the depressed 1930s, the Wobrock enterprise collapsed. Marga contributed to family woes by having a fling with a Greek hypnotist. The Wobrocks separated in 1935.

It was the foretaste of a grim scenario. Von Hindenburg had appointed Adolf Hitler as Chancellor in 1933. Anti-Semitism now asserted its cancerous hold on German society. Scottish-born Jessie had married not just one Jew, but two in succession. Though the husbands had departed the scene, the clientele at her Hamburg hairdressing salon remained largely Jewish. Under the pall of persecution these customers now faded away just when Jessie needed the money. As if that were not enough, the authorities had told Marga to forget about resurrecting her stage career unless she could prove she had 'Aryan' ancestry on her mother's side.[2]

At this point, a stroke of luck seemed to intervene. Jessie received an offer of employment in her native Scotland. She decided to gift her Hamburg business to Marga and to take up the post, making this the opportunity to certify her ancestry and thus her daughter's. She booked a berth on a vessel bound for the port of Leith, adjacent to Scotland's capital city, Edinburgh. The boat was scheduled to depart on 2 February 1937 and on that day Jessie left the family home to catch it.

To Marga's dismay, her mother now disappeared for several days. Unbeknownst to her, grandmother Jessie had acceded to a change of plan. She missed the boat and became a spy.

The Scottish–German spy Jessie Jordan would play an instrumental role in events that created a great stir in far-off America. She had experienced a less than privileged life. Her maternal grandparents came from humble Protestant origins in County Down, Ireland. Grandfather John Wallace worked as a labourer after arriving in Scotland. John's Irish-born daughter Lizzie Wallace gave birth to Jessie in Glasgow in 1887. The name of Jessie's father, William Ferguson, did not appear on her birth certificate as he had escaped to America, leaving Lizzie to fend for herself.[3]

After Jessie's birth, her mother married John Haddow, a widower who worked as a train engine driver. Jessie Wallace became Jessie Haddow as she grew up and by 1907 was a chambermaid in the east coast manufacturing city of Dundee. There, she met a German waiter who was a couple of years her junior. When her eyes first fell upon him, his brother had just died in London and Karl Friedrich Jordan was in tears. Jessie put a comforting arm around Karl and, as they say, one thing led to another. The young suitor had to return to Germany to do his compulsory military service, but he called for Jessie and the couple married in 1912.

On 29 July 1918, Karl died in Hamburg, his death certificate stating lung collapse as the cause – he may well have been a victim, therefore, of mustard gas poisoning on the Western Front. In the meantime, Jessie had become a German citizen and she continued to live in Karl's native land until 1937. Marga later asserted, 'My mother has always said, I am German. I love Germany. I would die for Germany and I would like to be buried in Germany.'[4]

One might be tempted to believe that Jessie pined for Karl and that it was his death in the cause of the Fatherland that prompted his widow to spy for Germany twenty years later. If such an emotional tug existed, it must have been weakened by Jessie's discovery of a cache of letters her husband had sent from the Front. They were addressed to another woman.[5] Jessie just had no luck with men. In 1920 she married Karl's cousin Baur Baumgarten. He, too, had a roving eye. The marriage did not work out and the Baumgartens divorced in 1923. Jessie became Frau Jordan once again.[6]

Jessie responded by becoming a successful Hamburg businesswoman. The city epitomised Germany's determination to overcome the economic disaster of the First World War. Its shipyards built great ocean-going liners that rivalled those of Scotland's Clydeside. The Hamburg America Line (Hapag) was the world's largest shipping company, rivalled only by North German Lloyd in the nearby city of Bremen.[7] The resultant prosperity created opportunities and Jessie saw one in the cosmetic industry. Her chance for success arose from the introduction of machinery such as the hair drier and the rise of the cheap 'perm'. Jessie acquired hairdressing skills and, at a shop she opened in 1923, specialised in a setting known as the 'Viennese wave'. With the return of affluence to her Hoheluftstrasse quarter of Hamburg, customers, especially from the Jewish sector of the city's population, flocked to her salon and she opened a new branch to accommodate them.

In spite of this success, or perhaps because of it in a nation riven by racial jealousies, Jessie Jordan was by the 1930s susceptible to intimidation. Quite apart from the vulnerability of her daughter and granddaughter, her son Werner was in military training in Germany and in a position to be victimised. These factors, as well as economic necessity, lay behind her decision to reconnect with her native Scotland.

So what did happen to Jessie Jordan on that February day when she set out with her baggage for Hamburg's harbour? Marga recalled the sequence of events as follows:

> When my mother missed the boat she did not come home. Later I found she stayed with friends called Ostjes. Herr Ostjes is a member of the Gestapo, the German secret police, and it was he who made the suggestion to my mother that she should confirm information of military importance when she came to Scotland and which was already known to Germany.[8]

Ostjes, an acquaintance of a friend rather than an actual friend as Marga was led to believe, had learned of Jessie's predicament and plans and arranged for her to be intercepted on her way to the docks. Over the next few days, officials persuaded Jessie Jordan to spy for Germany's foreign intelligence service, the Abwehr.

The officials offered a carrot as well as a stick – Jessie would be paid for her services. However, there was more than fear and finance behind her decision to spy. She had split loyalties, even fragmented and destroyed identities, because of her background – her family migrated from the factional northern counties of Ireland to Scotland, then she married into German society. On a more positive note, Jessie Jordan loved the 'Great Game' of international espionage. She was a voracious reader of crime stories and spy thrillers. Explaining her espionage later on, she wrote 'excitement and change … were life's blood to me'. Those who commented on her appearance did not see the slouched form of a victim, but a woman of proud and charismatic deportment. Her character helps to explain why she was not just a spy, but also an enthusiastic one.[9]

Jessie's new spy friends detained her for eight days before dispatching her to catch her boat. When finally she contacted Marga to tell her that all was well, Jessie did not mention what happened at the grey, forbidding building that housed the Abwehr offices in Hamburg's Harvestehude district. It was there, at 14 Sophienstrasse, that Jessie received her instructions and some rudimentary tuition on tradecraft. The new recruit learned that she was to address correspondence to 'Sanders' at Post Office Box 629 in Hamburg.

The name derived from a past alias of Hilmar Dierks, whom we encountered in the previous chapter as the tutor of Niki Ritter, the spy who delivered the Norden bombsight secret. Dierks was until 1937 in charge of air force intelligence in Hamburg. A professional soldier who fought in the First World War and spied for Germany more or less continuously from 1914 until his death in 1940, Dierks had at one time used the cover name 'Richard Sanderson' and this evolved into the code name 'Sanders'. In the words of a post-war British intelligence report, 'SANDERS … was almost certainly a generic name … as was the cover-address Post Box 629, Hamburg 1.' Spy correspondence was addressed to 'Sanders' regardless of the identity of the intended recipient.[10]

Jessie Jordan was a mere agent, not a trained intelligence officer. Like Hermann Goertz and Otto Karl Ludwig, precursor German spies sent to the UK and exposed in November

1935 and April 1937 respectively, she was expendable. With little regard for her inexperience, she had been thrown in against MI5, a professional counter-espionage agency.

One could argue, it is true, that there were limits to MI5's competence. Maxwell Knight, who took over as its director in 1931, was an ardent anti-communist who in the preceding decade had expressed fascist sympathies. His agency left itself open to the charge that it took the communist menace so seriously that it neglected the Hitler menace. Another charge, made in a later age, was that MI5 was blinkered on the subject of women. It did not employ female officers in the 1920s. When the Soviet trade delegation ARCOS began supplying cover for spies in the same decade, the MI5 leadership became obsessed with the number of women ARCOS employed, but suspected them only of being femmes fatales laying honeytraps for British victims – not of general competence in matters of spying. In 1931, Knight did employ Olga Gray to penetrate a communist spy ring at the Woolwich Arsenal. When she proved to be effective, her chauvinist employers gave her scant reward and she emigrated. In sending Jessie Jordan to spy in Britain, the Abwehr potentially played on a British weakness.

In the event, Jessie did not stand a chance. There has been some exaggeration of the degree to which she was under surveillance: we can disregard an account that appeared in the *Empire News*, claiming that an MI6 agent personally witnessed the Gestapo's approach to Jessie – 'then, buttoning up his coat and pulling down his hat, he followed them'. More reliably, we do know that because of its previous dealings with yet another German spy and double agent, Christopher Draper, MI5 had known about Box 629 since early 1936. MI5 did not have blanket authority to intercept and read private correspondence, but it could do so on the authority of a Home Office Warrant (HOW). It used this procedure to keep tabs on what went to Box 629 and this meant MI5 would soon know about Jessie Jordan.[11]

The unsuspecting Jessie was a busy spy. Once having arrived in Scotland, she at first lived with her half-brother, William Haddow, in the Friarton district of Perth. It was he who had offered her employment, as his wife Mary had died and he needed someone to housekeep for him and his two children. But it occurred to Jessie that Marga could perform the house-keeping and mothering role. She summoned her daughter to Scotland and that freed her to go on her travels. In England, she visited the military town of Aldershot. Hairdressers make good listeners and Jessie chatted to soldiers in the local bars, making notes and drawing sketches. She visited Southampton and spoke to sailors in that strategic port.

She now travelled to Talgarth, a village nestling in the east-ern foothills of the Brecon Beacons range of hills in South Wales. Once the seat of an ancient Celtic kingdom, by the 1930s Talgarth was a sleepy backwater with a half-decent rugby team and not much else, and Jessie could be forgiven for imagining that her activities there would arouse no suspi-cion. She had chosen the village for a family reason. Mary Jean Mackay Wallace, her mother's sister, co-owned a nearby coun-try house, Felin Newydd. Mary had for many years earned a living looking after infirm clients and in 1925 had established Felin Newydd as a convalescent home.[12]

In June 1937, post office personnel acting on behalf of MI5 intercepted a letter sent to 'SANDERS, Post Box 629, HAMBURG', the address that the security service had under surveillance. The postmark on the envelope was 'Talgarth, Brecon'. The letter described the officers' mess and barracks at Aldershot. MI5's Colonel William Edward Hinchley Cooke later reported: 'As it appeared to be a very feeble effort at espi-onage I allowed it to go forward for delivery in due course to the addressee. It was obviously the effort of a beginner.'[13]

Before June was out, an opportunity arose for the now-doomed Jessie to establish what she thought would be enduring 'cover' when she spotted a notice in Dundee's newspaper *The Courier* offering for sale the goodwill and contents of Jolly's salon at 1 Kinloch Street, Dundee. Jolly was an acronym for 'Jesus Our Lord Loves us Yet', and the selling proprietor was a godly citizen by the name of James Curran. On 7 September 1937, Jessie purchased the going concern for £75. She then spent a reputed £300 refurbishing it as a hairdressing enterprise. When later questioned about the money, she told the Dundee police that it came from Mary Wallace. In espionage terms, however, Mary was a fictitious cover. When MI5 obtained a letter purportedly written by Mary to her niece Jessie offering financial support, its handwriting expert declared it to be a forgery. Perhaps guessing that she was being watched and needing an explanation for her expenditures should she be questioned, Jessie had written the letter herself.[14]

Now back in Perth, Jessie continued her correspondence with her German controllers. One of her missives was a letter to Hamburg, intercepted as usual by MI5. It was in an envelope that enclosed a further envelope containing a letter from 'Sanders' dated 16 July 1937. Posted from the Central Station in Amsterdam, this enclosed letter asked her to travel to The Hague 'for the purpose of discussion in detail all your business affairs which are still pending in Germany'. MI5 personnel took note of the enclosed letter, but found the inner envelope that encased it to be of greater interest. It bore the traces of writing that had been erased and experts applying special methods were able to make out Jessie's address in Perth. Accordingly, Hinchley Cooke was able to obtain a further HOW authorising the interception of all correspondence addressed to her there and from now on Jessie was under even closer surveillance.[15]

With her cover established as she thought, Jessie Jordan finally left Perth for Dundee, where the local post office took over the task of monitoring her correspondence. She acquired a flat with a view of the Tay estuary. Her new abode was a stone's throw from her freshly painted salon. She joined a local

Dundee library and indulged her taste for thrillers. She borrowed, for instance, E. Phillips Oppenheim's *The Evil Shepherd*, in which the character Francis Ledsam gets through whisky, champagne and liqueur in the first twenty-eight pages and meets his friends in a 'small white Georgian dining room, with every appurtenance of almost Sybaritic luxury'.[16]

In Scotland Jessie continued the spying activities that she had started in England. Forty miles to the south of Dundee lay a series of naval installations. The estuary on which they were situated (the Firth of Forth) was heavily fortified and crossed by a mighty rail bridge. Warships put in for repairs and sheltered under the guns of the 'inches', fortified islands strung along the approaches to the bridge and the dry docks beyond. The entire US Atlantic fleet had dropped anchor in the shadow of the bridge in 1918, lined up as neatly as the targets in Pearl Harbor twenty-three years later and were captured in an oil painting by the artist Sir John Lavery. The area had been a target of German espionage in 1912, when Armgaard Karl Graves claimed to have been tasked by the Germans to blow up the rail bridge – he turned out to have been a double agent and his book of the plot, much discussed in the American press, sold 100,000 copies on the eve of the First World War. The area for which Sanders told Jordan to 'confirm' certain details would suffer the first Luftwaffe attack of the Second World War.[17]

Travelling by bus, Jessie made sketches, took photographs and wrote notes, and then sent her reports to Hamburg. Although her efforts were amateurish and she could have conveyed to her German masters little that they did not already know, they confirmed the existence of a plan to provide German bombers with useful coordinates. Yet the assessment did not spur precipitous action. Hinchley Cooke and his colleagues were the inheritors of counter-espionage tradecraft and did not want to rush in and make an arrest that would have betrayed their knowledge of Box 629 and German methodology. Furthermore, the British government, like its American counterpart, was averse to actions that might provoke a deterioration in relations with Germany – the policy of 'appeasement', as its critics called it, was on the road to its apogee in Prime Minister Neville Chamberlain's agreement with Hitler in Munich in September 1938. MI5's policy was, then, wait and watch.

In pursuing this policy, Hinchley Cooke and his colleagues ran into two problems. The first was that the people of Dundee were onto Jessie Jordan. One story that gained currency was that the local postman became suspicious of the volume of foreign mail that arrived at 1 Kinloch Street and told his superiors that Jessie might be dangerous. In truth, his superiors already knew about Jessie Jordan. Whether or not because of the postie's vigilance, from 10 December 1937 at the latest, Alexander Jack, an officer in the General Post Office in Dundee operating under the authority of an HOW, steamed open envelopes bearing US stamps addressed to 1 Kinloch Street and photographed their contents.[18] That was necessarily a secret and not released to the press. The reality of MI5 surveillance would not prevent the humble postie from becoming a hero of the press when the story broke in 1938. Keeping a lid on patriotic posties was one of Hinchley Cooke's tasks and with news suppression as well as investigation in mind, he made regular visits north from London to confer with the Dundee police and senior postal officials.

Mary Curran was another potential inconvenience. She had worked for her brother-in-law at Jolly's and Jessie kept her on. She and her husband John maintained the appearance of friendship with Jessie, who spoke about politics with John, a tram conductor, and loaned him 'a book on anti-Jewism in Germany' together with a copy of one of Hitler's speeches. Mary's superficial cordiality masked her suspicions about Jessie's purchase of Jolly's, not a prime property as it was in a relatively poor district. The seemingly extravagant Jessie had paid for the premises in Bank of England £5 notes. (Could her German paymasters have been unaware that Scottish banks issued their own bank notes and that English 'fivers' stood out a mile, like £100 pound notes in a later day?)

Mrs Curran also wondered about the money Jessie lavished on the establishment and how she so easily imported from Germany specialist 'wave' equipment. Her frequent travels to Hamburg and her inquiry as to the location of the nearest military barracks increased the Currans' curiosity. Mary reported her suspicions to the Dundee police. The force were already tracking Jessie's every move and reporting back to MI5's Vernon Kell. Sir Vernon had been the founding director of MI5 and was anticipating retirement, but was still on an annually renewable contract and took an active interest in counter-intelligence as he had done in the First World War.[19]

On 7 December 1937, Mary Curran spotted Jessie's handbag resting on a table in the rear room of the salon premises. No devotee of privacy, she opened the bag and discovered a map. Handwritten numbers on the map identified locations in Scotland and the north of England. Mary showed the map to the police, who took photographs. Then she replaced it in the handbag.[20]

Eleven months later, Mrs Curran and her husband John tried to obtain financial reward from the government for their services to the nation. MI5 was aghast at the open nature of their request and resisted it. It noted, disapprovingly, that the Currans had in May 1938 received £25 for a two-day spread in the *Daily Record* in which they claimed to have cracked the Jordan spy case virtually single-handedly.[21] Of course they had not, as Jessie was already under surveillance. As Colonel Kell put it, 'We were fully aware of Mrs Jessie Jordan's unlawful activities as far back as July 1937, viz. over three months before the present claimants approached the police on 18 November 1937.'[22]

Kell was being overly dismissive, for it was Mrs Curran's discovery of the map in November that helped to persuade

MI5 to concentrate its vigilance on Jessie's Dundee business address, instead of on her recent Perth address, which was already the subject of an HOW.[23] The Currans' enthusiasm for disclosure was, nevertheless, an embarrassment to an agency whose byword was secrecy.

As for Jessie Jordan, her espionage was amateurish and trifling, yet also indicative. It signalled that in spite of its professed friendship with Britain, the Hitler regime had aggressive intentions. For Jessie did not aim to steal technological secrets to help Germany's defence. Rather, she supplied details such as bombing targets that would facilitate a military attack.

MI5's response to this was conservative. Its mission in autumn 1937 was to track a traitor while keeping a lid on the case in spite of the blundering efforts of amateur sleuths. It succeeded in that task – until events in America forced its hand.

Murder in the McAlpin

Situated on New York's Broadway and 34th Street, the McAlpin was the world's largest hotel. Run by well over 1,000 staff, it boasted progressive facilities that included a floor solely devoted to female guests and a pioneering ship-to-shore radio system. From certain of its windows, it was possible to gaze at the imposing structure of Macy's, the world's largest department store.

The McAlpin had been a favourite with German spies in the First World War and the hotel's reputation held into the 1930s.[1] It attracted operatives addicted to big-name attractions: grand hotels, state-of-the-art ocean liners, fast cars. Women met their Abwehr lovers in the McAlpin or its rival, the Taft Hotel. The size of the establishment offered spies a special commodity that they sought: anonymity.

In the early weeks of 1938, four Abwehr agents hatched a secret plot that would centre on the McAlpin. The conspirators took care to conceal their identities and, for the sake of convenience, we can call them Agents A, B, C, and D. Agent B, however, was just an assistant and withdrew from the scheme because of cold feet.

Agent A accepted his role, which was to induce Colonel Henry W.T. Eglin to visit the McAlpin. Eglin was the commander of a military facility on Totten Island in the approach to Long Island Sound. The plotters knew that the US Army officer was privy to American's east coast defence plans. The Abwehr agents' scheme was to get him into a McAlpin bedroom bearing documents that outlined those plans and then to relieve him of those documents, which they would send to the military command in Berlin.

The plot went further than earlier attempts by Lonkowski and his accomplices to steal the secrets of American military technology. It was an aggressive scheme reminiscent of what the Spanish Secret Service had tried to achieve in the Spanish–American War of 1898. Upon the outbreak of that war, Ramon de Carranza, Spain's military attaché in Washington, DC, fled to Montreal, where he established a spy base and sent agents to obtain the secrets of United States coastal defences. The Spanish naval command aimed to send five cruisers up the Atlantic Coast to bombard strategic targets that Carranza's agents had identified, for example Philadelphia's financial district. Admiral William T. Sampson's blockade of the Spanish fleet at Santiago de Cuba and the US Secret Service's arrest of Carranza's main agents defeated the Spanish plan.[2]

At least in 1898, Spain and the United States were already at war; there was no such excuse for the Abwehr agents' aggression in 1938. In that year, diplomats in Berlin and Washington were promoting the appearance of friendship between their respective nations. Contrary to that appearance, Agents A, C, and D acted in a spirit of bellicosity.

With the approval of Agent D, Agent A drafted a message for Colonel Eglin. Agent A would telephone the message, representing himself as an Adjutant of the Chief of United States Army Staff, Major General Malin Craig:

A secret emergency staff meeting is scheduled to be held at the McAlpin Hotel, New York, NY, on Friday, January 28,

1938. Your attendance is requested, and you are called upon
to observe the following details:

1. You will not divulge the nature or circumstances of the
   meeting to anyone.
2. You will appear in civilian clothes and arrive and leave
   unattended.
3. You will time your departure so as to arrive at the Hotel
   McAlpin at 12.20 p.m., Friday, January 28th.
4. You will sit yourself in the main lobby of the hotel and
   will await being paged as Mr. Thomas W. Conway. After
   identifying yourself as such you will be escorted to the
   meeting rooms.
5. You will bring with you all mobilization and coast
   defence plans in your possession, also pertinent maps and
   charts and a notebook for entries at the meeting.
6. It is repeated that the utmost discretion is expected of
   you in regard to this meeting, as no one is informed
   except those directly concerned.[3]

Agent C, who possessed nubile qualities, was to be held in
reserve to exercise her charm on the colonel if necessary. Agent
D, who had links with the Gestapo, was to be an enforcer. In
preparation for the entry of the unsuspecting Army officer to
the hotel room, Agent D would be standing on a sill, dressed
as a window cleaner. At the right moment, he would spring
into the room and assist Agent A in overpowering their victim.
Agent D would administer to Eglin the contents of a syringe
disguised as a fountain pen.

The American authorities learned of the plot in a round-
about way. Their enlightenment stemmed from the dual nature
of Jessie Jordan's spy mission. For, as we saw in the last chapter,
Jessie was not just a spy, but also a poste restante. She received
letters and parcels from agents in foreign countries and forwarded them to Germany. The Abwehr had added this mode of
communication to its system of ship-borne couriers. Sending

letters via Perth and Dundee instead of directly to Hamburg might cause fewer suspicions. There was another rationale behind the use of Jordan: if things came unstuck there would be a scandal not in target countries such as the United States, but more conveniently in the UK. As MI5's Guy Liddell later put it, the post box was in Scotland 'so as to throw the onus on the British in the event of unpleasant revelations'.[4]

A few of the letters that Jessie received or forwarded came from Czechoslovakia, into which Hitler was planning hostile incursions. Most of them, however, came from America. One such letter, translated into English from the original German by MI5's bilingual Hinchley Cooke, was postmarked Warwick Street Station, New York, 1 December 1937, signed 'Rt' and addressed to 'Mr. S', no doubt 'Sanders'. It acknowledged that future letters would be sent through Jordan and emphasised the sender's security consciousness: 'I have nothing in my possession which could lead to the conclusion that I am in any sort of contact with you or Germany. The copies which were enciphered some time ago have now been destroyed. The addresses I have memorised.'[5]

In January 1938, Jessie Jordan began to receive letters from an agent who called himself 'Crown'. They arrived at 1 Kinloch Street, Dundee. Possibly thanks in part to Mrs Curran, who had communicated her suspicions to the police, MI5 intercepted them and made copies. The letters covered a range of subjects. Crown constantly craved money, recognition and assets. In one letter, he asked for 'a very small Zeiss precision camera'. On 19 January, he asked for a supply of forged White House writing paper to help him to request the *Enterprise* and *Yorktown* aircraft carrier plans. In February, he complained about not having heard from his controller and said his brother in Prague had written, as promised, to 'Berlin'.[6]

MI5 made copies of these and other letters. They scrutinised the letter Crown's brother had written, posted from Prague and signed Hansjorg Gustav Rumrich. Dated 24 January, it offered Gustav's services as a spy and mentioned 'my brother G, who is active for the matter in the United States'. If this was a clue to Crown's identity, MI5 either missed it or failed to alert the Americans for reasons of their own. British intelligence had a long-standing policy of keeping their methods secret and of telling the Americans only what they wanted them to know.[7]

Another letter set the alarm bells ringing and at last prompted the British to send an alert. This letter was dated 17 January 1938. Addressed as usual to 'Sanders' via Jessie Jordan, the letter outlined Crown/Agent A's plot to obtain details of America's east coast defence operations.

The letter indicated the date of the apocryphal Emergency Staff Meeting to be held at the McAlpin Hotel – by now postponed to either Monday, 31 January or Tuesday, 1 February. It explained how Crown and his accomplices would handle Colonel Eglin: 'We shall attempt to overpower him and remove papers that he will have been ordered to fetch along. I shall leave clues that would point to communist perpetrators.' Crown admitted, 'the matter will probably stir up a little dirt, but I believe it will work out all right. The arrangements have been made with extreme care, every little detail has been reckoned with.'[8]

MI5 had no further details with which to assess the seriousness of the plot, but could not rule out the possibility that Crown and his associates would resort to murder. A memorandum in its files noted, 'this plot might easily have led to loss of life'.[9]

Still, it was not a foregone conclusion that MI5 would alert the American authorities. It was true that there was a presumption of transatlantic cooperation and shared information, and Britain had for some time cultivated a special intelligence relationship with America. Here are two examples. First, in 1898, the British had expelled Carranza from Canada to assist the Secret Service's counter-espionage effort. Second, in the

First World War, the British had shared cryptographic and battlefield intelligence with the Americans.

But information is power and the Admiralty code-breakers in the war had refused to share code-breaking *methodology* with their United States counterparts. Moreover, there was a cultural difference between MI5 and the FBI. When it saw malfeasance that threatened national security, the FBI's instinct was to make an arrest, but MI5 did not share this preoccupation. Its instinct was to follow a suspect, with the object of obtaining further information. Why not just let Jessie Jordan run, with this objective in mind?

There were also political problems. Did the British really want to alert America in such a way as to aggravate relations with Germany at a time when the London government was intent on preserving harmonious relations with Berlin? Until the beginning of January, the civil servant Sir Robert Vansittart had overseen British intelligence and had been keen on cooperation with America with a view to thwarting Hitler's plans, but he had been moved from his position as permanent under-secretary of state for foreign affairs to another post precisely because of his strong anti-appeasement stance. In the following month, Foreign Secretary Anthony Eden would resign over the same issue. Prime Minister Neville Chamberlain's government simply did not want to rock the boat.

For their part, the Americans were loath to receive potentially destabilising news at a time when Washington, too, was intent on getting along with the German government. President Franklin D. Roosevelt (1933–45) had just appointed Joseph Kennedy as Ambassador to the United Kingdom. He conceded that Kennedy was a 'very dangerous man'. On account of his Irish–American heritage, he might resort to the old Anglophobic tradition of 'twisting the lion's tail'. There was a suspicion that Roosevelt did not really approve of Kennedy and simply wanted to get rid of him from American politics. But there was another factor that played in the new appointee's favour. Kennedy was attuned to Prime Minister Chamberlain's policy of not confronting Hitler and this suited Roosevelt's purposes in early 1938.

Yet the time was in two ways propitious for MI5 to depart from its customary caution. First, Joe Kennedy had not yet completed the arrangements for his move to London. He would not arrive to take up his post until 1 March. In the meantime, the American Embassy was in a state of interregnum.[10]

Second, although Vansittart had officially moved on, his interest and influence lingered in his old domain. In his newly invented post of 'chief diplomatic adviser to the British government', he was meant to be a vaguely defined 'roving ambassador', but after a few weeks the devoted peace advocate Lord (Arthur) Ponsonby expressed concern that Vansittart might be running a 'duplicate foreign office'.[11] His successor as permanent under-secretary, Alexander Cadogan, expected Vansittart to 'make trouble'. He was 'annoying'. He was keeping up his contacts with the secret services. Later in the year, an *Evening Chronicle* journalist would observe that the permanent under-secretary was 'the only man who knows the name of every member of Britain's secret service.' Vansittart was not about to forget or to neglect the advantage that knowledge conferred.[12]

For months after his supposed removal from the permanent secretaryship, Vansittart continued to discuss Anglo-American intelligence cooperation with MI5 personnel. He continued to receive MI5 confidential reports. He obtained, for example, a copy of the 17 January McAlpin plot letter. He was not imprudent enough to interfere openly, but his continued tenure of high office and his intimacy with intelligence circles would have been an encouragement to those deciding on a tip-off.[13]

Crown's letter of 17 January arrived in Dundee on the 28th. MI5's Post Office interceptors immediately photographed it and put the film on the night train to London. It arrived at MI5 headquarters in London the next day and, in spite of the politically delicate situation, the decision was taken to send the Americans an urgent alert. After all, it was one thing to appease Germany and to keep the transatlantic cousins in the dark as part of the power struggle known as the Great Game, quite another to risk the Americans finding out that the British had allowed one of its officers to be terminated in cold blood without issuing any kind of a warning.

On 29 January 1938, MI5's Colonel Kell gave a copy of the letter to Colonel Raymond E. Lee, the US military attaché in London. Lee sent an urgent alert to the US Army General Staff, who transmitted a warning to New York to safeguard Colonel Eglin's life. MI5 also gave Lee a memorandum that outlined the nature of the plot. It noted that its prospective 'perpetrator is a German espionage agent (he may be of any nationality; he has a good knowledge of the English language) whose identity is unknown'. In an attempt to furnish clues as to Crown's identity, it added that the conspirator was knowledgeable about aircraft. For the US Army he had listed as his 'choice of station' three locations: two airfields in the USA and one in the Panama Canal Zone.[14]

Alerted to the situation, Department of State officials were still reluctant to be caught up in a spy case that might impair relations with Germany. The fact that Crown's identity was a mystery suggested a way out, the delegation of responsibility to an investigative branch of government. They thus urged the FBI to enter the fray. Director J. Edgar Hoover at first dragged his feet and for good reasons.[15] Several government agencies as well as the military were involved and there was a possibility of jurisdictional buck-passing and warfare. Hoover also explained that his initial reluctance sprang from the fact that the story was already in the press and, as one FBI agent ruefully remarked in retrospect, 'discretion is the very essence of an espionage investigation'.[16] In spite of these difficulties, Hoover changed his mind. The United States faced a clear danger of foreign penetration that threatened its security interests. It would have reflected poorly on the FBI director if he took no action and, in any case, Hoover was not one to shirk a task that, if allocated to others, might diminish his agency's standing.

MI5's tip-off memorandum had insisted, 'It is of the utmost importance that in any action which is taken on this information, no indication whatever should be given of the fact that it was obtained in Great Britain.'[17] The counter-intelligence agency was here being true to a tradition exemplified by the affair of the Zimmermann telegram. Sent in the spring of 1917, German Foreign Secretary Arthur Zimmermann's encoded top-secret telegram had promised Mexico restoration of the territories the United States had wrested from it in 1846 in exchange for Mexican loyalty to Berlin should America enter the war then raging in Europe. When exposed, the Zimmermann telegram had inflamed American opinion, contributing to US entry into the First World War. At the time London, not wanting Berlin to know it had broken German codes, had insisted that there should be no disclosure that the telegram was a British intercept. A similar principle applied in 1938 – MI5 wanted to keep secret its knowledge of how Germany's post box system worked.

In its handling of the McAlpin plot, MI5 continued its policy of restraint. It did not arrest Jessie Jordan, choosing instead to follow and observe her, hoping for American discretion. Jessie continued to operate as a spy in ignorance of her watchers. She had no idea that the proverbial can of worms was about to open in America. It was her misfortune that the clues supplied by MI5 were being turned over to the FBI's greatest detective.

4

Enter Leon Turrou

On 30 January 1938, military intelligence told the FBI about Crown's plot to kidnap Colonel Henry Eglin.[1] Needing a lead investigator, J. Edgar Hoover turned to one of his most gifted special agents. Leon G. Turrou's mastery of seven languages had impressed the FBI boss as early as 1921. FBI director of personnel Clyde Tolson, whose views reflected Hoover's, noted Turrou's reputation for having 'an uncanny knack of securing information'. Another manager observed that Turrou was simply the 'best investigator of criminal violations in the Bureau'.[2]

Turrou was remarkable in that he overcame the prejudice directed against him. One of his promotion assessors said he was 'not very impressive looking'. Another scrutiniser remarked on his 'somewhat foreign physiognomy'. Still another noted the 'foreign accent' that went with features that bore 'the stamp of his foreign birth'. Turrou's own observation was that he had a 'Slavic cast of countenance' and the 'typical high-cheek-bones oval face of a Russian'.[3]

An objective description of Turrou's physique came from Walter F. Stillger, MD, who performed a medical examination on behalf of the FBI. He described a man, 5ft 8in tall, weighing 143lb, whose teeth were 'in good condition several gold-capped'. His genitals were 'negative', a reference to their good health. His left leg was also 'negative', but, accounting for his slight limp, his right leg showed a 'healed scar ... due to shrapnel wound'. Turrou's body may not have impressed his colleagues, but it had a history.[4]

The later Turrou–Hoover feud that broke out in July 1938 gave Turrou's detractors a renewed opportunity to air their views and FBI opinion fell in line with the director's lead in turning against the agent. For example, Special Agent Louis Loebl's officially commissioned account of Turrou's life focused on his habit of exaggerating and on his unreliability. Loebl began with Turrou's account of his childhood, which he said was 'a lot of hooey'.[5]

Turrou's account of the first twenty-five years of his life is indeed erratic to the point of invention. He once told a breakfast club in Los Angeles that by the time he reached his first birthday, both his parents were dead, a claim that gave the impression that he had limited means of ascertaining what happened in his very early years.[6] In reality, his mother Rebecca survived. She settled in Singapore's Jewish community for a while, perhaps accounting for Leon's fluency in the Malay language. Then in 1916 she travelled via Yokohama to Seattle, on her way to Brooklyn, NY. On the ship's manifest of the SS *Sado Maru* she had struck out the word 'Russian' opposite her name and inserted instead 'Hebrew'. Leon also had two surviving brothers who could have jogged his memory.[7] Rebecca was a wanderer in more than the geographic sense. As her granddaughter delicately put it, she was 'evidently before her time'. She engaged in several relationships, including a brief marriage in Brooklyn. There was considerable family debate about the identity of Leon's 'real father', with family rumours variously posting him as a count and as a native of Alsace; Turrou recalled in his Los Angeles talk that his father might have been a French musician.[8] To help cope with his complex past, Leon appears to have invented certain facts about it and to have allowed invention to develop into a habit, especially when that was to his advantage. His capacity for invention earned him a great deal of criticism, but may also have been an asset in that it helped him to recognise other people's mendacity.

Leon was born on 14 September 1895 in the town of Kobryn, which is today in Belarus. Historically, this community was located in Poland. At the time of his birth, though, it was under Russian control, as it had been since the partition of Poland by Russia, Prussia and Austria in the 1790s. Although at one point Leon claimed that his late father's name was 'George Turrou', the name 'Turrou' was in fact a simplification of his mother's name, Turovsky.[9]

Turrou's descendants hold DNA evidence indicating that he was 75 per cent Jewish.[10] In his lifetime Turrou denied this: 'I happen *not* to be a Jew, either by birth or faith.'[11] How do we interpret this remark? Turrou was not brought up in the Jewish faith and was not very religious, but there was more to his denial than that. Fear and opportunity played their role – fear in Eastern Europe, a land of pogroms, and opportunity once he left home and wanted to pass himself off as a gentile to ease his career. Our story will reveal, however, that his denial was a paradox – he claimed to be a gentile to strengthen his campaign to save Jews and the rest of humanity from the evils of Nazism.

As narrated by Turrou to his Los Angeles audience, this is what happened to him in his childhood. On his mother's death, her next-door neighbours adopted him – Turrou either failed to remember their names or chose to obscure them. The husband was a musician and took his adopted son on a 'tour of the world', visiting Australia, China and Japan to name just a few of the countries they visited. In Egypt, according to Turrou's fabricated or real account, his new father placed him in a Jesuit school, where he remained until he was 8 years old.

'Give me a child until he is 7 and I will give you the man' is the reputed Jesuit maxim and, even if he developed an agnostic outlook, perhaps Leon did acquire his exceptional literacy skills at this early stage. When he was 11, the young migrant found himself deposited in Berlin for further education and learned German. By the age of 13, he spoke five languages. At this point, Turrou recalled, 'I was abandoned in Berlin by my foster parents and it was necessary for me, at that time, to make my own living.'[12]

This would take us up to 1908. Continuing his story, Turrou said he now got by in Berlin by selling newspapers, in the meantime continuing his education, and then migrated to London. At the age of 17, he departed for the United States. Immigration records show, so we can at least be sure of this, that he passed through the Ellis Island processing depot on 12 March 1913. Turrou told his Californian listeners that, once arrived, he 'sold newspapers and did odd jobs'.[13]

Leon fell in love with America. Along the way, he also fell for a girl called Olga. It did not work out. Joseph Davidowsky, Olga's brother, vetoed their engagement 'because Olga was a Greek [i.e. Orthodox] Catholic and Turrou was a Jew'. The hoped-for marriage did not take place.[14]

According to Davidowsky, Turrou was 'in despair' when things fell through with Olga.[15] So what does a young man do when true love fails to run its course? As any reader of *Beau Geste* will tell you, he joins the French Foreign Legion. P.C. Wren's novel was published in 1924 and it may well have influenced Turrou to romance his First World War experiences when he related them in later years. The FBI's chronicler Louis Loebl accepted Turrou's Foreign Legion story, though Turrou gave various conflicting accounts of his military service, none of them verifiable. Loebl estimated that Turrou was with the French unit from August 1917 to November 1918 – a period when the Legion took heavy casualties on the Western Front.[16] Turrou never explained why he risked his

life with the Legion, but it might be surmised that the growing American support for Poland influenced him. President
Woodrow Wilson befriended Jan Paderewski, the Polish
pianist and future prime minister, and in his 'Peace Without
Victory' speech to the Senate on 22 January 1917, then in his
war aims Fourteen Points address on 8 January 1918, singled
out the partitioned nation for special treatment, demanding 'a
united, independent and autonomous Poland'.[17]

When recovering from wounds in a Paris hospital, Leon met
a girl called Teresa, the sister of another wounded Pole. Teresa
Zakrewski was a Catholic. Given his experience with Olga
and the intolerance of the times, Leon may not have revealed
his Jewish origins to her parents – it was another reason for
being discreet on the subject. Teresa's mother and father lived
in China and Leon travelled there to marry her. Soon they had
two boys, Edward (born on 19 November 1918) and Victor
(9 December 1919). The family took up residence in Siberia at
the Russian terminus of Turrou's new employer, the Chinese
Eastern Railway.[18]

Misfortune now struck. Following their triumph in the
Revolution of 1917, the Bolsheviks sealed the border:

> … there was a Civil War going on in Russia. My wife
> got stranded on the other side of the gate, while I was in
> China, and for two and one-half years I was unable to com-
> municate with her. My inquiries at the American Consul
> indicated everyone in that little village where she was living
> was eventually massacred. I gave them up as dead. It was
> then I decided to return to the United States.[19]

Back in America, Turrou joined the Marines in a non-combat
capacity serving in France and Belgium and in 1921 petitioned for naturalisation. With that paperwork completed, he
became officially 'Turrou' and not 'Turovsky'. A new opportunity now arose. In 1919, Congress had approved the funding

for an American Relief Administration (ARA) with the aim
of addressing some of the hardship in war-torn Europe. Two
years later, famine struck in Russia, where civil war still raged
four years after the Communist takeover of 1917. The ARA
sent a task force of 300 Americans under the leadership of
Colonel William N. Haskell. Turrou served with the mission
from September 1921 to February 1923 and was Haskell's
interpreter and assistant in Moscow. A historian of the relief
expedition, Bertrand Patenaude, has noted that Haskell 'raved
about Turrou's talents'.[20]

A few years later, Turrou recalled how, in 1922, urgently
needed American wheat was not getting through on the
Soviet railway system. After five years of wartime neglect,
'engines rusted at the sidetracks for lack of vital parts'. More
frustratingly, Communist Party officials were not letting supplies through the vital junction at Balashov in the Lower Volga
region. Hundreds of cereal-laden cars stood motionless in side-
lines, some of them diverted there for personal gain by Soviet
soldiers. Furious, Colonel Haskell demanded that the responsible officials should appear at his office. When they arrived,
their spokesman was Felix Dzerzhinsky, the Soviet Commissar
for Transportation, who doubled, more significantly, as the
head of GPU, the State Political Directorate or secret police.
In the ensuing discussion, Turrou was the translator and took
a risky line by making Haskell seem more aggressive than he
was. The outcome was satisfactory. Dzerzhinsky turned to his
comrades and gave an order 'with not a trace of emotion on
his deathmask face': 'The trains will move and if you fail the
supreme punishment is waiting for you.'[21]

In Russia, there was an even more important outcome for
Turrou. He discovered that his wife and boys were alive and
well – even if little Edward had searing memories 'of people
hanging by the necks from telephone poles, killed by the
communist revolutionaries'.[22] Turrou took his family back to
the United States, where Teresa's mother joined them. Joseph

Davidowsky, who continued his turbulent relationship with Turrou, recalled, perhaps imperfectly, that 'he always spoke Jewish to his mother-in-law'.[23]

Turrou never articulated his reason for wanting to join the FBI. He came from a part of the world that had long experienced ambivalent identities and the chance to assume different roles and guises in undercover work may have been an attraction. One can speculate that his difficulties in finding his long-lost family may have helped to persuade him of the need for an effective detective service. Here, the FBI was an attractive choice. It already had the reputation of being an all-American institution and, for a relatively new arrival in the USA, joining the Bureau would be an affirmation of patriotism and of a new-found identity. Turrou's shrapnel-pierced leg meant that active military service, another way of accomplishing that goal, was not an option and the Bureau offered a life of risk and adventure for which Turrou had developed a taste in the course of his restless youth. The high profile of organised crime in the Prohibition era may have helped to make the attraction of a career in the FBI irresistible.

J. Edgar Hoover had always wanted to appoint Turrou. As deputy director he had recommended his appointment in 1921, only to be overruled on the ground that Turrou did not possess the usual requirement for a special agent, a law degree.[24] After further fruitless applications and a long delay, political events tipped the balance in Turrou's favour. In 1928, the Republican Party nominated as its presidential candidate Herbert Hoover, who had directed the ARA. Turrou expressed his admiration for what Hoover had done for Russia and volunteered to work on his behalf in the Russian-speaking precincts of New York. He spoke in several languages at public meetings in support of his former employer. At the general election on 6 November Hoover gained an overwhelming victory against his Democratic rival, Al Smith. It was time for Turrou to claim his reward and his supporters petitioned

Assistant Attorney General William J. Donovan. Soon after Hoover's inauguration on 4 March 1929, Donovan sent Turrou his letter of appointment – it arrived in the same envelope as a letter from J. Edgar Hoover containing the standard injunction that there should be 'no publicity'. On 1 April, Turrou entered into active service as a special agent in the city of Chicago.[25]

Between this date and the start of his investigation into the Crown affair in February 1938, Turrou worked on around 3,000 FBI cases, giving him experience that was not only extensive, but also in some instances germane to the great investigation that would bring him fame.

Turrou's language skills gave him an operational advantage. The tale of his very first case illustrates the point. Chicago's Special Agent in Charge (SAC) Earl Connelley had asked him to track down Ignatz Skropinski, an immigrant from Kraków, Poland, who had escaped from Leavenworth prison having been sentenced to five years for his part in a violent US Mail robbery. More experienced agents had already interrogated Mrs Skropinski on several occasions, to no avail. Connelley told his new recruit to try once more. The rookie arrived at the Skropinski apartment in an old tenement on Cicero Street. Mrs Skropinski reluctantly admitted him to her home and then stalled him during a desultory conversation, in the course of which, Turrou later recorded, she 'suddenly rattled off a quick burst of Polish. She was staring directly at a big potato in her hand, but she was talking to her daughter.' She told the girl to go to the barbershop and 'tell Poppa not to come back for a while'. It never occurred to Mrs Skropinski that an FBI agent might understand Polish. Turrou exited the tenement, found a Chicago policeman to assist with the arrest and stunned a deeply impressed Connelley by delivering the escaped convict to his office. This won Turrou the first of many commendations for his detective work.[26]

Another of Turrou's early cases saw him working under cover on the completion of the USS *Akron*, otherwise known as ZRS-4. The *Akron* was a pet project of the US Navy, a helium-filled, rigid-construction airship designed to be a mother vessel that launched and recovered F9C Sparrowhawk fighter planes in mid-air. With its sister dirigible the *Macon*, it was well over 200m long and compared with the German hydrogen-filled airship the *Hindenburg*. The *Akron* crashed into the Atlantic Ocean during a gale off the coast of New Jersey, killing seventy-three of its seventy-six passengers. The *Macon* met a similar fate two years later and the consensus was that the experimental craft were not airworthy. According to Turrou, there had been a Soviet plan to sabotage the *Akron* by means of faulty rivets installed by a communist worker, who then disappeared. In his report on the matter, Vice Admiral Charles E. Rosendal found that the 6 million rivets had been sound. Nevertheless, in July 1941, to a fanfare of press publicity, Turrou revealed his role in trying to prevent sabotage at the time of construction.[27]

The *Akron* met its fate in April 1933. In November of that same year, Turrou was personally involved in another crash, one that revealed to his colleagues the self-boosting side of his character. At the time, he was helping in the search for the Kansas City Massacre gunmen. On 17 June 1933, three men had tried to spring Frank Nash, an escaped federal convict who was being escorted by local police and the FBI to Leavenworth penitentiary. Outside the Union Railway Station in Kansas City, Missouri, Vernon C. Miller, Adam C. Richetti and Charles 'Pretty Boy' Floyd shot dead three police officers and Nash also died from bullet wounds. The case ushered in the FBI's fully armed war on crime (Turrou had just undergone machine gun training). Although the perpetrators were Midwestern rural bandits rather than big-time urban gangsters, the investigation was important to the propaganda war on organised crime being launched by Attorney General Homer Cummings and J. Edgar Hoover. Turrou was pursuing lines of inquiry on Vernon Miller when, early on the evening of 14 November, he was driving his brand new Rent-a-Car Chevrolet from Memphis, Tennessee, to Paragould, Arkansas. There are two versions of what happened next.

Investigating the incident, the FBI's D. Milton Ladd reported a conversation with a witness, B.R. Harris, at the Judd Hill Plantation near Truman, Arkansas. Harris said that Turrou's car overtook him 'at about thirty-five miles per hour', then 'cut back to the right-hand side of the road and in doing so slipped on the loose gravel on this highway and that he noted the rear end of the car was swaying badly' and when 'about one hundred feet in front of him it went over the embankment'. Harris stopped his own vehicle and went to the FBI man's assistance, for the Chevy had turned over twice, landing on its wheels in the water. Harris flagged down another approaching car, whose driver took Turrou to the nearest hospital.

Turrou gave Ladd a different version of the incident. Stopping for petrol and to ask advice on his route, he half-noticed there was a black Buick or Cadillac lurking nearby. He left on Highway 63 heading towards Jonesboro driving at about 25mph. About 3 miles east of Truman, 'he heard a loud honking in the rear and at the same time a black Buick or Cadillac coach drove past him at about fifty miles an hour, cut in and pushed him over an embankment'.[28]

It was a good story. 'Attempt Take Life US Officer Fails' ran the *Jonesboro Daily Tribune* headline. The next day, the paper reported J. Edgar Hoover's promise to pursue 'every possible clue' to identify the 'gangsters' in the assassination plot. With slightly more scepticism, the *Memphis Press-Scimitar* headline ran its account under the tag 'US Agent Blames Gang for Highway Death Plot'.[29]

After agents had inspected skid marks at the scene of the accident and reviewed all the evidence, R.H. Colvin, the SAC at Oklahoma City, concluded that 'there were no facts developed to substantiate to the slightest degree the story told by Agent Turrou as to his having been forced off the highway by two men who had followed him from Memphis'. He added that SAC Ladd of the St Louis office believed 'there was absolutely no merit in Agent Turrou's claim'. He reported to FBI director Hoover that Turrou had entertained the press at his hospital bed to give out the stories that appeared.[30]

The ambitious Turrou had been unwilling to accept culpability for the car crash and had summoned the press to massage and embellish the news. Hoover was at this stage willing to tolerate this and kept assigning his brilliant agent to major cases.

No case was bigger than that of the Lindbergh kidnapping. Charles A. Lindbergh was a 25-year-old airmail pilot when in 1927 he flew the *Spirit of St Louis*, a monoplane he had personally configured, from Long Island to Paris. The first solo nonstop crossing of the Atlantic, it made him world famous – and a target for the kidnapper who, on the night of 1 March 1932, used a ladder to access a bedroom in the Lindbergh home near Hopewell, New Jersey, and kidnap 20-month-old Charles Lindbergh Jr. The Lindberghs agonised over a $50,000 ransom note left by the kidnapper and paid up through an intermediary. Two months later, the boy's body was discovered in a shallow grave.

Turrou later wrote, 'Not since Paris abducted Helen and precipitated the Trojan War has a kidnapping had so many repercussions.' When Roosevelt became president, he insisted that the Bureau must find the killer. Accordingly, Hoover formed a 'Lindbergh squad' that included Turrou. At first the squad made little headway, but a tip-off from a member of the public led to the arrest, on 20 September 1934, of a suspect, Bruno Richard Hauptmann.

Turrou sat with Hauptmann for hours. On this occasion as on others, he displayed his uncanny knack of winning the confidence of a suspect. Turrou was able not only to spot mendacity on the other side of an interview table, but also to win the trust of persons who looked back at their interrogator and saw someone with shared characteristics. It is quite remarkable that he caused those whom he questioned to incriminate themselves, at times in a manner that amounted to a self-imposed death sentence. Turrou persuaded Hauptmann, against his better judgment, to transcribe long passages from the *Congressional Record* and the *Wall Street Journal*. The same quirks and spelling errors that appeared in the ransom note began to crop up. Hauptmann was convicted and died in the electric chair on 3 April 1936.[31]

By this time, a familiar alarm bell had rung in Washington. Hoover complained that 'there appeared in the press considerable publicity concerning Special Agent L.G. Turrou'.[32] The Boss saw a continuing problem with Turrou's love of the limelight. However, he held back partly because he empathised with the publicity instinct and partly because what made the FBI look good made Hoover look good. It helped that Turrou at every turn gave the impression that he was devoted to Hoover, sending the director frequent and well-received suggestions about how the FBI might improve its performance.

Hoover and his FBI colleagues were as one in their verdict that Leon Turrou was a truly gifted detective. The Crown case that Turrou began to address in February 1938 would test his gifts anew.

Crown Identified

At first, Turrou made little headway chasing down Crown's identity. When he asked for checks to be made on Crown's military profile, the Army drew a blank. Other lines of inquiry yielded only half-clues. For example, Turrou had noted that Crown posted his letters from a location in the Bronx, New York. This identification of a particular area reminded him of the way in which he had helped to track down Hauptmann, the killer of the Lindbergh toddler. Here, though, the trail ran cold.

Turrou surmised from Crown's relocation to a first-floor apartment (mentioned in a letter) that he might be married with small children. The text of the letters suggested good education. The typing indicated that he was familiar with a keyboard but self-taught – uneven digital pressure had caused some letters to be more pronounced than others, meaning the typist did not use all of his fingers. But all that was clutching at straws. 'Baffled,' Turrou recalled, 'we settled back to wait for a break.'[1]

When that break came, it was the accidental result of a police operation. Late on the afternoon of 15 February 1938, detectives John S. Murray and Arthur J. Silk of the New York

Police Department (NYPD) hovered within sight of the King's Castle Tavern on Hudson Street. They awaited the reappearance of a Western Union messenger who had disappeared into the tavern. A boy now entered the pub and emerged shortly afterwards carrying a parcel. Watched by the detectives, the boy approached a street corner. On hearing an expected whistle, the boy paused, then moved towards the whistler and handed over his package. It was at this moment that the detectives made their arrest.

The police officers took the whistler to a room at the Post Office Building on 33rd Street and Eighth Avenue. The sibilant parcel receiver confessed to being the person who, pretending to be Secretary of State Cordell Hull, had called Ira F. Hoyt, the New York chief of the Passport Division, with a request to prepare a parcel containing thirty-five passport application forms addressed to Mr Edward Weston, Under-Secretary of State. It had been a weak effort, not just because Hull had an inimitable Tennessee accent, but also because the real name of the Under-Secretary of State was Sumner Welles. Seeing through the ruse, the Passport Division had alerted the NYPD.

The State Department's security staff had made up a dummy package for the Western Union messenger to collect and take to the appointed place of rendezvous and the arrested man had fallen into the trap. He now faced a battery of interrogators from the NYPD, State Department and military intelligence. He admitted that his real name was Guenther Gustave Maria Rumrich.

For the next few days, the Army held 'Gus' Rumrich prisoner at its facility on Governor's Island, 800 yards off the southern tip of Manhattan. Major Joe Dalton, the assistant chief of staff at G-2 (Military Intelligence) who had received the original MI5 tip-off about the McAlpin plot, was based there. For several days, he interrogated Rumrich along with State Department special agent T.F. Fitch and the NYPD detectives. The interrogators were not unfeeling and on 17 and

18 February, they escorted Rumrich to his home so that he could see his wife and 2-year-old son, Gerald.

A certain feature of the affair indicated it should not be considered as an isolated incident. At the time of his arrest, Rumrich had been carrying a briefcase. He later explained that he always carried this when he left his home, lest his wife inspect its contents and discover what he was up to. The briefcase contained low-level, open-access intelligence such as Army and Navy registers and other odds and ends. Of particular interest among those odds and ends was a rough pencil draft of a telephone message Rumrich had been planning to deliver. It addressed Colonel Henry W. T. Eglin, Commanding Officer of Fort Totten: 'A secret emergency staff meeting is scheduled to be held at the McAlpin Hotel, New York, N.Y. ...' The text would have been familiar to anyone who had studied the Crown correspondence and Dalton had been one of the first to know about the McAlpin conspiracy. Confronted with the scrap of paper, Rumrich confessed to the intelligence officers that he was connected to the plot against Colonel Eglin at the McAlpin Hotel.[2]

The State Department agents attempted to extract more details from Rumrich. In exchange for full disclosure, they asked, what guarantees would he want? Rumrich demanded promises of safety for himself and his wife and children. He did not want to be deported, as his fate back in his native Germany might be dire. He wanted all criminal charges against him to be dropped and asked for his personal indebtedness to be wiped out.[3]

The Department of State's officials refused to accept these conditions, but faced a dilemma. They did not want to prosecute Rumrich over the theft of the passports, because Secretary of State Cordell Hull would have to appear as a witness and that would strain relations with Germany. Rumrich was a US Army deserter and the military could prosecute him for that instead of for espionage, but it seemed too benign a response in relation to the gravity of Rumrich's activities and would not have got to the bottom of what was going on. Like his State Department collaborators, the Army's Major Dalton was keen for the FBI to take over the case.

Leon Turrou learned of the arrest on the morning of 17 February from 'badly garbled' accounts in the metropolitan newspapers. Though he had not yet seen the incriminating note, he suspected right away that there was a McAlpin connection and wanted to be in on a case that might help him solve his own, more urgent inquiry. J. Edgar Hoover at first hesitated, but at 9 a.m. on Saturday, 19 February, State Department agent Fitch in company with NYPD detectives Murray and Silk went to the Hotel New Yorker, where Rumrich was being held, and told him he was being handed over to the FBI. Rumrich protested to Fitch that 'he did not appreciate being pushed around and turned over to another agency', but it was to no avail. From 10 a.m. that morning, he was in the hands of Leon Turrou, the FBI's top detective.[4]

Sensational and erratic accounts of the arrest continued to appear in the newspapers, apparently fed by an NYPD leak. Within days, details of the passport scam were public knowledge. Temporarily, the press observed the polite fiction that an unnamed foreign power was behind the plot. This allowed the *Hamburger Nachrichten* to publish on its front page, no doubt to the accompaniment of local mirth, an account indicating that 'a large international spy ring' was responsible.

Although Turrou made no public comment, by the end of the month details of his widening inquiry had appeared in the American press. Reed E. Vetterli tried to calm the situation. As Special Agent in Charge, New York, Vetterli ran the local FBI office while Turrou ran the Rumrich investigation. When quizzed, he denied there was a threat to national security and declined to say which foreign power was involved. The American press had not really needed to ask that question as it had already deduced the source of the espionage

– the *Washington Post* noted the 'Teutonic appearance' of the arrested man and Germany was unambiguously in the frame. In vain did Under-Secretary of State Welles impress upon the British Ambassador the US Government's view that the 'news had got into the press prematurely and that the authorities wanted its importance to be minimised'.[5]

The leaks had reduced the chances of uncovering any wider spy ring that may have existed and of bringing the spies to justice. To Turrou's dismay, German intelligence diverted ships carrying spies, destroyed evidence and told its agents to run for cover. There was a danger that the full working apparatus of Germany's American spy network would remain undetected and continue to operate.[6]

Contemporaries and historians wondered at the way in which Turrou nevertheless succeeded. The FBI special agent-turned-historian Raymond Batvinis wrote that, 'Turrou, with seemingly no effort, gained admissions from practically everyone he interviewed.'[7]

Turrou had the gift of being able to make people talk. For illumination on this point, Turrou's book *The Nazi Spy Conspiracy in America* is a first-hand source.

In drawing on this book, we need to remind ourselves that Turrou spared no effort in trumpeting the role he played. 'Who was this man before me?' he asks, in his account of the passport scam interrogation. 'Was this – could this be "Crown"?'[8] By this stage, it must have been abundantly clear that Rumrich was Crown. His brother in Prague had referred to him in one of the intercepted letters included in the Crown batch, copies of which were by now in Turrou's possession. There was the pencilled note Rumrich had so carelessly carried in his briefcase, and other interrogators had already connected Rumrich to the McAlpin plot.

Here, it should be interjected that in its American operations, at least, German foreign intelligence displayed certain weaknesses. It allowed its agents to use the same hotel as in the First World War, gave a pivotal role to the same shipping line, Hamburg America, and resorted to similar tactics, such as fraudulently acquiring American passports. Repetition made for predictability, and predictability is the enemy of security. Rumrich and his colleagues were asking to be found out and it was only the historical amnesia resulting from the absence of a continuous US counter-intelligence service that afforded them a temporary reprieve.[9]

It was disingenuous of Turrou to suggest that he made the Crown–Rumrich discovery through his own, solo, brilliant analysis of the evidence. His book *The Nazi Spy Conspiracy* nevertheless provides an insight into the psychological tactics that Turrou used in extracting vital clues from the arrested agent about the German spy network. Rumrich was by this stage Prisoner 13 at the Guard House on Governor's Island. Each day, he would be delivered to the FBI's interrogation room in Manhattan. There, Turrou would interview him in the presence of just one other FBI special agent – Turrou wanted no more leaks. So Rumrich suffered questioning in claustrophobic conditions, cut off from the public and from sources of human support. The German authorities made no attempt to extricate him from his situation, leading him to believe he had been abandoned, a circumstance that encouraged him to talk in order to procure a deal from the Americans.[10]

The room in which Turrou questioned his suspect was on the sixth floor of the United States Court House on Foley Square, Manhattan. Only one door gave entry into the 20 sq ft chamber. Yellow walls surrounded a floor covered with red linoleum, alleviated by a grey rug. A row of chairs along one wall gave Turrou's colleague a choice of viewing angles. A flat-topped desk at the other end of the room accommodated a chair for the interrogator and opposite, slightly to one side, was a large and comfortable chair designed to make the suspect feel at ease. A few moments after Rumrich entered the yellow room for the first time, Turrou motioned to him to sit down and rang for coffee, sandwiches and cigarettes. While Rumrich was still standing, he ran his eye over him and formed an impression of his character.

The detective saw a man of 5ft 11in with a military bearing and high forehead. Pulling himself to his full height, the prisoner demanded to know why he was being dragged around from one place to another. His manner of speaking suggested to Turrou that he was proud to the point of weakness. He played on that and suggested to Rumrich that he was an intelligent man who had cleverly played the fool to keep the full story from the stupid NYPD detectives. He indicated that a conversation would now occur between equals. Revealing his credentials, he said he knew about the code words employed in the Crown letters, for example the use of the word 'furs' to indicate secret plans.[11]

Having played the pride card, Turrou deployed an empathy ace and arranged for Mrs Rumrich, now pregnant with the prisoner's second child – the future Robert Rumrich – to visit together with toddler Gerald. Though showing emotion towards his weeping wife in a patriarchal sort of way, Rumrich fobbed her off with the story that he was being questioned about a minor fraud back in the Midwest. Softened by Turrou's approach, Rumrich talked that same day and on into Sunday, 20 February, until 2 a.m. On Monday, 21 February, he signed a confession. Thereafter he continued to talk – and talk and talk. He lied and withheld information, but gradually a picture emerged about his life, his espionage activities and his accomplices.[12]

Rumrich's signed confession opened with his life story. He had been born in 1911 in Chicago, where his father Alphonse served as secretary of the Austro-Hungarian consulate general. His paternal grandfather had been mayor of the city of Turn, near the spa town Teplitz-Schoenau, in Bohemia. His maternal grandfather had an estate in the Hungarian township of Drávatamási and was a professor at the Royal Hungarian

University, Budapest. Rumrich boasted he was able to trace his Hungarian ancestry back 1,000 years, yet his exalted ancestry was also a source of low self-esteem, bred of high family expectations and indifferent achievement.[13]

The biographical portion of Rumrich's confession to the FBI charted a troubled life. In 1913 he and his younger sister Lillian had moved from Chicago to the German city of Bremen, where their father took up a new post. Upon the outbreak of war there were further family disruptions, for Alphonse served as an artillery officer in Russia, then moved to Italy and after that Budapest. Another upheaval in the life of the young family occurred in 1918 with the 'Chrysanthemum Revolution', the short-lived social democratic overthrow of the Austro–Hungarian Empire. They sought refuge in the newly formed republic of Czechoslovakia, settling in Teplitz-Schoenau and nearby Turn, where Guenther attended school but did less well than his younger brother Gustav, who went on to study chemistry at the University of Prague. In the meantime, Alphonse suffered a business failure and had to fall back on his relatively modest imperial consular pension. In more peaceful times, the brothers Rumrich would have benefited from the rich cultural tapestry of Central European life. As things stood, they were casualties of war, revolution and imperial collapse. Gustav became a fascist. Guenther found himself adrift in a sea of uncertain identities.

Aware that he qualified for United States citizenship on account of his Chicago birth, Guenther Rumrich went through the necessary procedure and sailed for New York in 1929. Reaching the required age of 18, he joined the US Army. An Associated Press journalist observed that 'although he had gained a brilliant technical education during his student days in Germany, he enlisted as a $30-a-month roughboy in the Medical Corps'.[14] Within a few months he was in debt and went absent without leave (AWOL). After being court-martialled he served a prison sentence, then resumed his military career and rose to the rank of sergeant, spending some time serving on Governor's Island where he would later be held in custody. He moved west with the Army and, in November 1935, he married a girl from Missoula, Montana.

At 16, Guiri Blomquist was almost nine years his junior. Rumrich's insecurity meant that he could only have married an innocent. Possibly in the knowledge that she was already pregnant, her parents approved of her marriage to the Army sergeant. Rumrich now took to drinking heavily and got into debt. He told the FBI that at this point there occurred 'some irregularities with the hospital fund, which I administered'. On 3 January 1936 he again went AWOL. He went to New York City, where he worked as a dishwasher and then as a German teacher at the Berlitz School of Languages, before finding a job as a translator with the Denver Chemical Manufacturing Company at a salary of $22.50 per week. He sent for his wife and their baby, Gerald, who had in the meantime been born, on 22 June 1936, back in Missoula. He borrowed money to buy furniture and settled with his young family in the Bronx.[15]

It was in January 1936, while still washing dishes, that Rumrich made his fateful move. He wrote to the official Nazi organ in Germany, *Völkischer Beobachter*, enclosing a letter to be forwarded to Colonel Walter Nicolai and offering to serve as a spy. Rumrich knew of Nicolai because he had read the colonel's memoir about his activities with German military intelligence in the First World War. The prospective spy asked to be contacted under the name Theodore Koerner through a notice in the advertisement columns of the *New York Times*. That notice duly appeared on page 3 on each of the days between 6 and 10 April 1936: 'THEODORE KERNER – letter received, please send reply and address to Sanders, Hamburg 1, Postbox 629, Germany'. The FBI later ascertained that the letter commissioning the ad was written on the stationery of the North German Lloyd shipping company.[16]

Once Rumrich had supplied his address, Nicolai's successors sent him a letter 'in which a great deal was said about patriotism and in which stress was made of the fact that Germany was very glad to be in a position to be helped by foreigners who recognised the injustice being done to Germany'.[17] The Abwehr continued, for a while, to receive Rumrich's communications through the 'Sanders' P.O. Box 629 in Hamburg and soon sent him $40 for information about artillery units in the Panama Canal Zone, where its newly recruited agent had spent time with the Army. Late in 1937, the Abwehr instructed Rumrich to communicate in the English language using the name Crown and to write via an intermediary in the UK. The address of his new 'letter box' was Mrs Jessie Jordan, 1 Kinloch Street, Dundee, Scotland.

Why did Guenther Rumrich spy for Germany against the land of his birth? It was not because of a pressing invitation or threats by the Gestapo. Unlike Jessie Jordan, he was a volunteer. Money was a factor, but there was more to it than that. A woman who knew him in later years observed, 'He always tried to be a "big shot".'[18] Guenther Rumrich was the self-doubting product of an insecure upbringing who desperately wanted to take on a mission that increased his sense of worth and self-importance. Like other spies, he was capable of 'splitting' and living two parallel lives, a reflection of his background in ethnically divided Czechoslovakia, reinforced by a life split between two continents.[19]

In the course of interrogation, Rumrich divulged some information on how the Nazi spy ring operated. For example, he explained how he would receive one half of a torn postcard, to be reconciled as a means of identification with the other half when borne by one of his fellow agents. He did not, however, reveal many names. Rumrich was a minor cog in a greater machine and knew less than his more senior colleagues. Furthermore, as he explained to Turrou, Germany's spies in America were kept in ignorance of one another –

standard practice in a professional intelligence organisation. This policy of compartmentalisation meant that if any agent were captured, he or she would be able to reveal only limited details to interrogators.[20]

Rumrich achieved the fame that he craved. The covert network that embraced him came to be widely known as the 'Rumrich spy ring'. The FBI's case files almost without exception are headed 'Rumrich', reflecting the fact that he was the first to be exposed. Turrou's report of 27 February 1938 based on his questioning of Rumrich came to be the template for most of the later FBI reports on the spy case and agents continued to head their memoranda 'Rumrich' long after the investigation had widened to take in more important spies. It was not just a matter of filing convenience. The more accurate title 'Nazi spy ring' was too strong a label when America's leaders were shying away from a confrontation with Hitler's Germany.

Guenther Rumrich's spying activities were limited and ineffective. In a first phase, ranging from the summer of 1936 to the end of 1937, the Abwehr tested his reliability. After sending information on Panama in June–July 1936, he sent further data on troop dispositions and other military matters that he obtained from open Army and Navy sources and from newspapers. The intelligence was, as he later pleaded in an attempt to minimise his offence, 'available to anyone'.[21]

Trusting him a little more, in a second phase the Abwehr provided him with what were meant to be the more secure addresses, a new address in Hamburg as well as Jessie Jordan's. From November 1937, it paid him a monthly retainer of $30.

In December, Karl Schlueter contacted Rumrich. Schlueter was a long-serving German spy. It was he who had been the intended recipient of Lonkowski's ill-fated parcel on board the SS *Europa* in September 1935. More recently, Schlueter was the Abwehr's replacement for Karl Eitel, who had lost his post on the SS *Bremen* because of embezzlement. Schlueter asked Rumrich to find out about the latest US aircraft carrier designs. It was he who then asked for passport application forms, explaining that the Abwehr wanted US passports to give false identities to German secret agents who would pose as American sailors when attempting to penetrate the Soviet Union.[22] A further agent, code-named Ruth, would be in touch to arrange for the collection of the passport forms and the fee for this job would be $300.

On 1 January 1938, a certain N. Spielman sent Rumrich advice on how to be a spy. In a letter sent from Bordeaux, Spielman wrote in the guise of a businessman and issued various cautions about tradecraft. There were words of encouragement: 'I believe that in time you will get acquainted with European business procedure.' There were instructions on discretion followed by the injunction: 'If you wish to become a good merchant you must pay heed to these little things and hints.' Spielman's representative Jenni would soon be in touch about the price of 'furs'.[23]

An agent improbably called 'Schmidt' now got in touch. The FBI never ascertained his first name and evidence not available to the FBI at the time indicates that 'Schmidt' was an alias used by Schlueter.[24] It was Schmidt who requested the east coast defence plans and outlined the McAlpin Hotel kidnap scheme as a means of obtaining them. The Abwehr now began to pressure Rumrich, threatening to cut his funds if he did not produce results. It gave him further tasks, finding out about an Army effort to synchronise anti-aircraft fire with searchlights and stealing heat-detection technology that would help identify incoming aircraft. To pacify his employers, Rumrich used a false identity to obtain figures on venereal disease in the armed forces – figures that incidentally revealed how many troops there were and where they were stationed.

To help him with his tasks, Rumrich recruited a further agent, Erich Glaser. Turrou described Glaser as 'a strapping six-footer of about twenty-nine, rather handsome, with dark brown hair and dark, stupid eyes'. A native of Leipzig in Germany, Glaser had served in the US Army in Panama, where he first met Rumrich. He was in awe of his fellow soldier, whom he admiringly described as 'an intelligent young man with a good education and background'.[25] When Glaser left the Army, his former comrade invited him to New York and in January 1938 he moved in with the Rumrichs living rent-free. At Rumrich's request he re-enlisted – with the US Army Air Corps at Mitchel Field in Long Island. He stole some minor codes and plans and delivered them to the Abwehr via Rumrich. He agreed to help with the kidnap and passport plots.

In his confession, Rumrich supplied the sought-after details of the 'Schmidt' McAlpin plot. The honeytrap element of the plan fell through at an early stage – in Turrou's words, Colonel Eglin 'was not the type of man who could be lured to a hotel room by a woman'. It fell to Rumrich to impersonate the Adjutant to General Craig and make the phone call to summon Colonel Eglin. Glaser would book the room to which the unsuspecting victim would be led and would hide in a closet ready to leap out and help overpower the Army officer. 'Schmidt' would assume his position on a window ledge, his pen-syringe at the ready. Once the deed was done, the three-man crew would exit the scene with the sought-after plans, leaving behind the crumpled body of Colonel Eglin, together with a copy of the *Daily Worker* to indicate that the communists were to blame.[26]

Turrou described Rumrich as 'a minor figure in this vast spy plot' and as a 'sap' hung out to dry by unscrupulous Nazi agents who creamed off the money due to him. He insisted that there existed a 'Nazi' espionage operation that was far more sinister than the limited manoeuvres of a lowly pawn.[27] It was indeed true that, except for the McAlpin Hotel coastal defences plot, Rumrich posed no real threat to the United States. Even the McAlpin plot would come to nothing. The British tip-off that risked exposing the secrets of MI5 turned out to have been unnecessary, for the Abwehr never authorised the scheme.

Turrou was right, then, to dismiss Rumrich as a minor character. Yet Rumrich/Crown still had real significance. For Rumrich's confession led to further arrests and revelations – beginning with the unintended apprehension of a red-headed beautician.

Tales of Hofmann

Another ship, another German spy. The *Europa* was due to berth at Pier 86, Hudson River, on Thursday, 24 February 1938, and Rumrich had said that the Abwehr's Karl Schlueter would be on it. Turrou decided to intercept the steamer before it docked. He requisitioned a Coast Guard cutter and waited. At last, the great ocean liner approached its destination. Entering the world's busiest port, it slowly manoeuvred into Quarantine, at which point Turrou and two colleagues drew alongside. They clambered aboard. By prior arrangement with the authorities, they represented themselves as immigration officers.

When the FBI men examined the ship's passenger list, they seemed to be out of luck. There was no passenger named Schlueter, nor was there any sign of another person Rumrich had told them to expect, 'Jenni Hofmann, flirtatious *aide* to the wily Schlueter'. Turrou now wondered whether the spies were disguising themselves as crew members. He inspected the ship's manifest and the words leapt out at him: 'Karl Schluter ... steward' ('Schlueter' was variously spelled Schluter and Schlüter). The detective's elation was short-lived, for there was a line through the name and alongside was the handwritten note, 'Did not sail.' Schlueter had been due to depart with the ship from Bremerhaven, but heard about the FBI probe in America and disembarked before the vessel put to sea – according to Turrou, the Abwehr put him on a battleship for his own protection.

Deflated at first, Turrou continued to inspect the ship's manifest, this time in search of crew members, and now he found his reward, the entry 'Johanna Hofmann … hairdresser'. Turrou and his fellow special agents decided not to rush in and make an immediate arrest, but to ascertain what Hofmann looked like and then to follow her. By arranging a parade for the inspection of boarding passes, the detectives were able to obtain a visual sighting of each member of the ship's crew. And there she was. Turrou was either greatly taken by Hofmann's appearance or decided to dwell on it to give greater impact to his later account of the event. He would write about how she stood, in her trim white uniform, 'an attractive girl, poised and sure of herself, but with a carriage and glance which revealed, even in these impersonal circumstances, that she was quite sensitive to, and aware of, men'. Hofmann was 5ft 6in tall, with a mass of wavy, auburn hair, a trim figure, fair skin, deep-blue eyes and wore dress sizes 14 and 16.

Turrou already had a man posted on the dock and, once the hulking vessel had nudged its way to its allotted berth and tied up at around 5 p.m., he and his colleagues joined him. Together they watched the human cargo from a dictatorship disgorge itself into the Land of the Free. They waited in the hope that Hofmann would lead them to other German agents. At 7 p.m. she disembarked, wearing just a light coat against the winter evening's chill. She walked a few paces towards the steps at the end of the pier and stared beyond. A frown appeared on her face. Her anticipated lover or spy, or 'combination of both', had not appeared. She made as if to return on board.[1]

Turrou with two other agents approached her. The FBI's crack detective asked her if she knew Schlueter and Rumrich.

She denied all knowledge of them. The agents arrested her and took her to the United States Court House in Foley Square. According to Hofmann in a statement she made at her later criminal trial, Turrou at this stage told her that 'if I would sign for him a direction to the first officer of the S.S. *Europa* to deliver to him, Turrou, certain articles, namely a brown suitcase and a light-brown leather handbag, I would be allowed to depart for Germany upon the sailing of the S.S. *Europa* the following night'.[2]

Equipped with his note, Turrou boarded the *Europa* and in company with the ship's captain Heinrich Lorenz visited what he recalled was Jenni's cabin on D deck (according to Jenni, it was Cabin 67, A deck). It later emerged that Lorenz had cooperated with the Abwehr and had helped the German secret service establish its original links with Rumrich. He must have been filled with trepidation when the FBI man boarded his ship and made his request. There was, however, another side to this story.

Though penetrated and controlled by the Nazis, the German shipping lines did retain traces of their original pedigrees – the person who had built the Hamburg America line into the world's largest shipping enterprise had been, after all, a self-made *Jewish* businessman, Albert Ballin.[3] Bullied as they were by the Nazis, senior officers serving on the North Atlantic run were in some cases lukewarm if not antagonistic towards Hitler and Turrou was able to build friendly relations with a few of them. In her autobiography of 2017, Captain Lorenz's daughter Marita painted a sympathetic portrait of her father. While he liked to wear a sword on ceremonial occasions, he was not a militaristic expansionist. He was married to an American of distinctly anti-Nazi inclination – born Alice June Lofland, Mrs Lorenz had acted on Broadway under the stage name June Paget and both she and her daughter would later spend time in a Nazi concentration camp (Alice was held on suspicion of spying for the United States).

Marita maintained that in 1938 her father was apolitical but anti-Hitler. She furthermore claimed that he became a double agent acting for Turrou and the FBI and that this was the reason that he was allowed to continue to sail after being interrogated in New York. In the interest of balance, it should be noted that Marita had a traumatic and colourful life that potentially affected her judgment. An American Army sergeant raped her when she was just 7 years old. She later fell in love with Fidel Castro. She claimed that the CIA recruited her when she was Fidel's mistress and that she declined the agency's commission to poison the Cuban dictator. Marita's recollections may have been tinged with melodrama and her memories of her father's politics are second-hand for she was not born until 1939, the year after the Nazi spy scandal. However, she was very close to her father and when she wrote about his views it is reasonable to suppose that her voice is that of Heinrich Lorenz.[4]

Back to our story. Turrou found a brown leather bag under Jenni's bunk and, in the left-hand drawer of her bureau, a key to fit it. He decided not to open it there and then, but to maximise the psychological effect by doing so in Jenni Hofmann's presence. Returning to his office and finding her in the same chair where he had left her, he got her to confirm that the bag was hers and then opened it. It contained $70 and a package. As he opened the package, Jenni gave him a 'Mona Lisa look'. It contained letters, all in code. She said she had no idea how to decode them. Just as she uttered that disclaimer, Turrou's colleague discovered in a recess of the leather bag a scrap of paper with the key to the code. Jenni later said she was supposed to have learnt the code by heart and then destroyed the paper on which it was written, but had neglected to do so. It was not the finest moment in the history of the German secret service.

The letters in Jenni's package were all from Schlueter and they gave Turrou some new names. One letter, addressed to a 'Miss Moog', explained that Schlueter was 'on vacation' and

that Jenni was standing in for him. It indicated a premedi-
tated decision to send the expendable Jenni to meet her fate
in lieu of Schlueter, her treacherous lover. Another letter was
for Rumrich, saying the $70 was for him, that $1,000 would
be forthcoming for the aircraft carrier plans, giving various
instructions and asking for a progress report. Further missives
of a more cryptic nature were addressed to Martin Schade and
Dr Ignatz Theodor Griebl, both of New York City. These were
names for the FBI to investigate.

Turrou prided himself on his interview technique. He
prized from Jenni the secret of an unhappy love affair she
had had when very young. She was sensitive on the subject
of unhappy romances, as her younger sister had killed herself
when jilted by a German naval officer. Turrou tried to take
advantage of her emotional state, but at first it did not work.
Claiming to be an unwitting courier, Jenni denied knowing
about the contents of the letters. She also repeated her claim
to be ignorant about Rumrich. Turrou now tried one of his
trademark tricks. After one of her more vehement professions
of ignorance, Turrou signalled to an agent standing at the back
of the interview room, near the door. Following his gaze, Jenni
turned to look at the door. As the door opened, she heard
Rumrich's voice saying 'hello Jenni', then the man himself
walked in. Jenni screamed and went sheet-white.

Although Jenni later retracted the confession she made on
25 February, it was useful to the FBI investigation at the time.
It was a succinct admission of the role she had played. The
next day, Rumrich, Glaser and Hofmann appeared in court
and were charged under the terms of the Espionage Act. Bail
in each case was set at $25,000 and as none of the defendants
were able to pay this amount they were all remanded in custody pending the convening of a Federal Grand Jury.[5]

It was now clear to a widening circle of officials and
journalists, and indeed the general public, that the German
spy ring extended beyond Rumrich and his immediate

accomplices. German officials began to panic. Dr Richard Bottler had just arrived in New York to be counsellor at the German Consulate General Office. Turrou described him as 'a pompous, officious man with red cheeks', adding that he was 'typically Nazi'. Immediately after Jenni's arrest, the consulate had received a report on the event from Captain William Drechsel, who was in overall charge at the German shipping line piers. Reacting to the report, Bottler took on the task of damage limitation.

The FBI allowed Bottler to visit Jenni on condition that Turrou would be present. Not realising that Turrou spoke German, the counsellor raged at Jenni for revealing too much in her confession and told her to divulge nothing more. Calming down, he arranged for Jenni to receive a weekly stipend to allow her to buy what she needed and supplement the prison's dietary rations. She would also have legal representation in court. Not long after Bottler's visit, George C. Dix took on the task of being Jenni's defence counsel. Dix's relationship with Turrou would be, as the detective put it with rare understatement, 'personal'.[6]

Higher up the diplomatic chain, there was a reaction from the German Embassy in Washington the day after Jenni's arrest. Ambassador Hans H. Dieckhoff's secretary, Baron von Ginan, was in New York at the time. He arranged to meet Captain Drechsel and told him that the ambassador was acutely worried about the spate of publicity that had followed the Pier 86 arrest. Drechsel replied that the New York executive officers of the Hamburg America Line and North German Lloyd shared the embassy's concern about the impact of the case on German–American relations and were worried about the potential loss of business by their companies. This last point was a serious one. By 1938, French and British ships had taken the Blue Riband for fastest Atlantic crossings and commercial competition was intensifying just when passengers were finding the on-board atmosphere on German ships to be distasteful. A high-profile spy scandal was the last thing the German ships needed.[7]

Drechsel, like Lorenz, was a man in a quandary. He was 58 years old, was about to receive his pension, wanted to settle in the United States and was expecting his naturalisation papers to arrive soon. He was afraid that the German authorities would cancel his pension rights if he did not cooperate with fascist designs. He confided these concerns to Turrou. He enlightened the investigator about the nature of the Nazi grip on German shipping lines. He explained how the Berlin government dictated who should be given jobs on German ships and designated a member of the National Socialist Party to be the political officer on each ship, stipulating that he should be superior in authority to the ship's captain. Drechsel had been subjected to all kinds of intimidation and threats and had been forced to expedite the work of William Herrmann, who was in charge of the Gestapo in New York. He worried about the future of his company and made the rather unlikely claim that he was going to lobby his company's bosses back home to limit any reputational damage by refusing to facilitate Nazi spy operations.[8]

The Germans were right to worry about the arrests' repercussions. The day after Jenni's detention, J. Edgar Hoover issued a press release. He said he had 'unearthed' a 'widespread plot' and promised further arrests. The nation's journalists wrote stories that sparked international coverage. An informed account of the affair appeared in London's *Daily Mirror*, which claimed, 'G-man Hoover and his lieutenants have now turned their backs on crime investigation to search for more alleged spies who have gravely jeopardised America's safety.' The *Mirror* reported that a top-level emergency meeting of Army officers was addressing the security issue. The paper hinted at sympathy for the 'red-haired German girl' who now languished in solitary confinement, where she received no friends and no messages. Back in America, *Time* was distinctly less sympathetic towards 'spy Hofmann, who spoke no English and

whose orange-colored hair showed traces of dye'. The magazine reported that 'plump' Jenni had been part of the plan to
'lure' Colonel Eglin to the McAlpin hotel.[9]

Actually Jenni Hofmann was more victim than seductress
and was, like Rumrich, a minor cog in the Nazi spy ring. But
her story did throw further light on the workings of that ring.
Born in Dresden in 1911, she was the middle of five siblings.
She attended a local trade school, where she learned the art
of hairdressing. Unlike Rumrich, she seems to have had no
bad habits and the FBI found in her history no evidence of
a criminal record. Yet she was adventurous as well as passion-
ate, and left her inland city for a life on the high seas, joining
the North German Lloyd Line in 1931 and then again, after a
lengthy spell back home, in 1936.

Jenni first met Schlueter on a Far Eastern voyage on the SS
Gneisenau and later sailed with him on the *Europa*. She had
the potential to be a useful courier, but there was more to
it than that. With Jenni, Schlueter talked of getting a divorce.
No doubt he engaged in similar discourse with the tall young
blonde from Queens whom he also dated.[10] Jenni was at first
attracted to him. The Abwehr operative was of similar height
to Jenni and a few years older, with a son in the Hitler Youth
and a long scar across the top of his head made more visible by
his closely cropped hair. Possibly she was more drawn to him
ideologically than physically – historians write of the appeal
of Nazism for some women who were drawn to an image of
an idyllic German past, now under threat from a toxic mix of
industrialisation and communism.[11]

Schlueter's lifestyle helped to reel Jenni in. He took her to a
Japanese restaurant near Times Square and promised her a date
at the cabaret. Once she was roped into his schemes, there was
no turning back. When he wanted her to undertake a more
risky enterprise and she suffered from cold feet, he turned
nasty. He told her that if she did not cooperate, her father's
pension would be at risk.[12]

Although the American press told lurid tales of how Germany's redhead had assisted in the nefarious Nazi plot, Jenni's activities had been mostly mundane. She had promised Schlueter she would carry letters and he undertook to enroll her as 'a member of the German Military Intelligence'. In company with Schlueter at first, she delivered missives to German spies in New York, including Ignatz Griebl, Martin Schade, Kate Moog and Guenther Rumrich. On one occasion, she played with Rumrich's little boy and listened to the men discussing a number of espionage plans and objectives – from such overheard conversations, she was able to give the FBI some additional leads. She played her espionage game under supervision until that fateful day when Schlueter told her he was taking a vacation and she would have to courier alone.[13]

Perhaps wishing to inflate the importance of every arrest he made, Leon Turrou argued that Jenni was much more than courier. He referred to letters she received from the 'mysterious spy chief in Bremen' who signed himself 'N. Spielman' and who referred to Jenni as 'my agent' in a manner that indicated implicit trust and the fact that 'Jennie was far from a blind dupe'. Making his claim for Jenni's importance, Turrou noted that she 'was entrusted with the task of looking over and signing up a Nazi spy in Czechoslovakia while Hitler was "softening up" that country for conquest'.[14]

The spy in question was Gustav Rumrich, our chemistry student at the prestigious German University in Prague. On 20 December 1937, Gustav wrote to his brother in New York, saying he needed money and was looking for a job. He was thinking of signing up to fight for the fascists in the Spanish Civil War. Guenther said no. Though it is unlikely that he knew that Admiral Canaris was flooding the Sudetenland with secret agents, he told his brother he should instead spy for Germany in Prague. He should mail a typewritten letter addressed to Jessie Jordan at 1, Kinloch Street, Dundee, opening with the words 'very esteemed Mr S. [i.e. Sanders]' and giving his particulars. Guenther enlisted the support of Schlueter and Hofmann, and equipped them with photographs of Gustav.

In January Guenther wrote to Hamburg via Jessie Jordan saying to expect his brother to be in touch, and Gustav duly wrote to the same address on the 24th. Guenther explained there was some urgency to his request as he was due to be conscripted into the Czech Army later in the year. MI5, of course, intercepted and read the letters.

On 15 February (the very day of Guenther's arrest in New York), Schlueter and Hofmann visited Gustav in Prague. They represented themselves as Mr and Mrs Schlueter and as good friends of Guenther, and agreed to meet the next day at the Hotel de Saxe in Teplitz (now Teplice) near the German border. At the hotel, Schlueter checked in showing a German passport that indicated he was born in Bremerhaven in 1905 and gave his profession as businessman.

At the de Saxe on the 16th, the pseudo-married couple gave Gustav a letter from his brother advising him to be 'sensible'. Jenni and her 'husband' then confessed they were fellow agents and not a married couple, and proceeded to brief their new recruit. Gustav would receive expenses and payment for his spying services. Jenni would be his minder and paymaster, but he would receive written instructions from the Irish capital, Dublin. Though he had been writing to Dundee, he would in future communicate with the Irish poste restante, Mrs G. Brandy of 14 Willow Terrace, Dublin. He was to pose as a philatelist, so that instructions could be sent to him concealed in stamp collections. Schlueter gave him a cipher on a small piece of paper concealed in a cigarette.

Gustav was soon arrested on suspicion of espionage and the Czech police found the cipher when they raided his house. In his confession to them, Gustav Rumrich explained his mission. In the words of an MI5 translation, he was to obtain 'information regarding the Czech Communist Party and the relationship between Czechoslovakia and the USSR'. Hofmann confirmed that the recruiting duo persuaded Gustav to join the Communist Party in Czechoslovakia. Undoubtedly, the Abwehr had an anti-communist mission. However, the mission description was also designed to please, for the Americans, the British and the Czech government were all opposed to communism. Moreover, Gustav admitted to being tasked in a further way: 'If found suitable, it was proposed to use him for military espionage against Czechoslovakia.' As Turrou noted, he was one more weapon in Hitler's annexation armoury.[15]

Turrou depicted Jenni Hofmann as a dangerous spy. Potentially, perhaps she was. In the event, the efforts of the British and American counter-intelligence services stopped her in her tracks. For this reason, she was less important for what she did than for the consequences of being caught and of telling what she knew. She was an asset to the FBI in that she revealed more about Germany's spies and about the workings of the ship-borne courier system. Her arrest and those of Rumrich and Glaser were steps towards the exposure of the wider Nazi spy ring.

However, because the American press was onto the story, the arrests and ensuing confessions were also problematic. As we shall see in the next chapter, this was acutely so for British.

Avoiding an Edinburgh Trial

The arrests in America presented the British authorities with a dilemma – what to do with Jessie Jordan? Three factors had hitherto dictated that they should do precisely nothing. One was to do with tradecraft. Barring an imminent threat to national security, it was so much better to follow a spy suspect around and find out what she was up to, without alerting the Abwehr to the extent of MI5's knowledge about its operations. The second factor promoting nil action was the perceived advantage of not giving offence to Hitler's Germany. A third factor, at least according to one contemporary newspaper, was the desire to give Leon Turrou time to do his job, without creating publicity that would alert the Abwehr to too many clues.[1] The overall challenge was, then, how to avoid a sensational trial of Jessie Jordan in Scotland.

The arrests of Rumrich, Glaser and Hofmann and their New York court appearance on 26 February meant that MI5's knowledge of Jessie Jordan's activities could no longer be completely concealed. There was indeed a distinct possibility, as later events would confirm, that Jessie Jordan would be required to testify in upcoming US espionage trials. The possibility sharpened MI5's dilemma. For while the Anglo-American special intelligence relationship was important, it was also subject to limitations: Jessie was MI5's intelligence responsibility, and not to be trusted to the vagaries of the American court system. All this pointed in one direction: the British would have to arrest the Dundee hairdresser to keep her away from the American justice system, but an open trial was at all costs to be avoided and the traitor would have to be silenced.

Responsibility for the hush-up fell to Colonel Hinchley Cooke, whom MI5 dispatched to Dundee in time for the arrest. Cooke had overseen Jessie's surveillance and had already made several trips to Edinburgh. He was an experienced officer – in the First World War he had questioned German women who passed through British ports, sometimes passing himself off as a German, and operated with sufficient effectiveness to be awarded the OBE while still in his twenties.[2]

Cooke travelled to Scotland to take care of the fallout from the American revelations. City of Dundee Chief Constable Joseph Neilans prepared the ground by obtaining search warrants for Jessie's business premises at 1 Kinloch Street, as well as for her half-brother Frank Haddow's house at 26 Strathmore Avenue, Coupar Angus, Perthshire, the home of Haddow's daughter Patricia, who worked at Jessie's shop. On the morning of 2 March, two police cars bore Cooke, Neilans, Detective Inspector Thomas Nicholson and Policewoman Annie Ross to Kinloch Street. Their guide was Detective Lieutenant John Carstairs, who had started a dossier on the Jordan case back in November 1937.

At the street corner, the approaching officers saw a double-fronted salon, one window of which was painted over with black lacquer, while the other promoted beauty products. A sign above the shop announced 'J. Jordan, Hair Specialist'. The five-strong raiding party entered the salon, finding Jessie, whom they detained, and 14-year-old Patricia. The police searched for evidence. They dug up the drains, raised the floorboards and inspected Jessie's former apartment at 23 Stirling

Street. The evidence they found, however, lay unconcealed, in a cubicle-cum-bedroom, off the beauty salon, where Jessie was currently spending her nights.[3]

According to one version of events, the cubicle contained a see-through bag containing airmail letters. In his report on the raid, Joe Neilans made no mention of these – from the outset, the American dimension of the case received discreet handling. The police officers did record their discovery of Jessie's passport, her military sketches, a road map of Scotland, Admiralty handbooks and Ordnance Survey maps of areas of possible strategic interest. MI5 and the police were intent on uncovering evidence to confirm what was in fact easy to prove, that Jessie had personally spied on the British defence establishment.[4]

At noon, the officers placed Jessie under detention in the policewomen's section of their Dundee headquarters. They then departed to inspect the residences of two of her half-brothers. Before proceeding to Frank and Patricia's home in Coupar Angus, where a number of their colleagues had already assembled, they had another call to make. They visited William Haddow's establishment at 16 Breadalbane Terrace, Perth, where Jessie's daughter Marga Wobrock was housekeeping and child minding. By the time they arrived at 1.25 p.m., local police were in occupation there, too.

The Breadalbane Terrace raid was the lead story on the front page of the *Daily Express*. Though Jessie was the spy, she received only a small, separate paragraph. The main spread was about her photogenic daughter. Marga told the paper's staff reporter, 'Two men and a policewoman came to my flat. The policewoman took me into the bedroom while the men went through all drawers and cabinets and examined all my papers. The woman searched the bedroom, looked into the pockets of my clothes – even the pockets of the dressing gown I was wearing. I had just come out of the bath.' Neilans reported that his men found no additional evidence in either Perth or Coupar Angus.

The *Express*'s reporting was sympathetic. There was a head-and-shoulder photograph of Marga suggesting a woman of beauty and sensitivity, with mention of her singing career and a heart-tugging reference to her little girl. All this reflected the fact that the proprietor of the *Express*, Lord Beaverbrook, was a supporter of Prime Minister Neville Chamberlain's determination not to provoke Hitler. It was the editor of the *Express*, Arthur Christiansen, who later in the year authorised the infamous headline, 'There will be no war'. With its unrivalled circulation running into the millions, the *Express* helped to shape public opinion. But it also reflected British opinion, which had not yet turned decisively against Nazi Germany.[5]

The next day, while crowds gaped at the suddenly infamous salon at 1 Kinloch Street, Jessie Jordan made a one-minute appearance in court, during which she was charged with offences under the Official Secrets Act. Facing blanket secrecy, the *Courier* reporter on court duty had little to go on, so simply recorded that she was 'attired in a smart black coat with fur collar and a little green hat adorned with a feather', and that she looked 'pale and anxious'.[6] A few days later, Jessie made a further, four-minute court appearance in a sealed-off courtroom. As a backstop, she was further indicted under a 1920 law for having failed to register with the Post Office as a forwarder of mail. At the same hearing, her solicitor John R. Bond successfully pleaded for her to be kept not in Perth but in Dundee, where her defence could be better prepared.[7]

The day after her first court appearance, Jessie went on a journey. That morning, she left Dundee Police Station in a large car. It rolled on to the Firth of Tay ferry (there was no bridge in those days), and, once across the mile-wide Tay estuary, began to traverse the County of Fife. The police car wound its way through the sodden fields and green hills of an ending winter. It growled through sullen mining villages ravaged by the unemployment of the Great Depression.

The driver headed for another great sea inlet, the Firth of Forth. From that firth's northern shore, Fifers could gaze across the water at Scotland's capital city, Edinburgh, shimmering in power and rectitude in the rays of the low-slung southerly sun.

Jessie was one of six occupants of the vehicle. The driver was a police sergeant. Next to him in the front seat left was the knowledgeable Detective Lieutenant John Carstairs. Immediately behind Carstairs and the driver were two backwards-facing folding seats. On the left-hand folding seat sat policewoman Annie Ross. Next to Annie, Jessie occupied the right-hand folding seat. On the left at the back seat of the car was Chief Constable Joe Neilans. Although the senior police officer in the car, he on this occasion occupied little more than a ceremonial role.[8]

For sitting at the right rear, directly facing the woman he was questioning, was the man who had travelled up from London, Lieut Col William Edward Hinchley Cooke. The son of a British father and German mother, Cooke retained a hint of a German accent when speaking English. Contemporary photographs reveal him as a portly man squinting at life through a pair of heavy glasses. This was not good enough for the spy-crazy press corps. Cooke impressed a journalist from the *Evening Standard* as a 'tall, middle-aged Englishman' of 'benevolent' appearance with 'twinkling eyes' who had 'the knack of turning up in odd places during interesting political and semi-political events'. He worked for 'the mysterious MI5', an organisation based in a nondescript London house 'I am not allowed to say where' (actually the top floor of Thames House, Millbank, SW1).[9] A local Dundee newspaperman thought Cooke 'looks as though he might treat spies on the "Hardly cricket, my dear fellow" principle.'[10] More recently, MI5 historian Nigel West described 'Cookie' as a 'sweetie'.[11]

Col Cooke worried that Jessie might become famous. Starved of more substantial information, the national and local press had so far commented only on her appearance. The *Empire News* was a popular Sunday paper that did not like traitors and accordingly had her down as a '51-year-old ash blonde' who on the occasion of her court appearance donned the same 'shabby, old-fashioned plumed hat' she had been seen wearing at the time of her arrest.[12] Dundee's *Courier* stood up for its local lass, its 'small and full-figured blonde'. Whether the pressmen were pro or con, they would be sure to demand more and preferably sensational details. The MI5 plan was to suppress the story.[13]

The driver of the Dundee police car followed a route based on the cross-marked map found in Jessie's premises. What went through her mind with all this evidence against her? She does not appear to have been affected by a confessional urge. Perhaps her interrogators might believe one of her two stories, that she was settling an argument with a Hamburg friend about the state of Scottish coastal defences and that she had been sending the men in Hamburg merely corroboration of what they already knew. At the same time, she entertained the hope that her cooperation would result in leniency.

Cooke knew that he was pushing on an open door. He engaged in no bullying. He did not call upon the Dundee police to be the hard men to his Mr Nice Guy. The more gentle approach reflected Cooke's personality, his experience as a long-serving officer and his appraisal of the situation. It still made for a bizarre scene; a traitor who was willing to talk and a questioner with a keen interest in the truth but a matching hope that he could conceal the truth from the wider world.

As the car wound its way south, Jessie turned over recent events in her mind. What would happen to Marga now, she wondered, and to the little granddaughter who bore her own name, Jessie? And how had she been caught out? She had no idea that MI5 had kept her under surveillance for months on end. Perhaps she wondered about the 'postie' (postman) who had alerted the Dundee police to her strange correspondence. Her suspicions must have fallen on false friends, such as John Curran and his wife, who had taken such a close interest in her affairs.

Cooke's mind focused in the meantime on the task of detailing the evidence of Jessie Jordan's guilt in terms of her personal espionage, as distinct from her facilitation of the Crown correspondence. He was interested in questions as well as answers. To know what questions the Abwehr was asking was to gain an insight into what the Abwehr knew. So in spite of being already in possession of overwhelming evidence, Cooke continued to probe for further information, exhibiting in the meantime a disarming and confidence-building curiosity about Jessie's background and feelings.

As he faced his travelling companion, Cooke found himself sympathising with a person whose life had been a catalogue of misfortune, a woman who, in spite of her proactive personality, had been as much a victim of the Nazis as their servant. Being half-German himself, he knew what prejudices one could encounter in the UK.

As the police car visited locations along the Forth coastline, Jessie identified the places she had spied on. At Crombie, just beyond Rosyth, she had illegally photographed the Admiralty Pier at the Royal Naval Armament Depot.[14] Cooke asked her why she had written '3 Castels' against Fife Ness, and concluded that she had mistaken some derelict aircraft hangars for fortresses.[15] Cooke summed up her spying as 'obviously the effort of a beginner'. Her data collection efforts were paltry.[16]

By the time the police limousine turned north to head back to Dundee, the conversation had become desultory, for Cooke had other things on his mind. How could the whole affair be hushed up? More than four decades were to pass before the British government even admitted the existence of MI5 and it was desirable to conceal details of its modus operandi and the extent of its knowledge of the Abwehr. Might it perhaps be possible, in spite of pending American court cases, to prosecute Jessie Jordan on the basis only of her own espionage and without reference to the Crown affair? It was a tall order, but the less the Abwehr knew about what MI5 knew the better. When the car finally returned to the Dundee Police Station after an absence the *Daily Herald*'s reporter described as 'mysterious', MI5's challenge was only just beginning.[17]

There were options available for tricking the Abwehr into believing that MI5 was less competent than it was. One was to point to accidental disclosure, such as the curious postman's discovery of letters from abroad arriving at 1 Kinloch Street. Another was the Zimmermann option. In 1917, the British had pretended that Americans discovered the Zimmermann telegram with its fateful contents. Now, in 1938, information appeared in the press suggesting that the FBI tipped off MI5 about the Nazi spy ring, not vice versa. Newspapers on both sides of the Atlantic reported that evidence unearthed by the FBI was helping the British to realise what German spies were up to in their own back yard, for example stealing the design secrets of revolving gun turrets under development at Parnall Aircraft in Tolworth, Surrey. The story placed the FBI in a good light, never a bad thing from J. Edgar Hoover's perspective, and potentially removed MI5 from dreaded scrutiny. If only the Americans could be seen as kissed with genius, MI5 could languish in obscurity.[18]

A couple of weeks after her arrest, Jessie Jordan released a little bombshell that threatened to unravel any such plans for blanket secrecy. She wrote a letter to the Secretary of State for Scotland from His Majesty's Prison, Perth, requesting permission to write her memoir. No doubt wishing to ensure his client's ability to pay his fee, her solicitor John Bond had arranged a publishing contract for her in spite of the fact that prison rules restricted the free speech rights of inmates. Bond entered a plea on behalf of Jessie that, as she was pleading not guilty, she should be considered in the meantime innocent and free to write. The opposed parties reached a compromise. Jessie undertook not to publish until after the trial: 'Mr Bond my Law Agent would take care of this artickle untill I am tryed.'[19]

Here was a conundrum that would foreshadow events in America: in a free country, can you gag those who want to tell their story on the ground that their freedom of speech would injure the public interest? It was a pressing matter from Jessie's viewpoint. She needed to fulfil her publishing contract in order to pay her lawyers. The governor of Perth Prison supported her case, saying there would be widespread interest in her story. He added that she was poorly educated and would be unlikely to use her opportunity to send out coded messages. However, he suggested that MI5 should approve the texts before they were sent out for publication. On 27 April her solicitors, saying the matter was now 'urgent' as the trial was imminent and they could not instruct counsel without promise of payment, agreed to honour an arrangement whereby 'the biography would be carefully scrutinised'. The Scottish *Sunday Mail* did in due course publish a sanitised version of Jessie Jordan's life story – it appeared in serialised format between 22 May and 19 June.[20]

The sanitisation of the memoir was just one aspect of the concealment effort. The British authorities still had to contend with the problem of publicity arising from legal proceedings. The Edinburgh High Court trial promised to be a drama. Mrs Curran relished the thought and is reputed to have bought a new dress for the occasion.[21]

MI5 had other ideas, and prevailed. Mrs Curran's first disappointment came when the authorities decided to try the case in camera. Just a hand-picked few, such as MI5's director Vernon Kell, were to be allowed into the public gallery, and certainly no newspaper sleuths or photographers. A heavy police presence would restrict access to the courtroom area, including the lobby, and admission to the proceedings would be strictly rationed.[22]

The Crown prepared a formidable case, with forty-two witnesses and a mound of evidence ready for the High Court trial. A portion of the effort came to naught when Jessie's legal team challenged the 'relevancy' of the charges preferred against their client. As some of the offences had taken place outside Scotland, could they be tried under Scots law?[23] The prosecution responded by removing the English, Welsh, Czech and American dimensions from the indictment. The 'relevancy' objection was then withdrawn and at the same time – no doubt because of plea-bargaining and an intercession by the Security Service – there was a further amendment to the charges. Struck from the indictment was the clause 'having between 1st November 1937 and 2nd March 1938 acted as the intermediary for forwarding correspondence and information to ... foreign agents from persons in America and Czechoslovakia'.

The alterations to the indictment removed all references to Jordan's activities as a forwarder of spy mail. The case against her would focus on her well-documented personal espionage activities.[24]

The Solicitor General for Scotland, James C.S. Reid, MP, accepted a revised indictment that focused on her gathering of military information in Scotland between 14 February and 17 November 1937 – prior to the Crown affair. The *Empire News* recorded how the accused now pleaded guilty 'in a voice made harsh by long years of talking German'. The newspaper reported that there had been a secret deal – a guilty plea 'on the understanding that the indictment would be amended to exclude a number of particulars – none of which was made public'. In similar vein across the Atlantic, the *New York Times* noted that 'no hint of the connection between the [UK and US] cases had been allowed to appear in British newspapers.'[25]

The arrangement meant gains and losses for the parties involved. A certain amount of information was kept from the Abwehr, though its officials must have deduced that MI5 knew more than it admitted. From the diplomatic standpoint, the danger of an inflamed British public opinion leading to friction with Germany had been avoided – an outcome that pleased government officials at the time.

Jessie Jordan stood to be the loser. On the other hand, she expected some leniency because of her guilty plea and her advocate had an opportunity to strengthen that plea. Jessie's courtroom lawyer was the aspiring Conservative politician Arthur P. Duffes, KC. He was not and could not have been a specialist advocate, for spy cases were rare in Scotland and that meant that there had been no accumulation of courtroom experience. Duffes was making a name for himself in a very different sphere, as an automobile accident compensation specialist. In later years, the *Scotsman* marvelled at the logic of the accident specialist's claim that he had never travelled in a motorcar himself. Duffes described himself as 'the last of the pedestrians'.[26]

There was nothing pedestrian about Duffes' plea in mitigation: 'Having started as an unwanted child 51 years ago, she finds herself … once again an unwanted child as regards her native country and the country in which she has spent the greater part of her life.'[27] In another country at another time, Jessie might have been shot. But she had been defended by a competent advocate in a civilised democracy that was, so far, at peace with the world. She received a less-than-draconian sentence of four years in prison.

Though confined in a Scottish prison, Jessie Jordan remained on the FBI's 'wanted' list. The British authorities would take further steps to keep her out of what was by now a rapidly unfolding American drama.

What Griebl Knew

The FBI men who arrested Jenni Hofmann on 25 February 1938 seized the letters in her possession. Written by her manipulative lover Karl Schlueter, they addressed Guenther Rumrich and two others. In his letter to 'Miss Moog', Schlueter asked for news of Moog's impending divorce and urged her to trust his stand-in courier Jenni, 'since she is a good little skate'. The second letter haggled over the price of 'furs'. It was addressed to Dr Ignatz T. Griebl of New York City.[1]

As soon as they had decoded that letter, Leon Turrou with other FBI agents descended on Dr Griebl's medical practice in Yorkville, on the Upper East Side of Manhattan. Members of the team posted themselves at all exits to the premises and Turrou stepped into the waiting room. A crisply dressed and just as crisply mannered nurse told him to leave as it was after office hours. Turrou informed her that she had to tell Griebl he was from the Justice Department. The nurse squared her shoulders and went to get her employer. It gave the G-man time to peruse the waiting room's décor. On its walls were French etchings and a parchment of Griebl's commission in the United States Army Reserve.

A bespectacled 39-year-old emerged from his office. He nervously fumbled to undo the buttons of his white physician's garb, which he discarded in favour of a double-breasted coat that was too tight for his portly frame. His ashen complexion indicated that he was in the grip of fear. Turrou told Dr Griebl he was to come along with him to answer a few questions.[2]

In the course of many days of interrogation, Griebl at first held out. He denied all knowledge of Jenni Hofmann and said there was an 'innocent' explanation of his use of Schlueter as a courier. He stated that he had given Schlueter materials about communism and Judaism that he wanted people in Germany to see. Some of these concerned the Protocols of the Elders of Zion. These Protocols purported to show that in the previous century international Jewish leaders had met to hatch a conspiracy to dominate the world. A London *Times* report in 1921 had shown the Protocols to be a 1903 forgery by Russian fraudsters, yet Griebl claimed he had given Schlueter items that proved they were genuine. Another item he entrusted to Schlueter was *Salute the Jew*, an anti-Semitic book Griebl had written under the pseudonym William Hamilton. He added that Schlueter had delivered on his behalf correspondence regarding a real estate deal with a 'Hebrew' in Germany – it turned out that Griebl was in cahoots with the Nazi authorities to swindle the Jewish family in question.[3]

His defence was sufficiently vile to have the ring of truth. When G-men searched Griebl's office they did find voluminous anti-Semitic materials. Griebl had files on virtually all prominent American Jews detailing their ancestry, wealth and activities. His observations on individuals contained defamatory and obscene remarks. Among those who featured were Roosevelt's Treasury Secretary Henry Morgenthau, House Committee on Un-American Activities founder Samuel Dickstein, New York's Governor Herbert H. Lehman, New York City's Mayor Fiorello LaGuardia and the social reformer and Zionist Rabbi Stephen Wise. 'You are not a Jew,' Griebl told Turrou, 'so you will not be offended by what you find.' He could not have been more mistaken. However, the files had nothing to do with espionage and could not be used to advance the FBI's investigation.[4]

From his interviews with Jenni Hofmann, Turrou knew that Griebl was a spy. What he lacked was proof and a confession. The FBI man tried one of his stock tactics in an effort to break the suspect's resistance. Speaking loudly to drown the sound of an opening door, he said, surely the physician would remember an attractive, auburn-haired girl with blue eyes calling herself Jenni? Of course he would remember such a person, said Griebl, but he could not, as he had never met her. At that moment, he heard behind him the voice of Jenni, who had just entered the room. The voice stated that he had given her spy packages for transmission to Bremen. Shaken out of his aplomb by the courier's sudden appearance, Griebl flew into a rage and told Jenni she would be shot. But he still held out and denied his complicity.

It was time to play dirty. How, Turrou asked, did he get along with Mrs Griebl? Ignatz replied that she was an admirable, if sometimes difficult woman. Turrou asked if she was five years older than him and wealthy, and had recently departed on a trip to Germany? The answer was 'Correct'. The detective fumbled in his pocket for a scrap of paper on which he had written some dates. 'Dr Griebl, would it be too indiscreet for you to tell me about that tall woman who registered with you at the Taft Hotel about four times in the last month?'

Thus blackmailed, Griebl began to talk. He remained circumspect, objected to notes being taken and constantly demanded confirmation that there was no hidden microphone in the room – and like every spy, he told lies. But he squealed at length. Dr Griebl made Turrou and ultimately America aware for the first time that Germany's US spy network was extensive and that it had functioned without impediment for a considerable time.[5]

Griebl's background and history were now of considerable interest to the FBI and Turrou and his colleagues gradually pieced the story together. Born on 30 April 1898, Griebl was, like more than one spy, the product of a region of split identity. In his case, it was Strasbourg, the Alsatian city coveted by both France and Germany. Little emerged of his boyhood, but in the First World War Griebl was an artillery officer in the forces of Imperial Germany. An Austrian nurse called Maria helped him recover from a wound sustained fighting Italian forces. Thereafter, Maria travelled to America and worked to pay his expenses while he trained to be a doctor, firstly in Munich and then, once they had married, in Long Island University, where he graduated in 1927. In a tearful session with Turrou, Maria later complained, 'I slaved for him and worked my fingers to the bone for him, and then he ran after other women.'[6]

A few years after arriving in America, Griebl established his practice in the German–American community of Yorkville. He specialised in women's problems, but was a danger to them. The FBI dug out information on his troubles. It found that in 1933, a client threatened to sue him for 'serious and severe personal injury sustained by her as a result of an assault'. She did not go through with the suit, but her attorney denounced Griebl as an abortionist.[7] Then in 1935 he had a messy affair with Antoinette Heim, an independent businesswoman in her forties. Heim sued Griebl in the Commercial Claims Court, saying that after he made love to her, she paid him $300 a month to help him get a divorce and that after receiving thousands of dollars allowing him to build a summer cottage in Westchester County, NY, he dumped her. Maria testified to discredit the plaintiff, saying Antoinette offered to pay *her* to initiate divorce. Ignatz tried another story. He swore that the monthly $300 had been to pay for the brokerage rights in connection with the sale of a $15,000 painting. The court disbelieved the Griebls and Antoinette Heim won the case.[8]

The Griebls had no children on whom to spend their dollars, but Ignatz spent money on his lavish lifestyle and the
avoidance of trouble was not one of his strong points. To aug-
ment his income, he became an ambulance-chasing doctor,
testifying in court on behalf of injury claimants. He was, however, accident-prone himself. His car crashes of 1930 and 1936
left him open to suit and out of pocket, to such a degree that
Griebl contrived a legal fiction that he owned no property to
guard against the damages that might arise from a compensation case.[9]

All this was potentially relevant in showing that Griebl
needed the money he made from espionage. He never
explained his disloyalty to the Stars and Stripes he was fond
of displaying, but devotion to the Nazi cause as well as a thirst
for financial gain played their part. Griebl was connected to
the Nazi hierarchy through his brother, who had been close
to Paul Joseph Goebbels, Minister for Public Enlightenment
and Propaganda in the Hitler regime. In the wake of Hitler's
confirmation as Chancellor, Griebl became leader of the pro-
Nazi Friends of the New Germany. The Nazi leadership in
Berlin wanted to recruit German–American support. Griebl,
a flag-waving, English-speaking member of the US armed
forces, seemed a perfect choice for the job. And it suited him
commercially. He was already well known for his activities in
German–American social and cultural circles, and the new
post seemed to promise ever more lucrative medical work in
the German–American community.

At this point, however, Hitler's deputy Rudolph Hess
stepped in, saying Griebl would be too difficult to manage.
Friends of the New Germany gave way to the German
American *Bund* (association) movement, still a Nazi front but
less abrasive and more 'American'. Moreover, Griebl's local
Nazi rivals started a smear campaign, claiming that Maria was
Jewish (she was actually Gentile and anti-Semitic) and that
Griebl was a communist. Griebl lost his leadership position

and with it some earning capacity – though one historian has suggested that the Reich's sacking of Griebl was a ruse, for it made him available to spy.[10]

Griebl never ceased to agitate for the realisation of Nazi goals and that was anathema to Turrou. Yet in one sense Griebl's contemptible mentality was a side issue, for Turrou's task was to find how the Abwehr worked, so that he could hunt down spies. Interrogating Griebl, he made a breakthrough that was to shape his thinking:

T: When did spy activities in this country start?
G: In 1933, soon after Hitler came to power.
T: Who was responsible for organising the ring?
G: A man by the name of Wilhelm Lonkowski.[11]

And so it was that Turrou, hitherto in ignorance of Lonkowski and still unaware of the timeline and architecture of German spying in the United States, began to arrive at greater wisdom. To find out more about this mysterious character called Lonkowski, he decided to contact Joe Dalton. It will be recalled that this military intelligence officer had been privy to the MI5 tip-off about the McAlpin plot and had conducted the original interrogation of Rumrich when the spy was later arrested over the passport scam. What interested Turrou was the fact that the major had also been at his desk at the time of an earlier episode. This was the debacle of October 1935, when Lonkowski had been caught seeking to deliver a spy package to Karl Schlueter aboard the *Europa*, only to be released after interrogation by Dalton's colleague Major Grogan.

Dalton now showed Turrou the military intelligence file on the Lonkowski case. He defended his failure to have Lonkowski arrested by saying that with one exception (design details of an aircraft carrier detention hook) the materials contained in the spy package were in the public domain and harmless.[12] Turrou may have thought that Lonkowski's sudden flight suggested otherwise, but he was too tactful to suggest that.

Griebl told the FBI that Lonkowski approached him in 1933, asking him to spy for Germany, but said that he refused this invitation.[13] Be that as it may, he was certainly involved by 1935. It was in the spring of that year that the Abwehr's new chief, Wilhelm Canaris, ordered a hand-picked officer to establish a new substation in Bremen, a unit with the specified mission of spying on America. The officer's name was Erich Pfeiffer.

Griebl heard about Pfeiffer's special role and asked Schlueter to give him a letter in which he offered to spy for Germany. Pfeiffer took him on and wrote to him via the courier, Karl Eitel. The Bremen spymaster's letter arrived at 56 East 87th Street adjacent to Yorktown on the Upper East Side of Manhattan, and gave Griebl his general intelligence target, technical data on US Navy destroyers and on military aircraft.[14]

Pfeiffer subsequently sent Griebl more specific questionnaires via both Eitel and Schlueter. According to Pfeiffer, he received expenses and, on one occasion when he delivered blueprints of American warships and planes, a bonus of $200. According to MI5, however, Griebl received a handsome retainer of $500 a month, plus bonuses. Griebl's spy data came directly from Otto Voss at the Seversky plant, and sometimes from Lonkowski. Pfeiffer considered the latter to be improper 'poaching' because Lonkowski was supposed to report directly to Berlin, but he went along with it, and may have privately welcomed the procedure – German agents constantly vied with each other for the best intelligence coups.[15]

When asked about Lonkowski's escape, Griebl responded with his customary evasiveness. First, he said he had no knowledge of the event. Then he maintained that he sheltered the fugitive for the night, whereupon Lonkowski departed alone for the airport – whence the German aviator Ulrich

Hausmann flew him to Montreal for $800. Gradually, though, he admitted to full complicity. Lonkowski stayed the night with him in Yorkville, then Griebl drove him to his summer home in Larchmont, Westchester County. There, he gave him $100 for expenses and loaned him his car, with Hausmann acting as chauffeur. Thirty-six hours later, the car reappeared in Griebl's garage.[16]

The Lonkowski story was truly a revelation for Turrou, yet there were things that Griebl did not know. He was not in contact with Ritter, the spy who obtained the details of the Norden bombsight. He was ignorant of German intelligence operations on the west coast.

He did, though, provide Turrou with his arch villain. Turrou would find in Erich Pfeiffer not just an antagonist in the spy wars, but also a potent propaganda tool. The FBI detective rolled into one the identities behind the code names 'Spielman' and 'Sanders', making for a simple, understandable message about a German master spy. For Turrou's aims – not at the outset, but as the case rolled on – were threefold. He wanted to unmask the spies and arrest them, to identify who dispatched them and to tie in that person to the hierarchy in Berlin in such a way as to demonstrate the iniquity of the Nazi regime.

Oversimplified though it may have been, the image of Pfeiffer as the schemer at the centre of a joined-up evil web would strike home with the American public. Turrou would inflate Pfeiffer's image for publicity reasons, but he hardly needed to for the Abwehr officer was a formidable opponent. Pfeiffer was the product of both privilege and hardship. Born in the Rhineland–Palatinate town of Altenkirchen in 1897, he was the son of a mining director and received a Catholic education in local colleges. With the advent of war he joined the Navy and was in 1916 a junior officer on the *König* on the occasion when the battleship led the German line in the Battle of Jutland. That stalemate confrontation between the German and British fleets took the lives of almost 10,000 men.

If the patriotism of Erich Pfeiffer had ever been a half-built construct, the thud of heavy artillery and the screams of dying countrymen finished the job.

At the war's end, Pfeiffer married into his own social class. Elisabeth Helene Charlotte (Lotte, née Weimann) was the daughter of a university professor, a high-status job in 1920s Germany. Erich took a doctorate in national economy from the University of Freiburg and worked in the Essen chemicals industry. He stood as a parliamentary candidate for the centre-right and strongly anti-communist Deutsche Volkspartei and hoped for a political career.

Building his electoral power base, in 1925 Pfeiffer accepted trade union administrative posts in Altenkirchen and Koblenz. The contemporary political scientist Selig Perlman noted that by this time the German labour movement had 'shelved, perhaps for good, its former radical anti-capitalism'.[17]

However, a trade union background was still anathema to the Nazis, who consolidated their power with the rise of Adolf Hitler. With an eye to his future preferment, Pfeiffer re-enlisted with the Navy at half the salary he had earned as a union administrator.

In 1933 the newly installed Hitler regime signalled naval expansion and Pfeiffer accepted an invitation to take on an intelligence role. The regional intelligence hub was in Hamburg, a major port with strong international connections. Pfeiffer was dispatched to a coastal sub-branch, the Wilhelmshaven naval base. There, he first built up the Customs Service to be a counter-espionage force of around sixty men, and then spread his wings. In May 1934, he established a spy network in the Low Countries with the intention that it would be a springboard for the planned penetration of Britain.

An old-style naval officer and royalist who looked upon Hitler with distaste, Captain (later Admiral) Canaris took note of Pfeiffer's talents and genteel background. He decided to pull him out of Wilhelmshaven, which he regarded as too much of a naval enclave for an enterprising spymaster, and to install him in a new substation around 35 miles inland, in the ancient port and industrial city of Bremen.

Like his contemporary Nikolaus Ritter, Pfeiffer remarked on Canaris's frigid personality – the Abwehr chief 'coldly' crushed a Wilhelmshaven naval commander who was opposed to the Bremen transfer.[18] Yet Pfeiffer was Canaris's blue-eyed boy and in Bremen established an anti-American spy ring that was his pride and joy and whose competence he never ceased to defend. Pfeiffer set up his office on the third floor of a side-street building off Bahnhofstrasse that housed an American shipping company two floors below. His unit had its own identity and he could stamp his correspondence with its own seal – the legend 'Abwehrneben stelle Bremen', surmounted by the German imperial eagle and the Nazi symbol, the swastika.[19]

Pfeiffer took a house for Lotte and their pre-teenage sons Dietmar and Manfred at Friedrich Misslestrasse, a military facility next to a forced labour camp (thus he could have been in no doubt as to the nature of the Hitler regime). He appears also to have had a residence at Kronprinzenstrasse, possibly in association with his secretary, Hilde Gersdorf, who would be his long-term mistress.[20]

It was in Bremen that Pfeiffer developed his ideas on the espionage profession. He was a disciple of Maximilian Ronge. This renowned Austrian intelligence officer had first won attention in 1913, when he exposed his boss, Alfred Redl, as a double agent acting for the Russian Empire (opinion is divided on whether the Russians blackmailed Redl, who was gay, or whether they just paid him lots of money). Ronge succeed Redl as director of Vienna's Evidenzbureau and served through the First World War. Recently – in 1930 – he had published a memoir that expounded his philosophy. In *Kriegs- und Industriespionage* he presented espionage as, ideally, a way of preventing war. He deplored the demobilisation of intelligence after the last war, and the way in which spies who had done their patriotic duty were sometimes vilified. He had little time for amateurs or for espionage veterans who glorified their spy days by publishing colourful accounts. He placed great emphasis on the protection of operational secrecy. Building on his study of Ronge, Pfeiffer began instructing his own students. Abwehr officers travelled from far and wide to attend his spycraft courses.[21]

Pfeiffer's espionage against the United States played against a complex background that made it hard for Turrou to identify the lines of command. Bremen had no monopoly on the American show. Hamburg, the more senior spy station, sent agents to America with Canaris's backing and not always with Pfeiffer's full knowledge – Canaris clove to the intelligence doctrine that you only get to know what you need to know. Other spies took their orders from the Nazi hierarchy – information is power, and Hitler accomplices Reinhard Heydrich and Heinrich Himmler attempted to infiltrate the Abwehr and pressure it to further the Party's objectives. Canaris tried to resist this and had strong reservations about Hitler's militaristic policy. But he had to play a cunning game in order to survive. He was in no position to take an openly anti-Nazi stance and his failure to do so sent mixed messages to his subordinates.

Pfeiffer was in step with Party members as well as with Canaris in the years 1935–37. In the 1920s, Hitler had admired America's Nordic ethnicity and was in awe of Henry Ford and the US automobile industry. A close student of the United States, he saw that country as blessed with plenty of 'free' land (*lebensraum*) resulting from the extermination of the native population, something he sought for Germany at the expense of the Slavs to the east. He sought a sphere of influence for Germany on his side of the Atlantic that would match the advantages conferred on the United States by its generous land mass. He was determined to brook no American opposition to that idea and by 1941 was ready to contemplate military attacks on the United States. But earlier, he saw the

German–American population as an asset. In the early years of Hitler's regime, his Nazis aimed to spread their doctrines, exploiting people like Griebl and America's substantial population of German descent. In theory, this would be done without engaging in provocative behaviour. It was not until 1938 that Hitler declared the United States to be a 'Jewish rubbish heap'.[22]

Canaris was convinced of the importance of espionage against the United States. Giving a pep talk to Abwehr personnel early in his tenure, he told them that the United States was a 'key target', but not for aggression. The Abwehr chief understood that 1930s America had survived the Crash and Depression and had strategic strength: 'The USA must be regarded as the decisive factor in any future war. The capacity of its industrial power is such as to ensure victory, not only for the USA itself, but also for any country with which it may be associated.'[23] He wanted to steal military technology, but without making an enemy of America.

Briefing one of his agents, Pfeiffer similarly insisted that in relation to America the Abwehr engaged only in military espionage. A true pupil of Ronge as well as Canaris, he wanted to avoid war and persuaded himself that Hitler was of like mind:

> There was no question of war between Germany and America, and a situation such as had arisen in the first World War, where the USA came into the war against Germany, need never occur again. That was not just talk with me, but was my firm conviction; I think that at the time it was also HITLER's ... as regards rearmament, it was for us to see that Germany caught up as quickly as possible with the progress in the development of arms in the past 14 years by making use of the experience of others.

In practice, though, Pfeiffer admitted that he found it was impolitic to 'curb the enthusiasm of Party members' in the

United States and some of his agents would cooperate with the Gestapo and engage in extreme methods.[24]

Griebl was too prejudiced and ignorant to convey these nuances to his FBI inquisitors. However, that did not weaken Turrou's propaganda campaign. For propaganda depends for its effectiveness upon a simple message. That was why Turrou latched with such enthusiasm onto one of Griebl's tales that spoke of a simple perfidiousness on Pfeiffer's part. The awful tale had a further advantage in that it led straight to Berlin, allowing Turrou to point an accusing finger at the Nazi centre. Griebl's poisonous fable was about the propositioning of Miss Moog.

Miss Moog Says No

In May 1937, Griebl wrote to Pfeiffer asking for help with his proposed Jewish property deal. Pfeiffer replied that, if Griebl wanted to hasten the Jewish property transfer, he would have to come to Germany. At the time, the physician had several patients nearing confinement. He decided to shunt them off onto a colleague and made a reservation to sail on the *Europa* on 1 June.[1]

Maria observed his preparations to leave home and head for the ship. She put on her hat and made to carry one of his bags. He told her to stay at home as he hated shipside sentimentality and would see himself off. As soon as he had left, Maria's worries began to crowd in on her. It was not just Ignatz's philandering history or the hints and half-averted gazes from his clients. His secretary had told her there was someone, in particular, who was never off the phone to him. Maria had a premonition of finality.

Mrs Griebl had no maternal duties to inhibit sudden choices. She took a taxi to Hudson River's Pier 86, arriving an hour before cast-off. She stood on the pier wondering how to proceed. Suddenly she saw them, high on an upper deck, her husband and an attractive woman whose waist he fondled.

She stormed onto the ship. Confronted, Ignatz tried to fob off
Maria with an unconvincing story, but his wife left the boat
unhappier than she had been for years. It was not just that
Griebl was, as Maria put it, a 'born skirt-chaser'. The problem,
she later explained, was the double-strength spell that Miss
Kate Moog seemed to cast. It was she who ruined their lives
and got Griebl into his ultimate predicament with the United
States authorities.[2]

Turrou described Katherina 'Kate' Moog as tall, merry and
flirtatious, with a girlish voice. Another FBI agent said she was
'temperamental' and 'hysterical'. British intelligence noted
that she was 'well shaped'.[3] To elements in German intelligence, as we shall see, she had the potential to be a honeytrap.
To the FBI and Turrou in particular, she was a key witness and
her background invited scrutiny.

Kate's parents had been affluent enough in Germany to
send her to the United States to train as a nurse. In the 1920s,
according to an exaggerated if not fictitious account credited by the FBI, she had attended to the needs of Franklin
Roosevelt when the future president was struggling against
the onset of polio.[4] She told the FBI that she accepted an invitation to marry John Warwick Halsey, whose brother Edwin
was secretary to the United States Senate, and met a range of
senior politicians including Senator Claude Augustus Swanson
(Democrat, Virginia), who would serve as Secretary of the
Navy under President Roosevelt (1933–39).[5] When John
Halsey died, she moved to New York, where she married a
fellow German immigrant, Emil Busch (sometimes spelled as
Bush), from whom she subsequently separated. Putting the
failed marriage behind her, Kate Busch became Miss Moog
once again. She set up a nursing home business in New York,
where several of her elderly clients were Jewish. She proved to
be a capable businesswoman, and, on the basis of her earnings,
she was able to rent a fourteen-room apartment on Riverside
Drive and to pay the salaries of several servants.

It was in New York that Kate met Ignatz Griebl. She dazzled him with her looks, her charm and not least with a gilded
account of her high-flying days in Washington, DC. Ignatz
embarked on his customary seductive trajectory, but this time
it was not a fleeting relationship. The FBI documented the
occurrence of regular trysts in the Taft Hotel in the period
from January through December 1937. Following her separation from her husband, Kate had obtained a Mexican divorce
but, worried about its force in US law and with new expectations in mind, she now filed in the courts of New York (the
decree nisi would be granted on 27 June 1938).[6]

Kate and Ignatz sailed together on the *Europa* on 1 June
1937, distancing themselves mile upon nautical mile from the
bereft Maria. On board, the steward/courier/spy Schlueter
took them aside and said he would make the arrangements
for their meeting with Pfeiffer. Five days later, Erich Pfeiffer
met them as they alighted from the liner at Bremerhaven.
There were further meetings, some of them at locations
that were meant to impress Kate. There was the occasion,
for example, when all three dined at the Hotel Columbus in
Bremen, where they remained drinking until 3 a.m. the next
morning. Pfeiffer confirmed in the small hours that, in return
for spy services rendered, he would help Griebl with the
real estate deal, get him a post in the Air Defence Ministry
and procure for him his cherished Jewish-owned property.
Another time, Pfeiffer held forth in the Café Bremen on the
subject of his omniscience about American naval technology. According to Pfeiffer, the new generation of destroyers
under construction for the US Navy was built by overpaid
workers at too high a cost. The destroyers were 'suicide craft'
because of their thin hulls.[7]

In spite of this professed scorn, Pfeiffer exhibited a thirst
for US naval technology. Reflecting the stated needs of the
German Navy, he wanted details of the two aircraft carriers
under construction, the *Yorktown* and *Enterprise*. His agent Karl

Eitel had outlined to him a new arrangement on their flight decks, the use of 'arrester' equipment to slow down landing aircraft, and he wanted details.[8]

Pfeiffer later recalled that, in the course of discussion, Griebl offered him an asset. This was Kate Moog. His mistress might do useful work, but not in the manner of a male secret agent. Griebl asserted that she had high social standing in Washington and good connections with the White House, right up to her former patient, the President of the United States. She would be able to provide timely information about meetings between President Roosevelt and Secretary of the Navy Swanson, and about their deliberations over forthcoming shipbuilding contracts. Were Pfeiffer to visit the United States, she could arrange for him to be introduced to the 'best circles at Washington'.[9]

When quizzed in later years, the Bremen spy chief claimed that he had harboured doubts about Kate's utility as a spy. In his meetings with Griebl, he diplomatically refrained from mentioning these doubts. Instead, he indicated that it was Abwehr policy never to send its officers on visits to those countries on which they were spying, so it would not be possible for him to travel to Washington to meet Kate's contacts.

Pfeiffer valued written items and blueprints more than human contacts, and asked Kate if she could smuggle documents out of the White House. Kate could offer no reassurance on this point. The spymaster said he was not interested in political intelligence. While he appreciated any suggestions for future projects, he was really in the hunt for more concrete evidence about the capabilities of the US Navy. When seeking to exculpate himself under interrogation, he hinted that in espionage women could be of value only up to a point.[10]

Pfeiffer told Griebl there was no 'central agency' for organising the flow of intelligence to Germany via New York City.[11] He wanted to hold the strings in his own hand and to control Griebl's access to the Abwehr's Berlin hierarchy.

Then he discovered that Griebl had achieved that access on his own.[12] He said this had made him 'very angry'. He rationalised his ire, saying that it stemmed from a security concern: he was 'very much opposed to agents getting to know too many officers and vice-versa'.[13]

After their few days in Bremen the gynaecologist whisked his woman to Berlin by express train and the couple took up residence in a suite at the Hotel Adlon. The grand frontage of this establishment imposed itself on the Unter den Linden avenue, dwarfing the adjacent eighteenth-century Brandenburg Gate. Its luxurious rooms had accommodated guests ranging from Kaiser Wilhelm II to Albert Einstein (and in 2002, Michael Jackson would infamously dangle a baby from one of its balconies).

Within an hour of the couple's arrival, two men strutted past the baroque fountain in the hotel's lobby and ascended to their suite. A round-faced, balding man in his early fifties, Hermann Menzel was the Abwehr's director of naval intelligence. Canaris had entrusted him with sensitive tasks, such as brokering a deal with the arms manufacturer Krupp to exchange intelligence on foreign armaments industries.[14] The 41-year-old Udo Wilhelm Bogislav von Bonin was Menzel's deputy, entrusted with the duty of writing up intelligence reports for the High Command. The Breslau-born Lutheran was more debonair than military in his deportment, but was a ruthless man who had recently served in Spain as part of the Abwehr's mission to help General Franco's Falangists install fascistic dictatorship in that country. Since receiving intelligence training in November 1935, von Bonin, a convinced Nazi, had risen rapidly through the naval ranks.[15]

After a few minutes, the officers escorted the New Yorkers on a short journey. They skirted the Tiergarten woodland park so essential to Hitler's plans for an imperial remodelling of Berlin. Soon they arrived at 76–78 Tirpitzufer, today's Reichpietschufer. This was the site of the Bendlerblock building complex, an extensive military office facility. The foursome walked between Doric pillars onto the polished tiles of the entrance hall and braved the unreliable elevator to an upper floor, where chunky oak doors guarded the Abwehr offices. They finally arrived at the 'Fox's Lair'. Canaris sat at a desk on which sat a model of his former command, the battle cruiser *Dresden*. Behind him, tall windows and a French door gave onto a balcony overlooking the Landwehr Canal. There were just three photos in the sparsely decorated room: one of the Admiral's dog, another of an obscure Hungarian hussar and a portrait of General Franco whose campaign against Spanish democracy Canaris had materially assisted.

Canaris spoke to his visitors under the assumed name of 'Colonel Busch'. The admiral asked Griebl and Moog to spy for Germany in New York and Washington. Here is the FBI's summary of Griebl's version of what ensued in Canaris's office:

VON BONIN offered a plan whereby Miss MOOG would establish herself in a large, luxuriously furnished apartment in Washington. She would then cultivate the acquaintance of low-salaried members of the Army and Navy stationed in Washington, particularly junior officers assigned to the Army and Navy Departments. She would then entertain these officers lavishly, gain their confidence, and then notify Berlin. A suitable agent would be sent who would be introduced to these officers by her, and the Agent would thereafter attempt to get the information desired by the German intelligence service from them. VON BONIN emphasized that money was no object and could be spent fully to make the plan successful.[16]

The next day, as all accounts agree, Von Bonin and Menzel continued the briefing over lunch on the roof garden of the Hotel Eden on the opposite side of the Tiergarten. Griebl described an occasion that opened with a charm offensive on

Kate. The Abwehr officers then started to quiz her about her Washington social circle, before von Bonin cut to the point. They knew all about her and had done considerable research on US Army and Navy officers who lived in Washington. They knew who was embittered about lack of promotion and who had fallen into debt through one indiscretion or another. Such individuals might be induced to sell information to Germany.

What was needed was a suitable vehicle for approaching such men, and fine wine and beautiful women could be the key. How did Kate feel about the idea of a luxury salon in America's capital? There was a cautionary note: all Kate's expenses would be paid, but not those of her girls, for they would receive their money from clients. The proposal was for an industrial-scale honeytrap.[17]

There would be different versions of who mooted the brothel idea. At the end of the Second World War – when Nazis were running for cover and trying to exculpate themselves to escape punishment – many officials blotted out such episodes and invented convenient versions of the past. Von Bonin said he became involved at the time of the Griebl–Moog visit for the sole reason that he spoke English and the usual desk officer was away. He learned only in the foreign press about his and Menzel's alleged involvement in the brothel plot. He flatly denied that they made the proposal and claimed that Griebl invented the story in order to cover up his own complicity and escape prosecution in America. It was Griebl, he claimed, who made the proposal. He, von Bonin, had seen that Griebl was a swindler and had advised Menzel to reject the honeytrap salon proposal.[18]

Miss Moog offered her own version of what transpired upon the Hotel Eden's roof garden. Her account can be taken with a slight dose of salt, as she said that she and Griebl had found themselves fellow passengers on the *Europa* 'by coincidence', yet in important respects her narrative has the ring of truth. She said that von Bonin did make the offer to set her up in Washington, where she would entertain her old friends as well as 'young underpaid officers'. She confirmed that Menzel and von Bonin reiterated Pfeiffer's offer of help to secure the Jewish-owned home in Giesen in Lower Saxony. She added that there was a promise to give Griebl, on the conclusion of his period of service as a spy, a further home in Bavaria and a medical sinecure. She stated that with Griebl she left for Bremen on 27 June as they were embarking for the United States two days later, and on that day Pfeiffer took them to the Astoria Club. In a four-hour conversation he pushed the brothel idea, having been briefed by Menzel and von Bonin in the meantime. According to Moog, Pfeiffer now said that he would be the follow-up agent and would visit America to approach the pre-identified military traitors.[19]

Kate Moog said, 'We did not give [Pfeiffer] any affirmative answer but indicated to him that we would consider this matter and let him know later.'[20] Perhaps realising she was being exploited, she kept her counsel. Karl Schlueter made further approaches when she was back in America, and, she asserted, Pfeiffer kept up the pressure. Pfeiffer later contradicted all of this. He claimed, 'I certainly never told Moog she should become a second Mata Hari.' Loyal to his superiors, he added, 'nor would Kapitane Menzel have. Bonin would never have made such a stupid statement.'[21]

What seems to undermine Pfeiffer's assertion is that the German authorities stuck to their side of the bargain with Griebl. On 19 July 1937, the Jewish couple Isidore and Heln Berliner had to give up their house in Giesen, worth $50,000, in exchange for the $20,000 house in Peekskill, the staging post in Lonkowski's flight to Canada two years earlier.[22] Even that did not save them. They stayed on in Germany, and both died in the Auschwitz concentration camp in 1942, victims of the Holocaust like several of Isidor's siblings.

The honeytrap salon never materialised. Miss Moog in all probability said no. Yet, the aborted plot had both consequences and significance. Turrou either believed the Griebl–Moog version of events or pretended that he did in order to give further impetus to his anti-Nazi crusade. Whichever, it was a good tactic as the American press loved the story.

The Moog brothel story suggested the existence of a German Mata Hari mentality. Mata Hari was an exotic dancer of Dutch heritage who during the First World War mixed with high military and political circles in both Germany and France. A practitioner of *La Grande Horizontale* style of intelligence gathering (prostitution crossed with pillow talk), she faced a French firing squad in October 1917 having been convicted on a charge of spying for the Germans. The prosecution's claim that she was responsible for the deaths of 50,000 French soldiers testified to the contemporary belief in her espionage potency. The 50,000 death toll was improbable, but so was Abwehr chief Friedrich Gempp's claim that Mata Hari 'never did anything for German intelligence'.[23]

Mythology held that Mata Hari had offered to pose naked for the execution squad and blew them a final kiss before meeting the final hail of bullets. Cultural media exploited the legend. The German silent movie of 1927, *Mata Hari*, was an example, as was the identically titled American talkie of 1931, starring Greta Garbo. The celebrated Austrian director Fritz Lang had meantime created the silent film *Spione* (1928), about a glamorous Russian spy called Sonja Baranikowa. Such celluloid heroines rarely had agency, they simply performed pillow-talk duties.

Griebl may have concocted the brothel plan thinking that German intelligence officers would succumb to the seductive mythology. The cautionary memoir of one German intelligence officer hints at such a weakness. Oscar Reile, who was with the Abwehr from 1934 and worked for West

German intelligence after the Second World War, cautioned that women like Mata Hari were too unstable to be effective agents. Invisibility was a better attribute for female spies than the glamour and fame preferred by fiction writers. Reile considered it an opportunity lost that most of the Abwehr's women had been secretaries – he argued that there had been a general underestimation of the capabilities of women. He even claimed that women had superior instincts and intuition when it came to spotting 'fishy' behaviour.[24]

Anathema though they may have been to Reile, femmes fatales were ingrained in 1930s culture. The Mata Hari mystique gripped the American public as well as German naval officers. Sex scandal stories appeal not only because of the scandal itself, but also because of the subliminal sexual gratification experienced by the reader. When the *New York Times* decorously reported that Moog 'played a glamorous role' in the Nazi spy case, it might as well have added, 'read on …'[25] The Moog plot fizzled out as a spy plot, yet its significance was considerable. It could, of course, have been spun as a feminist parable. But for Turrou, the Moog story was a gift because of her charisma and the poor light in which it placed his main opponents, especially as it purported to show the line of command leading directly from Abwehr spies in America to the Nazi high command.

The brothel episode can hardly have enhanced the relationship between Kate and Ignatz. By the time Turrou interviewed the pair, in the spring of 1938, the relationship was showing signs of strain. In May, Ignatz told Kate that his wife was seeking a divorce in Reno, but Kate suspected he was spinning her a line. When she expressed doubt, Ignatz 'became very excited, slammed the door and left the apartment'.[26]

Turrou's questioning of Kate Moog in March 1938 enlightened him about her visit to Germany the previous year, but, although she was arrested and questioned, she was never charged. If she had accepted the Washington assignment, she might have become a reincarnation of Belle Boyd, the 'Siren of Shenandoah', who charmed her way into the confidence of Union soldiers in Washington during the Civil War and passed on their secrets to the Confederate leadership. But, at most, Kate was a minor spy courier. She was an insignificant figure – except as a witness.

As a witness to what happened in Germany and to the activities of Ignatz Griebl, she was, of course, invaluable. Listening to Kate and to Ignatz as he sang (and lied) about his own exploits, Turrou formed his views about German espionage. He was convinced it was essentially Nazi in character and had become a problem with the advent of Adolf Hitler.

The other lesson Turrou drew was that Eric Pfeiffer was at the nerve centre of German espionage against the United States. Pfeiffer would have liked to believe that too, but in truth he did not preside over a single, central-ised operation. Pfeiffer complained that sometimes even his own agents would work for Hamburg or take their orders directly from Berlin. And Canaris launched initiatives inde-pendently of Pfeiffer. As we saw in an earlier chapter, on Canaris's instructions Nikolaus Ritter had in 1937 obtained the Norden bombsight details in an operation that was con-nected to the Lonkowski–Gudenberg network only in an informal manner.

Right under Turrou's nose, even as he interrogated Griebl and other suspects, Ritter's brother was setting up another operation that was all but independent of the Gudenberg/Pfeiffer chain of command. Hans Walter Ritter lived in America from 1936 until his departure in early 1941. Charged with robbery in his first year in America, he was a rough type. He intimidated his US 'wife'/companion of five years by claiming that his brother Niki was a 'Gestapo agent'. The FBI later deduced that Hans directed his brother's spy ring in the

United States after Niki departed to take on further espionage roles in Europe.[27]

Hans Ritter helped to maintain communications with a San Francisco outpost of Niki Ritter's network. In the First World War, Germany had used Indian nationalists on America's west coast in an attempt to run guns to the Indian subcontinent and undermine British rule. In the 1930s, California figured once again in German strategic thinking and the consulate general in San Francisco developed secret-service links with Canada, Mexico, Brazil and Argentina. Although Germany had direct intelligence communications with South American nations, San Francisco was a significant lateral thread in the spider's web.

In June 1937, Baron Manfred Freiherr von Killinger, an ardent Party man and confidant of Hitler's, had arrived as the new consul general with the mission of stepping up espionage activity. San Francisco-controlled Abwehr agents now attempted to force local businessman Weston G. 'Pop' Frome, who was of German descent, to yield the technical secrets of his multinational corporation Atlas Powder, a spin-off from the chemicals conglomerate DuPont that Frome and his accomplices had set up. When he refused, the agents kidnapped Frome's wife and daughter. The evidence suggests that Hazel and Nancy held out and refused to pressure 'Pop' into making concessions to secure their release. In March 1938, the near-nude bodies of the two women were found in the Chihuahua Desert not far from El Paso. It was a botched and minor operation, but serves to illustrate the point that Pfeiffer's was not the only Abwehr operation in America, just the biggest.[28]

Turrou never cottoned on to the Ritter brothers' operations, but his interrogation of Kate Moog and Ignatz Griebl did make him wiser about the main Abwehr operation, run by Erich Pfeiffer. That gave him a trump card in future prosecutions and propaganda. Yet he was aware that there were still gaps in his knowledge of the Pfeiffer network. He wanted to know about its full extent and about the damage it inflicted. Griebl had given him a number of leads. Now, Turrou needed more evidence.

A Season of Inquiry

In March 1938, the FBI inquiry into the Abwehr spy ring gathered pace. By the beginning of April, its agents had extracted confessions and witness statements that enabled them to justify the convening of a Grand Jury. The jurors met on 16 May, held hearings over the next month and issued indictments that promised a political impact. The *Washington Post*'s Leland Stowe predicted that the 'Mata Hari racket' would be a 'major problem' for the government in the event of 'a second great war'.[1]

The role of German shipping personnel came in for scrutiny. Ignatz Griebl told of a conversation with Erich Pfeiffer regarding Captain Wilhelm Drechsel. The captain was chief marine superintendent of the Hamburg America and North German Lloyd lines, with responsibility for all German steamers docking in New York. Griebl alleged that Drechsel used his position to organise the secret transportation of spies and spy materials. He added that the official safeguarded German spy/couriers and liaised with Karl Friedrich Wilhelm (Willy) Herrmann, the New York Gestapo chief.[2]

Leon Turrou wanted to confront his suspect with a key witness, but decided to proceed with circumspection. Instead of pulling Drechsel in for questioning straight away, he arranged for Griebl to visit the captain at his Pier 86 office on a pretext. Ignatz would say he wanted to arrange a cheap passage to Germany for Maria Griebl, who was still working on the formalities of the Jewish property transaction. Griebl protested he was nervous about the plan. What if Drechsel realised he was cooperating with the FBI and had him kidnapped?

Turrou agreed to supply protection. When Griebl and Drechsel met on the morning of 20 March, Special Agent J.A. Berry lurked nearby. He kept Pier 86 under observation and was under orders to call for reinforcements immediately should Griebl not emerge from his meeting within half an hour. Griebl emerged unscathed after twenty-five minutes and the next morning visited the FBI office to give an account of his conversation with the maritime supervisor:

DRECHSEL: A cigarette, Doctor?

GRIEBL: Yes, please; why do you tremble so much, Captain?

D: You do not know the trouble I am [in], Doctor.

G: You speak of trouble? What should I say, Captain? I am under FBI surveillance for three weeks and I don't know if I am coming or going. They are trying to break me down mentally and that is the reason why I have come to you today. I want your advice.

D: Tell me who is involved up to this time and whose names have been mentioned?

G: Well, first of all, Dr PFEIFFER in Bremen.

D: What, Dr PFEIFFER? How in hell did they get his name?

G: That is not all. They also mentioned Col BUSCH [Canaris's alias], Captain Lt MENZEL and Captain Lt von BONIN of the War Department in Berlin.

D: My God, My God, how is this possible? Have they been warned?

G: No, of course not.

D. Well, then I will take care of it immediately.

It is hard to know whether Turrou scored an own goal by let-ting Drechsel find out from Griebl how much the FBI knew. But he concluded that at least he now had enough on the shipping manager to pull him in for questioning.[3]

Reed Vetterli joined Turrou in quizzing Drechsel. An able detective who had been promoted to Special Agent in Charge (New York) following his work on the Lindbergh case and a subsequent kidnapping inquiry, Vetterli was supportive of Turrou's early investigative efforts.[4] Drechsel explained to the two detectives his responsibilities at Piers 84 and 86 and freely admitted to partial responsibility in the matters Turrou and Vetterli were investigating – for example, he had facilitated the placing of the April 1936 advertisement in the *New York Times* that led to the recruitment of Rumrich.

Drechsel confessed to having supplied a free pass to Willy Herrmann, allowing the Gestapo man to board all German vessels berthing in New York. He took orders from high offi-cials in the National Socialist Party. One of these, whom he named as 'La Salle', was a director of the Hamburg America Line and took care of liaison between the shipping company and the Nazis. Seeking to exculpate himself, Drechsel insisted that he and his company were victims of the Nazi machine. After meeting Griebl on 20 March, he claimed to have sent a secret handwritten letter to his company's headquarters in Bremen detailing the pressures being brought on him. However, he had no copy he could show the FBI. Drechsel confirmed that after Hofmann's arrest, no spies were allowed 'to touch any American ports for the time being'. The FBI suspected the reason was that Drechsel himself had tipped them off.[5]

Under further interrogation by Turrou, Drechsel admit-ted that he had personally transmitted messages to Griebl, but said he had not kept copies of these communications. Turrou's reports noted discrepancies between Griebl's account of radi-ograms received and Drechsel's. By now, though, Drechsel was mounting his defence. In spite of his remark about La Salle, he claimed his employers were deeply upset by the use of their ships for espionage and feared a loss of business because of current revelations. He added that 'a vigorous investigation [was] now afoot by company officials at Bremen with the view of ascertaining the reason why Pfeiffer was permitted to utilise the confidential steamship company code for purposes other than those intended by the company'. Drechsel improbably claimed that the president of the now jointly administered Hamburg America and North German Lloyd firms had left for Berlin to launch a vigorous protest.[6]

Drechsel complained that there were Party enforcers on every ship. He said he lived in fear of the consequences of displeasing the Nazis who controlled the liners.[7] Drechsel claimed to have resisted pressure to bar a Jewish firm run by Simon Sarashon from operating on the piers he controlled, but he insisted he was in a difficult position. He had worked for Hamburg America for thirty-five years, expected his US citizenship papers to arrive soon and hinted he wanted to live in America when his pension matured in one year's time – he was terrified the Party might cancel his pension rights and was no doubt nervous that the FBI might stymie his citizenship application. Drechsel was clearly a fellow traveller who had facilitated Nazi espionage in significant ways, but he was sufficiently persuasive about his predicament to escape prosecution. He had contributed another piece to the jigsaw, and that, for Turrou, was enough.[8]

It was becoming abundantly clear that the shipping lines linked the top echelon in German intelligence with the lower levels. The FBI deployed its panoply of methods to uncover the truth. It interviewed, requisitioned telephone records and used the already disputed technology of polygraphy. Senior FBI official Edward (Ed) Tamm reported on other approaches: 'The mail of each alleged German agent is being covered, bank accounts are being reviewed, credit ratings established, associates determined and their income tax returns are being requested.'[9]

Abwehr officers – and they were literally commissioned officers in the German armed forces – sat behind desks in Berlin and in the Hamburg and Bremen branch offices. There, the middle-class men with duelling scars nursed the grievances of a lost war and directed the activities of their operatives through ships bound for the United States. The FBI's investigation left the Abwehr hierarchy relatively unscathed. The operatives were a different matter. These more exposed assets fell into four sometimes-overlapping categories: couriers, enforcers, agents and informants. The last group consisted, typically, of German–Americans with technical expertise who worked on American defence contracts. Apparently the Abwehr did not try to recruit Americans of non-German extraction. They did not need to as there was a sufficient supply of German–Americans with the right expertise who were willing to oblige.

Otto Voss was a leading example. He had been a colleague of Willy Lonkowski's and it was by investigating the Voss case that the FBI came to realise that the German secret service had got away with stealing US military technology for at least three years. After Griebl had fingered him, Voss was questioned on 10 March and charged the next day, eventually confessing to his role on 14 March. The FBI dossier on him noted that he had extensive training as a mechanic in Hamburg, fought in Finland and France with the German Army and had emigrated to America in 1928. His wife Anna was a domestic servant who opposed his involvement in espionage, but he ignored her objections and was an enthusiastic agent. According to one FBI report:

It should be noted that as far as the investigation of this [New York City] office is concerned, the information furnished by VOSS to agents in Germany was by far the most

damaging, inasmuch as he furnished confidential construction details of Army pursuit planes which are at the present
time the most advanced type in this country.[10]

Not every interviewee interrogated by the FBI was a spy, but,
innocently or otherwise, those questioned shed light on different aspects of the inquiry. German-born Johannes K. Steuer
was a case in point. Steuer was a mechanic who had moved
to the United States before the First World War. In 1917, with
fears of sabotage running high, he had been interned at Ellis
Island along with all other Germans who worked within a
mile of the Brooklyn Navy Yard. Along with the others, he
was released without charge and at the war's conclusion
he returned to work for his former employer, the Sperry
Gyroscope Company. He took out American citizenship.

By the 1930s, Steuer was Principal Inspector at Sperry, an
Anglo–American concern that designed and manufactured
military equipment. One of its projects was a bombsight. The
Sperry device would see only limited service as in the battle
for major contracts the firm lost out to Norden, whose plans
were being betrayed to the German authorities even as Turrou
launched his investigation into Sperry. These outcomes could
not have been foreseen at the time and the penetration of
Sperry would have been cause for serious concern. Turrou
questioned Steuer all day on 11 and 12 March, while two
of his colleagues searched the Steuer residence on Hudson
Boulevard, North Bergen, NJ, 'with negative results'.

Turrou worried that Abwehr agents were grooming
German–Americans with skills at the level of Steuer's, with
the purpose of using them as agents in situ, or inducing them
to return to work in Germany, where their know-how would
be utilised. He cited the example of another Sperry employee,
Irwin Backhaus, who had worked on government contracts in
his native Germany as well as in the United States. Backhaus
was internationally respected for his work on automatic pilot

planes, an antecedent to present-day drones. One day, an engineer from Germany met him at the St George Hotel, Brooklyn and offered him a contract in the Old Country. The money on offer was suspiciously generous and Backhaus realised he was being asked not just to work, but also to supply Sperry blueprints.

In a parallel case Griebl, with backing from North German Lloyd, offered a lucrative two-year deal to the naval engineer Christian F. Danielsen, who still had three daughters in Germany in spite of his thirty years living in America. When the North German Lloyd return ticket came through, it was for a one-month stay only, the idea being that Danielsen would pass on the secrets and then be let go.

In the event, the FBI could not pin anything on Steuer, but the principal inspector did shed light on security arrangements. US military intelligence had to give clearance to any foreign dignitaries who wanted to inspect the Sperry plant in Brooklyn. Steuer told a story that illuminated the weakness of the arrangement. Sperry's president had visited Germany and a German delegation subsequently arrived to see how the 3,000-part bombsight was produced. The delegates were not given access to sensitive assembly points and evidently there was some compliance with the demand for security. However, potentially even these precautions were rendered futile by the company's ambition to export for profit equipment that Germany's arms industry could have disassembled and imitated.[11]

There was a hot political background to all this. A significant number of Americans were convinced that arms manufacturers, the so-called 'merchants of death', had conspired to drag America into the First World War in order to swell their profits. They believed that the ensuing sacrifices by American GIs had been for nothing. They also held that the peace settlement on the conclusion of the First World War had been deficient, causing the sort of growing discontent that resulted in the rise of fascism in an embittered Germany. In a high-profile US Senate investigation between 1934 and 1936, chaired by Gerald P. Nye (Republican, North Dakota), the US arms industry came under a distinctly hostile gaze. Amidst the widespread conviction that self-serving profiteers had dragged the United States into a war that was inhumane and against the national interest, Congress passed a series of Neutrality Acts, the first signed on 31 August 1935, that imposed a general embargo on trading in arms and war materials.

All this was at odds with Secretary of State Cordell Hull's efforts to liberalise trade in an effort to pull America and the rest of the world out of the ongoing economic depression – as United States shipyards were already making money and jobs by building warships for Brazil and for Communist Russia.[12] However, any revelations that the weapons manufacturers were trading by the back door or allowing a potential aggressor access to their secrets, whether through negligence or not, would be politically explosive. America was divided and feelings ran deep on both sides of the debate.

Yet another Griebl tip-off led to the 15 March 1938 raid on the Wythe Avenue, Brooklyn, home of Johannes Kögel. A former German soldier who had served a mechanics apprenticeship in Darmstadt and had become an American citizen in 1931, Kögel was a skilled designer who worked for the Kollmorgen Optical Company, for whom he developed a pistol-drive periscope and other optical devices for use in naval warfare. When FBI agents found blueprints in his house, they took him in for questioning.

Defending himself, Kögel said he often brought work home. Nowadays it was doubly convenient, as he had to work in the evenings. In the depressed 1930s his firm had laid off men and he had to labour for longer hours to compensate and help his employers complete contracts on time. Asked to comment on the security risk of taking confidential materials away from the workplace, he tartly commented that they were making better periscopes abroad – Germany would learn little from American technology. Arguably, Vetterli, Turrou and the three other FBI special agents who interrogated Kögel were wasting their time. Perhaps Griebl was inventing Abwehr informers in order to throw Turrou off the scent. Just as likely, though, is the possibility that Griebl had a list of German–American mechanics regarded as *potential* informers. For such individuals, FBI inquiries may have been a deterrent.[13]

Turrou was keen to show that the German spy ring was uniformly Nazi and that it reflected the totalitarian character of Hitler's regime. The FBI did not have the means to investigate how the Gestapo might have intimidated individuals in Germany, forcing them to become spies. It did, however, look for examples of intimidation within the United States. For example, Turrou ascertained that Lonkowski had sent Senta de Wanger threatening letters after his flight to Germany, and that in the winter of 1937–38 Rumrich, using the pseudonym Frederick von Klotz, had attempted to terrorise Senta by making appointments to see her and then not turning up.[14]

In pursuit of evidence on intimidation, the FBI took an interest in the Gestapo's Willy Herrmann. Special Agent G.A. Callahan spoke to Herrmann at Griebl's house, confronting a man of medium height, aquiline features and greased-back black hair. The Gestapo man lived at a 75 West 89th Street apartment with Margaret Stevenson. She was a Works Progress Administration actor who innocently believed that her lover's job as a waiter in Brooklyn was his true vocation. Recalling what Pfeiffer had told him, Griebl had informed Turrou that 'Herrmann is charged with the enforcement and execution of orders sent to him from headquarters directly from Berlin and sometimes relayed from Berlin to Pfeiffer and in turn relayed to Herrmann in New York City'. He said that Herrmann's job was to ensure the 'trustworthiness' of German agents in America and to organise protection for the spy-couriers plying their trade on the Atlantic liners.[15] In an eight-page statement witnessed by Callahan on 28 March, Herrmann proclaimed himself a proud Nazi, acknowledged his Gestapo mission and confessed to knowing most of the spies identified by the FBI. He insisted he was doing political work, not conducting espionage.[16]

Herrmann tried to ingratiate himself with his interrogators by saying he was trying to close down communist murderers and bullies on the waterfront. One of his henchmen, Ewald Fritz Rossberg, told a more revealing story. He and Heinrich Bischoff, the Party enforcer on the SS *Europa*, went in pursuit of 'a German woman flyer' who 'had betrayed Germany'. This was the actor and athlete turned test pilot Antonie Strassmann, a strikingly beautiful woman who had become a focus of adulation in the Weimar Republic for promoting German aeroplanes in the United States. By the 1930s she had given up her involvement with Crown Prince Wilhelm von Hohenzollern, had taken up instead with Robert L. Hague, senior vice president at Standard Oil, and was a permanent resident in the United States.

Antonie, who was of Jewish descent, took business parties onto both the *Europa* and *Bremen* in 1937, where she evidently befriended crew members. Especially after one of them visited her hotel in a chauffeur-driven limousine, Herrmann suspected that 'the Strassmann woman' was trying to turn members of the crew. Rossberg and Bischoff were supposed to keep Antonie under observation and sabotage her anti-Nazi efforts. Like most of Herrmann's operations, this one was misconceived and ham-fisted. Antonie Strassmann continued unimpeded with multiple business and later Red Cross activities until she died in New York in 1952. Yet, Herrmann had brought to America a little whiff of the Nazi surveillance state.[17]

By the beginning of April, Turrou and his colleagues had gathered enough evidence to allow them to write the reports on which the Grand Jury hearings would be predicated.

However, much work remained to be done. There would be more testimonies as the story unravelled, in the words of a London *Daily Telegraph* reporter, 'piecemeal like a detective tale'. For example, Christian Danielsen, the naval engineer who had turned down Abwehr money, would be arrested as a material witness in time for the Grand Jury hearings. Yet only four spies were in custody, many of the interviewees told lies and all were reluctant to confess to criminal behaviour.[18]

This was not all. The FBI knew that the senior spies von Bonin, Menzel and Pfeiffer were beyond their reach in Germany. It continued to believe in the delusion that it should be hunting down the mythical 'Sanders' and 'Schmidt'. And there was another problem. The FBI knew of spies who had been operating in America but had not yet helped the Bureau with its inquiries. The reason was that they had gone.

The Flight of the Spies

The problem had begun in mid-February, when Karl Schlueter failed to board the SS *Europa* and allowed the besotted Jenni Hofmann to travel to America instead. Turrou would now have no chance of interviewing Schlueter.

The Abwehr had realised that the FBI was onto the case and set out to protect not just Schlueter, but also as many of its key agents as possible. One of these was Theodore Schuetz, alias Karl Weigand, described by Turrou as being 'a tremendously important Nazi spy contact man, ranking almost with Karl Schlueter'.[1]

Schuetz's day job was that of a steward aboard Hamburg America Line's steamer, the *New York*. When Berlin executed its protective plan, the *New York* was on a Caribbean cruise. The order came through to the vessel's commodore, Fritz Kruse. Schuetz was to return to Germany by any route, provided he did not set foot in the United States. The agent accordingly left the ship on 2 March 1938 when it docked at Havana.

The Abwehr top brass feared that the FBI would arrest Schuetz when the *New York* put in at its namesake's port and its fears were well founded, for Turrou immediately boarded the vessel upon its arrival in the United States. He found a line drawn through Schuetz's name on the ship's manifest – this is when the FBI's lead detective realised that a full-scale escape-and-evasion plan was in operation.

The Miami branch of the FBI laid plans to have Schuetz arrested in Havana, but he left for Mexico and there were potential diplomatic difficulties. Turrou pursued the case as best he could. Following his visit to the Schuetz-less SS *New York*, the detective asked to see the radiogram that had instructed Kruse to disembark his steward, but the 'lofty' commodore refused to produce it even when pressured to do so by the worried waterfront boss Wilhelm Drechsel. Commodore Kruse declared, 'I have got nothing to do with any of the activities of the personnel onboard the ship.'

It was a wretched admission by the chief officer of a passenger ship. So was his fellow-travelling afterthought: 'I am not involved in anything.' Abject fear may have been behind the disclaimer or a philosophy summed up in the title of antebellum America's Catholic-hating Know-Nothing Party.[2]

Later that month, Captain Drechsel met Consul General Bottler, members of his staff and two attorneys Bottler had retained to assist with Jenni Hofmann's defence. These attorneys, William J. Topken and Reimer Koch-Weser, were interim Reich-approved appointments who served until supplanted by George C. Dix, who saw his main duty as the defence of his client. Drechsel proposed a damage-limitation plan. Three wanted agents, Karl Schlueter, Herbert Janichen (a recent Pfeiffer recruit on the *Bremen*) and Theodore Schuetz, would return voluntarily to the United States and 'face the music'. They, together with Hofmann, would plead guilty.

Advocating a tactic that paralleled that of the British authorities in the Jessie Jordan affair, Drechsel gave it as his 'unquestionable' view that 'the matter could be perfunctorily disposed of in the United States District Court without giving the case the amount of publicity which would arise if the case should go to trial'. Drechsel argued that, 'Germany would benefit considerably by sacrificing three or four persons rather than revealing at the trial in detail' the full extent of German espionage and the names of other agents. Topken and Koch-Weser gave their 'tentative' assent, and the intention was that the plan would be promoted in Berlin via Ambassador Hans Heinrich Dieckhoff in Washington. Hinting at a double-agent role, Drechsel promised the FBI he would secretly inform it of the outcome.[3]

For the time being, Berlin ignored the proposal. It persisted with a policy of discontinuing agent voyages to the United States, defending those under arrest, denying everything – and extricating agents who were currently in America and not yet under arrest.

The most prominent example of such extrication was Ignatz Griebl. One day, when the swindler was sitting in Turrou's office and spinning him a line about how Germany was exchanging intelligence with Japan about the strengths and weaknesses of the United States Navy, he suddenly sighed 'Ach, Gott!' and covered his face with his hands. 'What is it?' Turrou asked, and received a bitterly intoned reply:

'Don't you realise, Mr Turrou, that what I am doing is sign-ing my death warrant in Germany? If they ever found out what I had told you – the secrets entrusted to me by von Bonin, Menzel, Pfeiffer and others …'[4]

Griebl made a chopping gesture, aimed at his neck.

The gesture helped to explain why Turrou never arrested or charged Griebl. He just wanted him to keep talking and the best way to do that was to let him run free. This was a tactical departure for the FBI from its ingrained 'arrest culture', and an indication that the Bureau was preparing for a new age with new challenges. At the same time, Turrou was acting in the apparently secure knowledge that Griebl would be too terrified to flee to Germany. This was before the scales dropped from his eyes.

On the evening of 10 May, Ignatz was unusually attentive to Maria and asked her to accompany him to Greenwich

Village to see a patient. After that, he said he had business on board the SS *Bremen*. It was 10 p.m. when they arrived at the waterfront and Maria could see the glittering lights of the *Bremen* and the *Hansa*, both berthed at Pier 86. Ignatz excused himself to use the men's room in a nearby saloon and then Maria saw her husband walk in the direction of the *Bremen*. He never returned.

There was another place to which he might have deviated at short notice, the Riverside apartment of Kate Moog. But at 6 a.m. on the morning of 11 May, Ignatz's other woman phoned Turrou in a panic: 'Ignatz – Dr Griebl – he has disappeared! … He has been kidnapped! They have taken him on a ship! They will kill him in Germany!'[5]

Griebl had left his physician's bag in the car and boarded the ship with no belongings, no passport – and no ticket, which made him a stow-away. He did have as means of identification a driver's licence and a gun permit, together with the sum of $180. He told Captain Adolf Ahrens he was fleeing America because of the espionage case. Ahrens allowed him to buy a tourist-class ticket for $156. And so it came to pass that the *Bremen* slipped through the Narrows past the unseeing gaze of the Statue of Liberty and headed out into the Atlantic bearing a man who would have been Leon Turrou's leading trial witness. On his first day at sea, he penned letters to his wife, complaining about his treatment on board, and to his mistress, claiming he was departing in order to conclude the Jewish land deal. He reassured Maria he would be back in time for the spy trial. He spent the rest of the voyage largely confined to Cabin 656, emerging only to dine at a table for one.

When the ship put in at Cherbourg, the US ambassador in Paris, William Bullitt, failed in his efforts to have Griebl taken off. Ambassador Joe Kennedy never really tried when the *Bremen* docked in Southampton – a person of Kennedy's political persuasion would not have wanted to offend Germany by engaging in such a provocative action. From Southampton,

Griebl cabled Reed Vetterli in impudent style: 'Stop trying to interfere will be back in due time arrange passport facilities for return through France with American Consulate Berlin.'[6]

Arriving in Bremerhaven, Griebl tipped his table waiter $5 (around $90 in today's values). He then went ashore and there to greet him was not a vengeful posse from the Gestapo, but Eric Pfeiffer. We have Pfeiffer's account of the course of events:

> There were no mutual recriminations: GRIEBL boasted that he had served Germany well to the last, surviving the most searching interrogations, 'the only rock on the shifting sands of German–American espionage;' and then he enquired urgently for monetary compensation … GRIEBL later went off to his home in Wurzburg, whence he bombarded PHEIFFER with new demands and threats, so that eventually a sum of between 50 and 100,000 Rmk. [between $350,000 and $700,000 today] was paid to him and arrangements were completed for satisfaction of his long-standing plans to exchange his property in New York for that of a Jew living in Giessen, with the latter's agreement.
>
> That was the last Pfeiffer saw of him. For Griebl now decamped to Vienna, to practice from the conveniently vacated premises of a departed Jewish gynaecologist.[7]

Compared with Griebl's flight, that of Werner George Gudenberg seemed less damaging to the FBI's prosecution case. Griebl – middle class, anti-Semitic and a consummate confidence man, had extracted major compensation from his Abwehr employers and made a similarly deep impression in America. Gudenberg's escape, while lower-profile, was nevertheless significant. He had enjoyed the confidence of premium defence contractors, and not just at Ireland Aircraft. By this time a United States citizen, in September 1932 he had married Veronica Karp, a pretty girl from Bristol, PA, who soon bore him an infant son. He was the epitome of upwardly mobile respectability. Between 1932 and 1936 he was a foreman in charge of thirty men in the cowling- and pattern-making departments at the military-contracted Curtiss Airplane and Motor Company, Buffalo, NY. The couple then moved to live in Bristol, where Werner ran the sheet metal department at the seaplane designers Hall Aluminum Aircraft.

Lonkowski visited Gudenberg in Buffalo in the summer of 1935. They had a few beers, Gudenberg boasted about his technical expertise, Lonkowski said that Germany needed him and the newly minted American citizen agreed to become a German spy. Gudenberg thereafter supplied blue-prints for Lonkowski to photograph or used his own Leica camera although it resulted in more blurry prints. He passed on information about Curtiss planes, such as their armament specifications and cruising range, and about a prototype 'scout bomber' being built in Buffalo. Some of the Curtiss blueprint reproductions were in Lonkowski's possession at the time of his detention by customs officers on 27 September 1935.

Turrou regarded Gudenberg as guilty but innocent, thinking that Lonkowski had led him astray. This was a lenient view or perhaps a rationalisation in light of Gudenberg's escape. As noted in Chapter 1, Gudenberg lured technicians to Germany so that they could there pass on the secrets of US military technology. According to Pfeiffer, Gudenberg's mission was no fleeting venture, for it was Gudenberg who took over Lonkowski's functions when the latter escaped to Germany. And there is further evidence against him. Nikolaus Ritter would later explain that when he operated through local contacts to steal the Norden bombsight plans in the course of his New York visit in November–December 1937, Gudenberg had been one of those contacts. Turrou had underestimated Gudenberg.[8]

To the distress of his wife Veronica, who was thrown into penury by his action, Gudenberg suddenly disappeared. He had already testified to the Grand Jury and was about to make

a second appearance on 27 May, a day when jurors were scheduled to hear evidence about Griebl's defection. Turrou was
grooming witnesses in the court's anteroom when Drechsel
burst in and announced that he had received a message from
Theodore Koch, captain of the SS *Hamburg*. At 4 a.m. the previous day, a steward had discovered, fast asleep in the third-class
lobby, a penniless stowaway who could produce no passport
or other means of identification except for a social security
card. His description, radio-telegrammed to Drechsel, indicated he was Gudenberg. Koch said he had had Gudenberg
thrown into the ship's brig and indicated he would turn him
over to the Gestapo to be disciplined upon the liner's arrival
in Hamburg. The German authorities telegrammed him fake
instructions, later produced in an attempt to deceive American
officials, to the effect that Gudenberg was to be kept under
lock and key for the whole voyage, unless the French authorities demanded his disembarkation in Cherbourg.

In the event, neither the French nor the British authorities
put the ship's captain to that inconvenience. American officials
had requested Gudenberg's detention, the State Department
briefed Ambassadors Bullitt and Kennedy that there was a
warrant for his arrest and District Attorney Lamar Hardy made
some urgent transatlantic phone calls. However, the *Hamburg's*
captain responded by moving Gudenberg to the ship's sickbay
and then asserting that he was too ill to be moved ashore in
either Cherbourg or Southampton. The Abwehr's repatriation plan had worked once again. Veronica, whose penniless
predicament had worried Turrou, was soon able to join her
husband in Germany.[9]

To what extent did the German escape plan work? When the
Federal Grand Jury issued its indictments on 20 June, it named
eighteen defendants. These were, as stated in the indictments,
Udo von Bonin, Hermann Menzel, Ernst Mueller, Erich
Pfeiffer, Schmidt (first name unknown), Sanders (first name
also unknown), Mrs Jessie Jordan, William Lonkowski, Karl

Schlueter, Theodore Schuetz, Herbert Janichen, Karl Eitel, Johanna Hofmann, Ignatz Theodor Griebl, Otto Hermann Voss, Werner George Gudenberg, Erich Glaser and Guenther Gustave Rumrich. A review of this list indicates that the FBI was not as lax as many have supposed.

Nine of the indicted were out of reach because they were abroad. Of these, Udo von Bonin, Hermann Menzel and Ernst Mueller were thought to have tasked the American spies from Berlin; Erich Pfeiffer worked out of Bremen; and Willy Lonkowski was safely tucked away behind an air force desk in Germany's capital. To indict such men with no chance of arrests being made was to invite a reputation for failure.

Here, it is of interest that the American authorities did not indict the person more responsible than anyone else for launching the spy ring, Admiral Canaris. He may have been too big a fish to fry for diplomatic reasons. But it is also the case that Turrou and his entourage had only a hazy concept of the German espionage hierarchy. The word *Abwehr* rarely if ever made its way into late 1930s FBI reports, and the name 'Canaris' never, though Turrou did know the admiral by one of his aliases, 'Busch'. In this ignorance, the FBI did not lag behind its approximate British counterpart. Authorised historians with full access to MI5 files for the 1930s note a similar deficiency on the part of the British counter-intelligence agency.[10]

A sixth indictee, Karl Eitel, had been caught embezzling and had been deployed to other duties in Europe, beyond the FBI's reach. A seventh, Karl Herbert Janichen, who had been a Pfeiffer courier when working as a waiter on the SS *Bremen* and had been questioned by Turrou, was also in Europe, far from the arm of American justice. An eighth, Schlueter, had been kept in Germany allowing Hofmann to be arrested in his stead. A ninth, Schuetz, had been diverted from American ports and made it back to the Fatherland.

Two more can be eliminated from our list. 'Schmidt', first name unknown, was never properly identified, and Rumrich seems to have used the name interchangeably with that of Schlueter. 'Sanders' was a generic alias. Being fictitious, Schmidt and Sanders can be eliminated from the list of those who eluded the FBI. Five were under arrest in the United States or Britain: Hofmann, Voss, Glaser, Rumrich and Jordan. That brings the total to sixteen. Of the last two, Gudenberg escaped when he was a witness and before he was indicted. Had he been more fully investigated, he might have yielded information about Lang and the Ritter brothers. Apart from that notable lacuna, it may be concluded that Turrou made just one serious error, his decision to trust Griebl.

Turrou's critics would claim that, in the words of historian Tim Weiner, he made the Bureau 'a laughing stock.'[11] They charged that he was responsible for self-serving, publicity-driven leaks that allowed mass escapes. To charge Turrou in this way is unfair, but it is certainly true that the leaks alerted the Abwehr and, for a while, kept spies from American shores.

The German escape plan did damage the American counter-espionage effort. Griebl's evidence, if only he could be made to tell the truth, would have been an asset for the prosecution. Furthermore, one can add to the roster of the absent a number of material witnesses, several of them ship-board couriers, who either decided to return to Germany or were persuaded to do so. For whatever reason, these potential witnesses smuggled themselves onto boats undetected. They included Ewald Fritz Rossberg, Wilhelm Boehnke, Walter Otto, Lutz Leiswitz and Johann Hart. Two ship's captains, Heinrich Lorenz and Franz Friske, were arrested as material witnesses and posted bail of $2,500 each, then absconded on a midnight sailing of the SS *Europa*.[12]

The *Los Angeles Times* attempted a political evaluation of the spy affair. It observed that the Grand Jury indictments had created a 'ticklish diplomatic situation'. In support of its view, it referred to what it described as the German press's indictment of 'American spy hysteria'.

This was a misperception. It was true that one German newspaper poured scorn on the American press: the *Hamburger Nachrichten* focused on the false arrest of an innocent German citizen in West Virginia, whose wife had been mistaken for a latter-day Mata Hari. Yet the account, though it was on the front page, was not a lead story. The official German response was a know-nothing silence. The official paper of the National Socialist Party, *Völkischer Beobachter*, appears to have mentioned the American spy affair not once.[13]

Public reaction at home to the spy-case developments was one of shock at the extent of German espionage, and at the way it appeared to have been orchestrated from the top levels of government in Berlin. It also involved finger pointing at the failings of Turrou and his colleagues. On Capitol Hill, pro-FBI legislators sprang to the Bureau's defence. To defuse potential criticism of its record, they trumpeted the FBI's success in fighting organised crime. Congressman Fred Crawford (Republican, Michigan) protested that the FBI was underfunded, giving licence 'to the yellow, lily-livered vipers of the underworld'. Henry F. Ashurst (Democrat, Arizona), chairman of the Senate's Judiciary Committee, reiterated his support for Attorney General Cummings' anti-crime campaign. Congressman Samuel Dickstein (Democrat, New York), the son of a Lithuanian Rabbi who was, we now know, in the pay of the Soviet intelligence agency the NKVD, was a prominent contributor to the debate. Destined to become famous for his opposition to both fascism and communism, Dickstein fulminated against Griebl and other spies, and welcomed the recent creation of the House Un-American Activities Committee.[14]

Turrou recalled the feeling among his FBI team that the Bureau's efforts had been 'checkmated'. But he cited the response of District Attorney Lamar Hardy:

The important point is that the American public must be made aware of the existence of this spy plot, and impressed with the dangers. Our Government and citizens must be awakened to the fact that it is imperative that we have an efficient counter-espionage service, to protect us against such vicious spy rings as this. We will go ahead with the case.

Hardy articulated goals that Turrou fervently espoused. Propaganda had always been important to the FBI detective. Speaking to the American people about the dangers of fascism was for him a primary, perhaps the primary, aim.[15]

As we have seen, there were only two escapes strictly defined, those of Gudenberg and Griebl. But should these have occurred, and should there have been a more immediate security clamp down that would have prevented the departure of other suspects and witnesses? Effective counter-intelligence was not without precedent in American history. In the War of 1898 and in the First World War, the US Secret Service and other government agencies had arrested spies and saboteurs and had held them in custody until they went on trial. Since then, federal enforcers had acquired stronger powers that were meant to make them even more effective. The Espionage Act of 1917 articulated the fact that the spy was a public enemy and spelled out stiff penalties, including death, for those found guilty under its provisions. In 1934, a reform package promoted by Attorney General Cummings for the first time gave FBI special agents the power to make arrests and the right to carry guns.[16]

But there were also impediments to Turrou's efforts. Not the least important of these was the fact that the German spying operations of the mid-1930s took place in peacetime. In peacetime there is a higher regard for the civil liberties of a suspect than exists during war – and the Espionage Act was in disrepute, because during the First World War and the ensuing Red Scare (1919–20) it had been misapplied to the persecution of dissenting minorities within the United States.

Another impediment in the way of effective detention was the United States Constitution, which, in peacetime especially, gives protection against arbitrary arrest and also guarantees free speech. Those who leaked information about the FBI's counter-espionage investigation may have done so for personal gain, but they did so secure in the knowledge that the right of free speech was enshrined in the First Amendment.

In further exoneration of Turrou, it can be reiterated that the leaks and open statements that permitted German spies and witnesses to remain abroad or flee originated with others. They went through three phases. Publicity about the original arrest, of Guenther Rumrich on 15 February, had been so great that director Hoover was initially reluctant to take the case. District Attorney Hardy and the police said they were incensed at the 'premature and about 75 per cent wrong' leak to the press, though it seems unlikely that the matter could have been kept under wraps indefinitely in an open society like the United States.[17]

The second blast of the publicity trumpet occurred on 27 February, when Hoover and Vetterli supplied the *New York Times* with a detailed account of the arrests of Rumrich, Hofmann and Rumrich's sidekick Glaser.[18] Hoover, who favoured publicity when it placed the FBI and its leader in an advantageous light, was on a promotional high, having earlier that month given his name to a book based on FBI case files, *Persons in Hiding*. (Shadow written by Courtney Riley Cooper, the book gave rise to four movies, including a February 1939 Paramount release, also called *Persons in Hiding*, that told the Bonnie and Clyde story.) Perhaps Hoover reasoned that the cat was already out of the bag and there was nothing to be lost in promoting the idea that the FBI was making headway on a major case. But there can be no doubt about the consequences. Nobody associated with the German spy ring could have failed to realise that the arrests signalled the need to make stayaway and getaway plans.

Against this background, Turrou embarked on a third course of action that put Germany's spies on alert – he warned his suspects and witnesses, Griebl included, that they would be called to testify before the Grand Jury in May. In April and May, at Turrou's request the Southern District of New York Court filed complaints against a number of witnesses requiring them to put up bail money. This meant that they retained their liberty and were free to leave the country.

Imprudent though this seemed in retrospect, Turrou remained for the time being Hoover's untouchable protégé. When Hoover released a diversionary blame salvo, he aimed it not at Turrou, but at Lamar Hardy.

A native of Meridian, Hardy was the 59-year-old son of a Confederate soldier, later a judge of the Superior Court of Mississippi. He had captained the football and baseball teams at Vanderbilt University, and, when appointed Corporation Counsel in New York City in 1915 with the mission of rooting out corruption, he had taken a firm stance – his first measure had been to fire his whole staff. Fiorello La Guardia (Republican mayor of New York, 1934–45) had accepted his recommendation that the city should have a commissioner of purchases to clean up the public contracting process. Hardy's record recommended him to both the mayor and President Roosevelt, who had appointed him District Attorney.[19]

This record failed to deter Hoover, who launched into full assault mode. On 1 June, the FBI director issued the following statement via New York Special Agent in Charge Vetterli: 'The responsibility for the disappearance of Dr Ignatz T. Griebl and the witness Werner G. Gudenberg is the responsibility of the United States Attorney and not of the Federal Bureau of Investigation.'

A little over four hours later, came the riposte from Hardy: 'I deny ... that the disappearance of these witnesses was in any way the result of negligence in the slightest degree on the part of my office.'

The *New York Times* reported the exchange as part of its coverage of what it termed 'the loss of two of the most important figures in the greatest attack on spies in peace time'.[20] All concerned recognised that the stakes were high. The blame game was in full swing.

Blame Games

The escapes sparked a search for scapegoats. At the time, FBI director J. Edgar Hoover was left relatively unscathed. He managed to persuade the White House that he was doing a good counter-intelligence job and gained the confidence of President Roosevelt just as he won the ear of every chief executive during his long tenure as the Boss.

In more recent times, Athan Theoharis has questioned Hoover's reputation for competence. Theoharis worked for the 1970s Senate inquiry into the FBI, CIA and other agencies, and then established a reputation as the chief authority on the history of the FBI. Theoharis, and more recently the historian Svetlana Lokhova, have pointed to an area where Hoover's FBI failed to stop foreign espionage or even to find out that it existed.

They were talking about Soviet spies. The FBI director put up a convincing *show* of being an anti-communist and, as Theoharis and others have shown, persecuted the American left. But when it came to the real threat against national security, he was less effective. In the 1940s, the world learned that Soviet spies had been active in the United States. In the 1990s, more information emerged, partly because post-communist

Russia temporarily opened its security files and partly because of the release of the 'Venona' decrypts of secret Soviet messages intercepted by the US Army's Signals Intelligence Service during the Second World War and in the early Cold War. The combined information confirmed some of Americans' worst fears about how Moscow's espionage damaged their nation.

We now know that in 1928, Joseph Stalin, General Secretary of the Communist Party of the Soviet Union, targeted US aviation technology. In 1931, the Soviet spy Colonel Stanislav Shumovsky enrolled at MIT. Together with accomplices, he successfully sought American military secrets over the next few years. Just as Lonkowski coordinated many of the Abwehr's US efforts, so Aleksandr Ulanofsky, a military intelligence officer operating under the alias Nicholas Sherman, directed a number of the Soviets' American operations in the early 1930s.

Moscow's objectives were in some ways similar to those of Berlin. Its agents hunted for and obtained State Department plans and details of military production. Pre-eminent among them would be a research physicist. Klaus Fuchs fled Hitler's Germany and some years later joined the Manhattan Project that developed an atomic weapon. When the British finally arrested him for passing on vital atomic secrets to the Soviets, J. Edgar Hoover fumed at London for monopolising the case, but the truth is that Fuchs was a giant-sized fish who evaded the security nets of both MI5 and the FBI until significant damage had been done.[1]

At least partly because Hoover opted for the easier task of persecuting radical minorities, the FBI remained blind to and even complacent about more serious threats. And the seriousness of those threats cannot be in doubt. Stalin's dictatorship would turn out to be as bloody as Hitler's. To quote a gruesome phrase, the Soviet leader presided over a 'population deficit' of approximately 48 million people, of whom only 22 million were soldiers killed in action fighting Germany and its allies.[2]

Given what we now know, the FBI's performance against the Abwehr has to be assessed in a wider context of counter-intelligence failure. In the 1930s, however, nobody knew enough about Soviet espionage to mount a serious challenge to the public narrative on FBI competence. The debate in the press and elsewhere was all about the Bureau's competence against German espionage and about who should be held to account for any deficiencies in that regard.

While the debates were vigorous and open in America, in Germany they were just vigorous. The government-controlled press kept the German public in the dark. Within the hidden world of officialdom, there was alarm over the Abwehr agents' exposure and its likely consequences. In Bremen, Erich Pfeiffer had access to US newspapers through his couriers and anxiously followed the stories about the debacle. He fretted that Ignatz Griebl was talking too much and erratically. He worried that the gynaecologist-spy was building Pfeiffer up into some sort of super-spy who could be blamed for the whole spying enterprise. When he heard that he was being accused of running the disastrous Jessie Jordan in Scotland, he breathed a sigh of relief, for he would be able to prove to his German superiors that she was instructed not from his base in Bremen, but from Hamburg.

Schlueter was another problem for Pfeiffer, though also an opportunity to divert the blame from himself. The Bremen chief portrayed his agent as a fanatical Party member and incompetent spy who had tried to show professional intelligence officers how things should be done. Schlueter had launched the inevitably exposed and very damaging McAlpin Hotel plot. Pfeiffer later recalled, 'The colossal ambition of Schlueter, combined with bad crime literature [inspiring Schlueter's actions] was at the bottom of the madness.'

Such was the power of the National Socialist Party that Pfeiffer could not hope to have Schlueter disciplined, so he sent him on a cruise instead. He arranged for the discredited agent to join the crew of a vessel engaged in the 'Strength through Joy' tourist and propaganda programme, organised by the Nazis, which sent more than 10 million Germans on seaborne vacations in 1938. Pfeiffer saw to it that Schlueter's ship was 'guaranteed not to call at American ports'.

Pfeiffer's efforts at self-preservation might well have failed, for powerful factions were out to get him. North German Lloyd complained that the American disclosures damaged its reputation and threatened its trade and profits. It was one thing to aid and abet espionage, but quite another to be found out. Its managing director, Pfeiffer recalled, 'demanded a full explanation' from him.

Worried about the impact of the scandal on German–American relations, Berlin's foreign ministry also expected an explanation from the Bremen spymaster. At the Abwehr's Berlin headquarters, Hermann Menzel raged at Pfeiffer's alleged indiscretions and ordered his junior to curtail his operations and concentrate on monitoring US press reports. Pfeiffer feared that too many forces were aligned against him. There was little support for him in Berlin. People were listening to hostile voices in America, not just the press, but pier master Wilhelm Drechsel with his complaints about the spy scandal's impact on shipping line profits.

Matters came to a head when Wilhelm Canaris ordered Pfeiffer to present himself for a dressing down in Berlin. The naval intelligence officer duly arrived at the Tirpitzuferstrasse military building. He ascended to the Abwehr chief's suite knowing that Canaris opposed the use of violence in intelligence operations and would be horrified by Schlueter's behaviour. He had always found his boss to be a cold fish and he feared he would be unable to wean the admiral away from censure over the controversial American affair, for 'in such cases [Canaris] used to go ahead regardless'.

Pfeiffer entered the boss's office. There, sitting as usual with his back to the windows overlooking the Landwehr Canal, sat the master of the master spies. Physically, Pfeiffer towered over the 5ft 6in chief, but psychologically he felt intimidated. He recalled, 'the atmosphere was that of a deathbed scene'.

Pfeiffer churned out his litany of excuses. It was Schlueter's fault, he was a rogue spy out of control, and had been insubordinate in reporting to Hamburg instead of solely to Pfeiffer in Bremen. Furthermore, Schlueter had used Hamburg cover addresses contrary to Abwehr policy. The 'stovepiping' principle had been breached – in the interest of security, one branch of intelligence was supposed to look after its own secrets independently of other branches, and Schlueter had ignored that requirement.

No doubt Canaris had worked all of this out for himself. He listened with forbearance. In spite of his intimidating summons, he had no intention of changing his view of the man he had hand-picked as a promising spymaster. Pfeiffer may have missed a twinkle in the admiral's eye when he asked, 'Well, Pfeiffer, have you got any complaint against me, too?' He now offered his junior a cigar, and at last Pfeiffer could relax, for 'it represented the pipe of peace'. Instead of punishing Pfeiffer, Canaris assigned him to other tasks.[3]

According to one of Turrou's newspaper articles some months later, Pfeiffer was actually promoted, the recognition being a reward for engineering the evacuation of Griebl from America.[4] Pfeiffer, as one might expect, was keen to defend his competence. He felt he had not really failed in his American mission, nor had he succumbed in his tussle with Turrou. To the extent that he had been brought down, he later told a British interrogator, it was because of collateral work by MI5 and not through good work by American counter-intelligence.[5] Post-war British intelligence assessments tended to agree with Canaris's view that Pfeiffer showed more competence than his colleagues in Hamburg, even if one such report noted that the quality of Abwehr intelligence made no difference anyway, for the leaders of Nazi Germany paid no heed to it.[6]

If a claim can be made for Pfeiffer's competence, does that reflect badly on the FBI? Must the Bureau carry the responsibility for the Abwehr's damage to national security? Although the degree to which Germany's espionage had damaged United States national security was never definitively ascertained, the FBI was worried. Its Washington paymasters never welcomed the theft of US national security secrets, and great volumes of military technology data were being smuggled out of the United States. Pfeiffer claimed that the information his agents obtained conferred military advantage. He gave as an example his spies' procurement of secret technology that improved the anti-aircraft defences of German pocket battleships.[7]

It may be added that the FBI ultimately took the view that Turrou's operation did not entirely wipe out Pfeiffer's spy ring. An FBI report sent to MI5 at the end of the Second World War noted, 'Dr Pfeiffer's activities in the United States were seriously disrupted in 1938 in the Rumrich case.' However, the report continued somewhat apprehensively, 'his representatives, if they actually existed, at Seattle, Washington, and Newport News, Virginia, have never been identified'.[8]

Turrou was pulled both ways when discussing the strength of the German spy menace. In extolling his own achievements, he had to show that the Pfeiffer machine had been overcome. But as an anti-Nazi publicist, he had to hype the monster. He recorded Pfeiffer's boast to Griebl at the high point of the Abwehr's operations:

> In every strategic point in your United States we have an operative. In every armament factory in America we have a spy. In every shipyard we have an agent – in every key position. Your country cannot plan a warship, design a fighting 'plane, develop a new instrument or device, that we do not know about at once![9]

Turrou said that 'vital defence secrets were being smuggled out on virtually every Nazi ship which left our ports'.[10] He knew that credible examples of German spying could be a way of defaming the Nazis. So he alerted Americans to the theft of blueprints for a new anti-aircraft gun under construction in Fort Monmouth, NJ, and of plans to strengthen US battle-ships. He warned them that Germany had obtained 'verbatim accounts of Cabinet conferences, secret military talks and Presidential telephone conversations'. The Abwehr's successes were too tangible to be dismissed as just a story concocted to promote 'European interventionist propaganda'.[11] Aware of the need for tightened security, the FBI hierarchy parroted Turrou's findings without criticism.[12]

Turrou detailed a variety of security breaches. For example, he wrote up the case of W. Starling Burgess. A Harvard gradu-ate who had served as a gunner's mate on the USS *Prairie* in the Spanish–American War of 1898, Burgess was further notable for having married five times, and for having designed the *Enterprise*, *Rainbow* and *Ranger*, racing yachts that all won the America's Cup between 1930 and 1937. Burgess had successfully used aluminium in the construction of his boats and now worked as a naval archi-tect for both the Aluminum Company of America and the Bath Iron Works, which constructed destroyers for the US Navy.

Burgess believed that if an aluminium–steel alloy could be used in the hulls of destroyers, it would enable them to achieve speeds of up to 50mph and help to retard corrosion. In December 1937, Burgess had the first of two meetings with President Roosevelt to discuss the project. After the first meeting, a report of the discussion appeared in a Bath, Maine, newspaper. It was a shocking breach of security – if a local journalist could obtain such information, what might the Abwehr be able to achieve? The FBI responded to the leak by demanding and obtaining lists of all those who had attended meetings to discuss hull technology. It was sending out a clear message about the need for security.[13]

It was not just a question of one isolated case. The FBI worried about Griebl's contention regarding Gibbs and Cox Company, naval architects. Griebl claimed that the German authorities clandestinely received monthly reports on the firm's deliberations in their office at 1 Broadway, New York City, and thus knew all about US naval shipbuilding plans. Accordingly on 15 March, Special Agents F.I. McGarraghy and G.A. Callahan began a string of interviews with Captain A.B. Court, a supervisor of construction for the US Navy who had advised President Roosevelt on naval procurement.[14]

Towards the end of the month, the Bureau acquired some confirmation of how the Abwehr operated. Vetterli and Turrou, in company with two other agents, cross-examined Jacobus Mauritz. The subject of this new inquiry was yet another German-trained mechanic who fought in the First World War, emigrated to America and ended up working on US defence contracts, in this case with the Newport News Shipbuilding and Drydock Company. The former artilleryman worked on the designs of the carriers *Ranger*, *Yorktown* and *Enterprise*, and on their aircraft arrester equipment, in which Pfeiffer and his superiors had expressed interest.

In August 1937, Mauritz had sailed on the SS *Bremen* to visit his mother and other relatives in Germany. The ship's hierarchy had been ready for him. Though Mauritz was travelling tourist class, Werner Jarren, the *Bremen*'s commander, invited him to dine at the captain's table. Jarren declared that Hitler was wonderful and urged Mauritz to read the dictator's testament, *Mein Kampf*. Mauritz said that at the privileged table he found himself in the company of three other pro-Hitler men. All three had doctorates and one of them quizzed him expertly about his defence work. Under later FBI interrogation, Mauritz insisted that he saw through the ruse, refused to cooperate and had never heard of Pfeiffer or Griebl. The FBI's examination of his personal finances, standard procedure with the object of identifying irregular money flows, came up blank.[15]

The upshot was no arrests, but more precautions. According to one of Turrou's reports, 'Captain Court advised that he considered the general system of handling ... confidential plans entirely too loose. He has taken several precautions; in fact he now has the waste paper destroyed.'

The effectiveness of such precautions was open to question. A worker at the Bath construction yard in Maine pointed out that all those who laboured on implementing a design had to know what the design was – tight security was easier said than done. Mauritz offered a parallel critique. After being grilled at some length about who held which cabinet key and who could see what plans, he lost patience with his questioners. He snapped out the view that the press usually found out about ship designs and that 90 per cent of the details of America's new aircraft carriers could be found in the British annual reference book, *Jane's Fighting Ships*. What Mauritz did not say, and what must have been evident to his questioners, was that a crucial 10 per cent was not and that this was the tenth that the Abwehr sought.[16]

The spy case did not change everyone's view. A *New York Times* editorial made a similar point to Mauritz's. It conceded that there were spies, but asserted, 'the spy problem is no real problem at all'. The frenzied effort by the FBI and by Army and Navy counter-intelligence officers was 'in itself symptomatic of the fear psychosis which has swept the world rather than of the alarming importance of the international spy'. There were few real military secrets. How could there be, when Brazil was building destroyers using plans supplied by the United States? The *Times* exhorted its readers not to support any proposal for a new super-spy agency, for spies such as Rumrich represented a low threat and could deliver only slim pickings, as so much technical knowledge had already been internationally disseminated.[17]

If Americans lived in an open world community with no secrets, espionage would indeed have been pointless and there would have been no need for blame games. However, while the *Times*'s vision was an attractive one, it was utopian. All the evidence points to the conclusion that the Abwehr obtained high-grade secret information (as well as a great deal of dross) about American military technology.

Yet if the Abwehr came away with booty, it was at a cost. In propaganda terms, it surrendered the last vestiges of American goodwill that remained in the German treasure chest. MI5's senior officer Guy Liddell saw this clearly. He emphasised not the damage done to American security, but the instructive character of the spy story: 'The most interesting feature of the case is the way in which the whole of the Nazi party machine … has been placed at the disposal of the German intelligence service for the purpose of espionage.' Drawing on a 'source', Liddell contended that the New York pier supervisor Drechsel, far from being an innocent party caught between a rock and a hard place, was the local representative of the National Socialist Party's Inspectorate, which had links with the Gestapo, and was 'closely connected' with Heinrich Himmler's *Schutzstaffel* – the notorious Protection Squadron, or SS. Like Turrou, Liddell saw the activities of the spies as drawing Germany into serious disrepute. Once that perception gained traction, it was destined to undermine relations between Hitler's Germany and the Anglophone world, making Pfeiffer and his colleagues a liability to their country.[18]

Turrou was determined to win the psychological battle by exposing the perfidious Nazi character of his target spies. He pointed an accusing finger at the Abwehr's agents in the United States. But he also wanted to complete his victory in the spy wars by securing the arraignment of those agents who were in custody. One day in June 1938, he achieved that objective.

Foley Square, in Lower Manhattan, was originally a swamp and was then named for a saloonkeeper with Tammany Hall connections. But times change, and, by 1938, it had a newer, cleaner image. The imposing dimensions of its recently completed United States Court House conveyed a stern message.

In that edifice, on 22 June 1938, Hofmann, Voss, Glaser and Rumrich were arraigned on charges of spying. Rumrich, Glaser and Hofmann were accused of stealing military codes and Voss charged with the transmission of secret information about Army aircraft designs. They all pleaded not guilty with the reservation that they might change their pleas later and all remained in custody. They were held in continuation of bail set at $25,000 each, an amount Hofmann's lawyer George C. Dix described as 'outrageous'. They could not raise the bail and no funds were forthcoming from the German consulate. It appears that the Berlin authorities had, after all, settled for the policy, suggested earlier by pier manager Wilhelm Drechsel, that a few should be sacrificed to protect the many.[19]

Assistant United States Attorney Walter N. Thayer stated that fourteen of the indicted were abroad. Jessie Jordan was in prison in Scotland and the thirteen others were in Germany, three of them serving in that country's War Ministry. His superior, Lamar Hardy, persuaded the judge to issue bench warrants for the arrest of all fourteen. No extradition would be possible, but the warrants would assert a moral point, would establish the fugitive status of those named and would render them liable to arrest if they returned to the United States. Such warrants had lifetime validity.[20]

The court charges followed the handing down of indictments by the Grand Jury two days earlier. In a press statement, Hardy put a positive spin on the outcome. The FBI had been investigating since February, he said, and the Grand Jury had conducted a five-week investigation. The inquiries unveiled 'a spy ring of extensive proportions'. German government officials residing in their own country had directed the spies, all of whom were of German extraction. He acknowledged the work of his own assistants, Lester C. Dunigan and John W. Burke, and singled out for special praise 'Mr Leon G. Turrou, a veteran agent who has worked unceasingly since the beginning of the investigation and has, in my opinion, done an extraordinary piece of investigative work.'[21]

Turrou was the hero of the hour. In his tussle with Pfeiffer he had emerged at least a part-winner, and his moral arguments were carrying the day. Unfortunately for his reputation, however, he was about to take action that placed him at the centre of the blame game.

Dismissed with Prejudice

The Grand Jury issued its indictments on 20 June 1938. That very day, Leon Turrou quit the FBI. In his letter of resignation to J. Edgar Hoover, he said he had finished his work as leader of the spy investigation. He had worked so hard to achieve results that his health had suffered. His physician had ordered him to rest and he owed it to his family to take the doctor's advice. Much though he loved the Bureau, he had decided to turn to a literary career. In his writings, he would be sure to convey his admiration for the FBI and for its fight against crime.[1]

It was a bold step. According to the *Washington Post*, Turrou was the 'highest-paid of the G-men'.[2] Barring a fatal shoot-out, if Turrou stayed on as a special agent he could look forward to job security, paid vacations and a pension. However, he was an ambitious person and wanted more than that. Being temperamentally unsuited to administration, he could expect to rise no further in the FBI. As was immediately apparent, he had his eye on an alternative source of future income.

On 22 June, the *New York Post* announced that, the following day, it would start publishing Leon Turrou's account of the spy case. One of America's great campaigning newspapers ever since Alexander Hamilton launched it in 1801, the *Post* was pro-New Deal and vigorously anti-Nazi under its new owner J. David Stern, but lagged in the circulation wars. The paper needed a good story, and Turrou's revelations looked like a sure bet.

The broadsheet devoted two whole pages to promoting its scoop. The spread included a fulsome biography of Turrou and promised 'the most astounding revelations ever published by any newspaper'.[3] The rewards for Turrou seemed ample compensation for the loss of his $4,600 per annum FBI salary. Press reports claimed that Turrou signed a contract giving him a down payment of $25,000, and a total of $40,000 on completion of a series of thirty spy stories. A few days later, there was a report of an advance of $1,500 from the Warner Brothers film studio and a promised $25,000 annual salary. The amounts had been exaggerated for journalistic effect, but Turrou would indeed be well paid. He had always wanted to promote his anti-Nazi message and now he would be amply rewarded for doing so.[4]

Such things take time to arrange and Turrou had been planning his exit from the Bureau for a while. In company with his New York boss Reed Vetterli, he had visited Stern in mid-May to scout the possibilities. In a later letter to Hoover's assistant Ed Tamm, he rejected the idea that in these proceedings he had been the 'vile and woolly schemer and Vetterli … the gullible lamb'. Vetterli, he said, had got wind of Hoover's own plan to publish a book on the spy case and sell the rights to Paramount Pictures for a reputed $25,000, and Vetterli had put it to Turrou that they should make a preemptive move.[5]

Be that as it may, Vetterli had then reported Turrou's negotiations to Hoover. The director did not like the *Post*'s attitude to the FBI and was displeased with the news. He praised Vetterli for telling the tale and, on 1 June, the New York SAC tried to ingratiate himself further when he suggested Turrou might be removed from the spy case team. Hoover took no action, but nine days later Tamm complained that Turrou was 'getting his picture in the paper too often' and was becoming a problem for the FBI. Though he blamed Lamar Hardy not Turrou for the escape of the spies, Hoover was now losing faith in his blue-eyed boy. Stern had required that Turrou resign his position before going to press, in anticipation that there would otherwise be trouble. He could not have anticipated just how bad that trouble would be.[6]

The *Post* was an afternoon paper and that did not give Lamar Hardy much time to react to the announcement of the Turrou series. He moved quickly. By 4.40 p.m., the district attorney had applied for an interim court injunction preventing publication of Turrou's stories. Two hours later, a signal came from Washington confirming that Attorney General Homer Cummings had approved the move. The press seized on the story. Journalists reported Hardy's argument that publication would have prejudiced the spy case. Hardy said the Grand Jury still had matters to consider, including possible additional indictments aimed at the officers of the German shipping companies. He averred that Turrou's articles would divulge information that might unfairly sway the minds of jury members. Stern was unimpressed. He expressed anger at the injunction, which, he claimed, was 'an unprecedented attempt to erase freedom of the press from the Constitution'.[7]

The next day, 23 June, Judge Murray Hulbert presided over a full hearing, in Room 506 of the Federal Court House in Foley Square, to determine whether the injunction should be made permanent. FBI observers reported back to Washington on the proceedings. They sent Hoover the good news that some papers were 'taking cracks' at Turrou.

The newly retired FBI veteran was, however, far from defenceless. One of his lawyers was Robert F. Wagner, Jr, destined to be a future mayor of New York. He was just starting his law career and played a secondary role on the day, but his presence on the team had psychological significance, for his father, the German–American United States Senator for New York, was a pillar of the New Deal and had famously sponsored the 1935 National Labor Relations Act, guaranteeing the right of workers to join trade unions. And Senator Wagner was right there, sitting in on the hearing. The pressure was well and truly on Turrou's opponents, as well as on Turrou himself.[8]

Turrou's senior counsel was Simon H. Rifkind, a Lithuanian–Jewish immigrant who had served a term as administrative assistant to Senator Wagner before returning to private practice in 1933. Rifkind argued that there was no precedent for prior restraint of a newspaper. It was, after all, a kind of advance censorship of the type that was to be found in unfree countries. John Burke, for the government, conceded the absence of precedent, but insisted that publication would prejudice a fair trial.[9] Further advancing the government's case, Don Burke said that Turrou had signed a confidentiality agreement. Rifkind said that he had not and that he had in any case resigned with immediate effect, giving up his right to vacation pay, which meant he was no longer, by any definition, an FBI employee, and thus not bound by confidentiality.

At this point Turrou displayed, for the first and almost the only time in his life, a willingness to attack the director of the FBI. He brought into court what was, in effect, a file on the Bureau's boss. He gave his attorney a scrapbook on the FBI's major cases and Rifkind showed it to Judge Hulbert, stating that 'the most prolific source' of crime story leaks to the press 'is Mr J. Edgar Hoover himself for Mr Hoover wants his picture in the paper'. To reinforce the point, Rifkind handed the judge a pile of articles Hoover had written in the *American Magazine*.[10]

Judge Hulbert may have been impressed. However, he was primarily concerned about the First Amendment prior restraint issue and with the question of whether a former government employee could be bound to silence. He ordered the lawyers to reappear the next day armed with precedents.

The case might have become a Constitutional confrontation, anticipating the landmark ruling in favour of the *New*

York Times in the Pentagon Papers case of 1971 (403 US 713). Instead, it yielded a compromise. Stern agreed not to challenge the restraining injunction during the course of the trial. There was still an issue, for his plan was for the *Post* to publish once the trial was over, whereas the government had not agreed to withdraw its injunction. Stern, through his suspension, had appeased President Roosevelt and Hardy could keep Turrou as an effective witness, a desirable outcome in the absence of the departed Ignatz Griebl. But there remained an unresolved tension over the issue of free speech. That which is hidden is so often treasured and the interest of the press and Hollywood in Turrou's suppressed story intensified.

While President Roosevelt found it politically convenient to blame Turrou, he also took on board some of the FBI veteran's arguments. Reacting to the threatened *Post* disclosures at a press conference on 24 June, he said that there should be a greater investment in counter-espionage and indicated that there would be more money not just for the FBI, but also for Army and Navy intelligence. He implied condemnation of Germany's behaviour in saying that the United States would not embark on foreign espionage – a mode of behaviour, he made clear, that was undesirable.

When a journalist asked him about the diplomatic repercussions of the spy case, the president sidestepped the issue, saying he had not recently heard from the Department of State. He resorted to distraction tactics, attacking an unnamed individual who was obviously Turrou. Revealing what the *New York Times* described as 'disappointment and chagrin', he repeatedly emphasised that a former FBI agent had displayed questionable patriotism and ethics by selling his story to a newspaper.[11]

By fingering an American scapegoat instead of criticising Germany, Roosevelt had avoided giving political ammunition to pro-neutrality critics such as North Dakota's Senator Nye. With mid-term elections looming, he had no intention of moving quickly against Germany. It was his good fortune that the trial of the four alleged spies would not finish until the elections were over. The postponement of the *Post* series helped to sweep the issue of Nazi espionage under the carpet – with the additional advantage that, once the elections were over, the trial and Turrou's now-available account of events would cause the espionage issue to re-emerge. This gave the president policy options, especially when the Democrats held on to their majorities in both House and Senate.

Hoover's dilemma was of a different order. He continued to rely on his former investigator's findings as set forth in his FBI reports – when the Director of Naval Intelligence demanded a briefing some days after Roosevelt's pronouncements, Hoover sent him two of Turrou's reports, as they were (and would continue to be) the best available.[12] However, he could not forgive the apple of his eye for, as he saw it, turning rotten.

It would have been inconsistent of Hoover to refrain from punishing Leon Turrou. There had been a high-profile precedent. On 21 July 1934, an FBI team led by Chicago's SAC Melvin 'Little Mel' Purvis had shot dead the mobster John Dillinger, who was known to have robbed ten banks and killed a policeman. There was intensive press interest, and Purvis, like Turrou, could be economical with the truth when narrating his own role. The diminutive agent made the error of publicising himself as an ace G-Man. He posed for a victory photograph at a Chicago train station with Attorney General Cummings, with the FBI director nowhere in sight. He even capitalised on his fame by marketing breakfast cereals.

Accordingly, Hoover took steps to reduce Purvis's image to that of a bit player, asserting that he had only a secondary role in the Dillinger incident. Purvis resigned from the FBI the following year. According to his son, he felt betrayed by Hoover, yet continued to love his boss, keeping a framed photo of the director in his office until the day in 1960 when he died of a self-inflicted gunshot wound.[13]

It is true, as his critics say, that in Hoover's view there was only one vacancy for the position of FBI hero and that he was determined to be the sole applicant. At the same time, the director had three responsibilities that help to explain his behaviour towards Turrou. First, he had to rein in those special agents who were publicity-mongers and who sought fame that would lead to more lucrative opportunities outside the Bureau. Had he failed to do so, the FBI would have haemorrhaged talent. Second, Hoover was responsible enough to know that mistimed publicity could wreck criminal trials. Hoover's final responsibility was for the integrity of counter-espionage work, which would be prejudiced if Abwehr officials could simply read all about the FBI's operations in the newspapers.

There was a danger that, by attacking Turrou, Hoover would discredit the prosecution's main asset. He took the risk regardless. The director claimed that his fallen idol had always been a 'problem child' who took advantage of a 'gullible public'. The press was not taken in. The *New York Times* thought Hoover was 'jealous' of a 'publicity rival' who had 'scooped' him.[14] When the Boss responded by publishing a searing indictment of the American press in *Collier's* magazine, one newspaper editor accused the FBI director of promoting 'off the record' publicity one minute, and abusing journalists the next.[15]

In the first spate of his rage against Turrou, Hoover recommended to the Justice Department that the former agent should not appear as a witness in the forthcoming spy trial. He said that the success of the government's case would be 'imperiled'. He had it on the authority of the FBI's New York office that other agents could testify instead. In the relatively few cases where Turrou had interrogated alone, the relevant witnesses could be re-interviewed by replacement personnel.

In a separate memorandum, Hoover asked the Justice Department's advice on how he might dismiss Turrou 'with prejudice'. One possible recourse was to the 1933 Act for the

Protection of Government Records. This law had been a reaction to the controversial case of Herbert O. Yardley.[16]

A poker-playing US code-breaker who could have given lessons to both Hoover and Turrou on how to be cavalier with the dictates of modesty and discretion, Yardley had directed a cryptographic unit known as the American Black Chamber (ABC). In the 1920s there were cutbacks in foreign as well as domestic security expenditure and in 1929 the US government closed down ABC. Upset by this decision, Yardley published a memoir entitled *The American Black Chamber*. The book shocked the Japanese, for from its pages they learned that ABC had been spying on them during the Washington naval conference of 1921. Publication of the book had contributed to a downward spiral in Japanese–American relations, just as the Nazi spy case now threatened German–American relations. When Yardley wrote a sequel called 'Japanese Diplomatic Secrets', the US government sought to limit the diplomatic damage, and impounded the manuscript. Congress backed up the executive branch by passing the Act for the Protection of Government Records, otherwise known as the 'Yardley Act'.[17]

Commenting on Turrou's resignation, an editorial in the *New York Times* noted that the former special agent's plan to publish in the *Post* had created a mess and speculated the Yardley Act might be invoked. Two hundred miles south at the FBI's Pennsylvania Avenue headquarters, Special Agent Percy J. ('Sam') Foxworth drew the editorial to the attention of his superiors, Ed Tamm and J. Edgar Hoover. Destined for high office in the FBI, Foxworth commanded the ear of the director and was regarded as politically astute.[18]

Fearing that federal attorneys had been unable to advance watertight legal grounds in the injunction proceedings against the *Post*, Foxworth took legal advice on the applicability of the Yardley Act. His advisers variously told him that nobody remembered the Act, that prosecutors were afraid of using it for fear of being accused of suppressing free speech and that in any case Congress had not agreed to the legislation. The last assertion was incorrect, but in any case Hoover and his advisers decided against invoking the Yardley law. It was just as well from their point of view, because the text of the law (of which FBI headquarters seemed to be ignorant) referred merely to an 'official diplomatic code or any matter prepared in any such code'. While the 1938 espionage indictments did refer to the theft of codes, the firing of Turrou had nothing to do with that and the Yardley Act was inapplicable to it.[19]

The United States lacked any equivalent of the UK's Official Secrets Act, so it was a problem when the government wanted to suppress information in the interests of a prosecution or of national security. Even allowing for that, the FBI was ill prepared for a contingency such as that created by the Turrou case. Had its lawyers been better versed, they might have considered referencing the 1876 Supreme Court case, *Totten v. United States*. In 1790, Congress had voted President George Washington a Contingency Fund, authorising unvouchered expenditure on spying. The practice continued and President Abraham Lincoln used spies in the Civil War. One of his agents, William A. Lloyd, accepted the mission of secretly penetrating the Confederacy in pursuit of military intelligence. His controller would authorise payment of a monthly salary of $200. But his supervisor never did so because he was assassinated. For this reason, Lloyd received only his expenses. At the war's conclusion, William Lloyd sued the Government for back pay. However, the Supreme Court found against him, stating that he was in breach of his secrecy contract: 'Both employer and agent must have understood that the lips of the other were to be forever sealed.'[20]

Totten was a potentially useful precedent and has since been cited, for example in the 2005 case *Tenet v. Doe*. However, there was no acknowledged criminal basis for the prosecution of those accused of betraying the secrets of the federal government. The contrast with the UK was stark. In 1932, the writer Compton Mackenzie published *Greek Memories*, a memoir of his time as a British intelligence officer. The authorities suppressed the book and Mackenzie was prosecuted under the Official Secrets Act. Such options were not open to the FBI or to any other branch of the US government.

J. Edgar Hoover did have one card up his sleeve. He had cautioned Turrou at the outset of his career that he should observe the 'no publicity' convention, but in 1935 the FBI director went one step further in the wake of the Purvis fracas. He made confidentiality a contractual requirement. Rifkind denied it, probably out of ignorance, but on 13 November 1935, Turrou did sign, in the presence of the Notary Public of Bronx County, NY, the following sworn statement:

> The confidential character of the relationship of the employees of the Federal Bureau of Investigation with the public is fully understood by me, and the strictly confidential character of any and all information secured by me in connection directly or indirectly with my work as a Special Agent, or the work of other employees of which I may become cognizant, is fully understood by me, and neither during my tenure of service with the Federal Bureau of Investigation nor *at any other time* will I violate this confidence, nor will I divulge any information of any kind or character whatsoever that may become known to me to persons not officially entitled thereto.[21]

Notwithstanding the fact that he had resigned from the FBI before signing his contract with the *New York Post*, Turrou had breached his 1935 undertaking to reveal no FBI secrets 'at any other time'.

On this ground, Attorney General Cummings and FBI director Hoover wrote to tell Turrou he was being released, with notices of the dismissal going to Special Agents in Charge right across the nation. The envelope containing the original of Cummings's letter was dated 25 June, but the letter within was backdated to 20 June, making the point that the government did not accept Turrou's resignation and that he was being fired. In February, Turrou had signed another contract stipulating that the resignation of a special agent should take place with immediate effect. At the time, he had welcomed the change, and even later he may have thought it would release him to start publishing right away. Immediate severance meant he lost his holiday pay entitlement and Hoover stipulated that he would also lose his pension. But in light of Turrou's writing contracts, this was less punitive than it would otherwise have been.[22]

There was, however, a sting in the tail. In his dismissal letter Hoover used the phrase 'with prejudice', meaning that Turrou was officially in disgrace. The director explained what he intended this to mean in practice: 'Turrou can never get back into any Government Department as long as he lives.' As punishment for breaking the code of *omerta*, Hoover's one-time favourite had incurred a *vendetta*.[23]

As Hoover intended, dismissal with prejudice was a real shock for Turrou, whose very identity was wrapped up with a patriotic attachment to his adopted country and with loyalty to the FBI and its leader. He tried to defend himself and continued to be, for a limited period, critical of the FBI director. He said the four accused spies had already signed confessions, so his published utterances could not affect the forthcoming trial. Succumbing to apparent amnesia about the oath he signed in 1935, he at first claimed, 'there exists no pledge, no rule, no statute and no regulation which forbids publishing any of the facts acquired by me'.[24]

Turrou then claimed that the 1935 oath was a supplementary order that Hoover rushed through in the wake of the Purvis affair: 'After Purvis resigned and wrote stuff, [Hoover] became jealous.'[25] He now asserted that he had signed the oath 'casually', scribbling his signature in haste on a whole bunch of official documents that had been presented to him for his authentication. His suggestion was that there had been an effort to trick him into silence.[26] He observed that Hoover had published stories with a view to educating the public, just as he intended to do, and that the director had been well paid for his contributions. What impressed the media was his charge of hypocrisy against his former boss. The *Washington Post* ran his defence under the headline 'Hoover Writes, Why Can't I?'[27] American newspapers were wedded to the principle of free speech and, from Hoover's perspective, there was a distinct danger that Turrou would remain a hero. Turrou's fame might have got him into trouble with the director, but it was also his shield. Hoover's publicity staff accumulated clippings with such headlines as 'Turrou, Ace of FBI, Cracked Hard Cases'.[28]

It was not a foregone conclusion that Turrou's trial testimony would carry all before it. For one thing, his amnesia defence over the *omerta* oath threatened to become a liability. On 1 July, the *New York Post* published yet another statement by him on the sworn promise to remain silent: 'I have no recollection of having signed this statement. Nor can I recall the circumstances.' Johanna Hofmann's lawyer George Dix seized on this professed memory lapse. In an affidavit filed in relation to the spy case, he stated:

> Since Mr Turrou admits he has a poor memory, and his recollection may be equally inaccurate in my client's case, I insist that it is all the more important that I obtain the testimony of witnesses having knowledge of the facts.

He claimed that Turrou had a financial interest in Griebl's departure for Germany, as the absence of the key witness licensed the detective to publish without fear of contradiction. Dix requested the setting up of a commission to interview Griebl and another key witness, Karl Schlueter, and he demanded more time to allow him to gather this and other evidence in defence of his client. The FBI had already dishonoured Turrou, and Dix was determined to complete the job.[29]

1. Wilhelm Lonkowski. Code-named 'Agent Sex', Lonkowski played a key role in setting up the Nazi spy ring before his dramatic escape to Germany in 1935. (Courtesy of the FBI)

2. The steamship *Bremen*. Holder of the Blue Riband for the fastest Atlantic crossing and the pride of the German merchant marine, the vessel and its sibling ships fell under Hitler's control and were vehicles for the Nazi spy ring. (Courtesy of DSM)

3. The Bendlerblock, Berlin. This military office building housed the headquarters of the Abwehr, Germany's secret service. Its director, Wilhelm Canaris, worked from a desk with his back to the balcony at the front façade, overlooking the Landwehr Canal. (Courtesy of Stefani Werle)

4. Jessie Jordan. The Scottish spy whose activities alerted first Britain's counter-intelligence agency, MI5, and then the FBI. Was she a conniving pro-German adventurer, or a sad and rejected woman in search of adventure? (Courtesy of TNA)

5. Felin Newydd. Mary Wallace, Jordan's aunt, lived in this country house, situated in Powys, Wales, not far from Y Gelli Gandryll (Hay on Wye), scene of the annual Hay Festival of Literature & Arts. She played an unwitting role in the Ring of Spies scandal. (Author's collection)

6. Talgarth postbox. Here, while visiting Felin Newydd, Jordan posted items intercepted by MI5. They included reports on military dispositions in Aldershot and a forged letter from her Aunt Mary offering to finance Jordan's deep-cover hairdressing business in Dundee. (Author's collection)

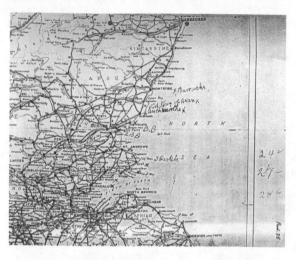

7. The Jordan Spy Map. A nosey employee, Mary Curran, found this map in Jessie Jordan's handbag. It revealed her treasonable intentions and her amateurism – her 'castels' and 'barracks' were mainly innocuous buildings. (Courtesy of TNA)

8. Guenther Rumrich. From a distinguished family in the old Austro-Hungarian Empire, he was an undistinguished spy. His service as an FBI informant resulted in a reduced prison sentence in the espionage trial of 1938. (Courtesy of FBI)

9. Heinrich Lorenz. A ship captain who helped the Nazi spies, Lorenz hoped to retire to live in the United States. The Nazis detained his wife Alice because they suspected her of spying for America. His daughter Marita slept with Fidel Castro and spied for the CIA. (Courtesy of DSM)

10. William Drechsel. An influential Nazi fellow traveller, Drechsel supervised German shipping in the port of New York and gave every assistance to spies and the Nazis, yet cooperated with the FBI's Turrou who refrained from arresting him. (Courtesy of DSM)

11. Erich Pfeiffer and friend. Hilde Gelsdorf was the secretary and mistress of the German spymaster in charge of purloining America's military secrets. Pfeiffer later won the respect of his MI5 interrogators. (Courtesy of TNA)

12. Mata Hari. Executed by the French in 1917 after being convicted of spying for Germany, the Dutch-born dancer and courtesan became a 1930s obsession of the media – and of Nazi spies. (Courtesy of FM)

13. Ignatz Griebl. A leading anti-Semite and womaniser, he promoted the idea of a 'Mata Hari' style honeytrap 'salon' in Washington, DC. He informed on his fellow agents and helped Turrou crack the German spy ring. (Courtesy of FBI)

14. Kate Moog leaving the Federal Court, NYC, 27 October 1938. Her lover Ignatz Griebl told German intelligence chief Canaris that she could run his envisaged Washington, DC 'salon', a vehicle for blackmail that would yield the secrets of American national security. (Courtesy of Historic Images)

15. Hotel Adlon. Viewed here from the roof of the Reichstag with the Brandenburg gate in the foreground, it was the venue of the Griebl–Moog love tryst on the eve of their meeting with Canaris, to whose office they travelled via the Tiergarten, to the right of the image. (Author's collection)

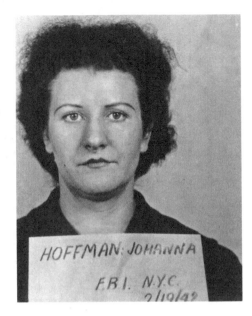

16. Johanna Hofmann. Her Gestapo-linked lover, Karl Schlueter, abandoned her to the FBI. The American press labelled her a 'minor' Mata Hari. Her imprisonment for espionage took away what remained of her youth. (Courtesy of FBI)

The Brown Pest

17. Jacob Burck cartoon, 'The Brown Pest'. The Poland-born Jewish-American artist and Pulitzer Prize-winner here gives an impression of the sinking reputation of the once-prestigious SS *Bremen* and its sister ships. The image appeared in the *Daily Worker* in 1935. (*Hunger and Revolt: Cartoons by Burck* [New York: Daily Worker, 1935])

18. Leon Turrou. Acclaimed in his day as the FBI's best detective, Turrou exposed the Nazi spy ring. (Courtesy of Bob Turrou)

19. J. Edgar Hoover (left) 'arrests' Louis 'Lepke' Buchalter (centre). This photo-opportunity apprehension of a criminal who had surrendered in advance without firing a shot typified the FBI director's determination to stay centre stage. That determination spelled the doom of high-profile Leon Turrou. (Library of Congress, LC 2004676730)

20. Farewell, German–American friendship. Germany's Ambassador Hans Dieckhoff had worried that the 1938 spy revelations would influence American public opinion away from the U and in favour of the UK. Here, on 22 November 1938, he bids goodbye to American journalists he had befriended prior to his abrupt recall to Berlin. (Harris & Ewing Collection, LC 20168744

Seeking the Evidence

Anti-fascists looked for a well-publicised trial and conviction of the four incarcerated spy suspects. Turrou's removal from the FBI had been a blow for the prosecution. It was another setback for them when George C. Dix secured a delay to the start of proceedings. To compound still further the difficulties of the prosecution and its supporters, the FBI's New York office was in disarray.

For in the wake of Turrou's severance, Reed Vetterli, too, quit the FBI. Tom Tracy, a former special agent now running a private detective business, was recruiting former colleagues. Turrou had refused to join him in September 1937, but now Vetterli accepted Tracy's offer of $12 a day. The former SAC also wrote for newspapers and irritated Turrou by asking for an introduction to Hollywood. J. Edgar Hoover charged Tracy with organising a conspiracy against the Bureau. Just after Vetterli's resignation on 22 August, the FBI director confided to his senior colleague Clyde Tolson that 'we have been having considerable trouble in our New York Division relative to mal-contents and griping'. Turmoil in the FBI's New York office did nothing to expedite a successful spy prosecution.[1]

The delay that Dix had achieved meant that all four of the accused languished in prison in a state of limbo. For Rumrich, the ultimate prospects seemed not too bad, as he hoped to be rewarded for testifying against the other three. His accomplice Erich Glaser could look forward to no such special treatment. Otto Voss, very evidently the most effective spy of the four in custody, was in serious trouble. Charles W. Philipbar was his attorney and in mid-July demanded full details of the charges against his client, no doubt with the object of picking holes in them. In the absence of provision of bail, though, Voss, like the other accused, had to stay in jail.[2]

Jenni Hofmann stared at the walls of her cell with one consolation. In George Dix, she had a fighting lawyer. Dix perceived from the outset that Turrou would be the main and indispensable witness for the prosecution. With the former special agent already under a cloud, he sought an opportunity to complete the destruction of his credibility.

Turrou saw Dix as a person who hated him with an irrational intensity and he reciprocated the animosity. In truth, the former detective and the lawyer shared certain characteristics. They both had a propensity to exaggerate. Each of them fought hard for his chosen cause. In the course of the Second World War, Dix would take on more than 300 civil liberty cases, at a time of intense patriotic fervour courageously defending citizens who had been detained as enemy aliens. All this lay ahead. In 1938, still a lawyer on the make, he defended Jenni Hofmann with formidable energy.[3]

When Dix appeared in court on 29 June, he supplied a foretaste of future tactics. The attorney charged that Turrou had been corrupted by the 'arrogance of office', and habitually lied. He levelled a charge that muddied the waters and delayed proceedings. Turrou, he claimed, had deliberately allowed Griebl to escape. When Judge Vincent Leibell asked him what proof he had, he said 'none, but I'll try to get it'. Questioned again by the judge, he confessed to his 'personal animus' towards the detective. Turrou was in court at the time, shaking his head in denial of the charges. The judge reprimanded Dix for impugning the reputation of a government official of many years' standing, but allowed him time to find his proofs.[4]

There ensued a battle by affidavit. Each side presented its arguments by this means to the court. Dix fired his next salvo on 2 July. He toned down his invective slightly, saying that he did 'not impute the receiving of a bribe', insisting instead that Turrou had been 'naïve'. He still argued that the former detective was 'glad that Griebl escaped', as 'Griebl, fugitive, necessarily would arouse more interest in such articles [as Turrou planned to publish] than Griebl as a witness who could or would not tell anything of importance'.

Dix took aim also at Lamar Hardy and Lester Dunigan. Neither the district attorney nor his assistant had interviewed Griebl or Schlueter. How could they assume that the evidence of these individuals, if given, would not have affected the outcome of the case? Dix claimed that Griebl could have been forced to testify. He could have been extradited from Germany on a charge of larceny – Dix did not specify whether he was referring to the Jewish land deal or to Griebl's sleight of hand over the automobile accident-damages claim. Because of negligence at the very least, he argued, the attorneys and Turrou had let slip an opportunity.[5]

Dix appealed for more sympathetic treatment by claiming that the odds were stacked against him. Complaining that Assistant US Attorney Dunigan told government witness Senta de Wanger 'I have a Texas judge here who will do anything I ask him to', Dix painted a picture of conspiring Texans, as Hardy also hailed from the Lone Star State. Judge T. Whitfield Davidson, in Manhattan on a temporary assignment, sprang to the defence of Dixie: 'We may be regarded as old-fashioned down in Texas, but we still believe in a God, we still believe in law and justice as expounded by John Marshall, and we are proud of a civilisation that has given to the Union such men as George Washington, Robert E. Lee, Andrew Jackson, Sam Houston, John Garner.' The judge held Dix to be in contempt of court.[6]

In a supplemental affidavit sworn on 22 August, Dix indicated that he was 'familiar with the German language'. He had been in touch with Maria Griebl, who on 4 August showed him a letter from her husband, mailed in Germany on 26 June. Dix quoted extracts from the letter in his own translation. In his letter Ignatz Griebl indicated what was perfectly true, that he had never signed a confession for the G-men. He told his wife he was not a fugitive from justice and had never been in contempt of a subpoena to appear before the Grand Jury. This was because the date for the Grand Jury meeting had been postponed from the original day of 5 May, and Vetterli had then phoned him to say his summons to appear had expired.

On 10 May, Turrou told Griebl and Kate Moog that a new date would be set for their appearance. It was on the following day that Griebl took action to ensure he would not be present to be served with a writ compelling him to appear in court. It was the day on which he made his unannounced disappearance, abruptly leaving his wife and his mistress to 'stowaway' on the *Bremen* with its obliging crew. In his conjugal letter he recalled that Turrou and Hardy were 'furious' at him, because by leaving the country he had taken out of their hands 'all possible legal control'.

Warming to his theme, Griebl claimed Turrou could not be a believable witness 'because he himself is the investigator'. There was no possibility of an objective trial and that was not the intention. The real aim was:

> to serve the American Public for breakfast a sensational 'Spy case' with highly interesting Anecdotes. What these G-Men, including Mr. Turrou, assert sounds like an interesting spy romance, which exists only in his brain, but never occurred. These little fellows are making themselves ridiculous …

[Turrou's] action is against the Ethics of a G–Man, and
therefore, not permissible.[7]

Griebl's letter encouraged Dix to believe that its author could
be deployed to destroy Turrou's credibility as a witness.

Dix's plan was for a commission to visit Germany to re-
interview Griebl, using the authority and facilities of US
consuls in Bremen, Bremerhaven or Berlin. In support of his
request, he had Johanna Hofmann file an affidavit suggesting
that Turrou had never regarded her as a prime actor in the
spy ring, merely as an accessory. To his formal application,
Dix attached three appendices. The first minuted a conversation he had had with Griebl on 30 April, saying that Griebl
refused to talk for fear of incriminating himself and that he
denied all knowledge of Jenni Hofmann. The second told
of Dix's encounter with Turrou on 21 June, the day when
Jenni Hofmann appeared before the Grand Jury. The lawyer
alleged that on this occasion Turrou implied Hofmann was
innocent, then assaulted Dix and threatened him with arrest.
The third appendix was an affidavit on the subject of an
interview he had conducted with Maria Griebl on 24 June –
unsigned, as Maria's lawyer had advised against it. In it, Maria
claimed that her husband was convinced that Turrou wanted
him to disappear.[8]

On 28 July, Judge Leibell ruled against the commission proposal and ordered Dix's supporting narrative struck from the
records of the court on the grounds that it was 'scandalous'.[9]
However, once he had dropped the provocative elements in
his plea, the persistent Dix got his way before a more sympathetic judge. Early in September, a commission did travel
to Germany. Lamar Hardy remarked that it was the first time
that a federal court in the Southern District had sent such a
commission abroad. Like the spies, the commission travelled
in James Bond-style luxury. They sailed on the SS *Champlain*.
A French Line ship constructed in Saint-Nazaire, the fast and

elegantly designed *Champlain* was one of the new breed of 'cabin liners'. The commission members who sailed on this well-appointed ship were George C. Dix, Hardy's assistants Lester C. Dunigan and John W. Burke Jr, and FBI special agent John T. McLaughlin.[10]

On 19, 20 and 21 September 1938, the commission interviewed Dr Griebl at the US Consulate in Berlin. The fugitive said he was prepared to return to the United States to testify on certain conditions: immunity from prosecution, freedom to publish his own account of events and all expenses paid, transatlantic fares and legal fees to be included.[11] The attorneys refused to agree to those conditions. Thereupon, Griebl offered to make a statement at the consulate, provided his wife, then under detention in New York as a material witness, be released. The attorneys agreed to this.[12]

Griebl insisted that Jenni Hofmann was a spy. McLaughlin reported that the former New York medic was trying to persuade the German foreign ministry to tell all four accused to plead guilty – if true, he was adhering to the Drechsel damage limitation plan. Griebl stated that Turrou had no credibility, as he was a Jew and a radical – no doubt Griebl had picked up on some of the spurious anti-Semitic stories about the ex-G-man being a communist. As ever, however, the trickster was enigmatic. Off the record, he confided to McLaughlin, 'You can understand what would happen to me here if I did not say that and did not contradict the things I told the FBI ... Personally, self-preservation has always been my god.'[13]

Griebl rambled on in a manner that the attorneys felt was 'silly' and 'half crazy', and finally supplied a written statement that ran to 17,000 words.[14]

Back at FBI headquarters, officials impatiently awaited reports from McLaughlin. The envoy later explained to Ed Tamm that the six messages he had sent via diplomatic pouch were the only communications he had been able to get out of Germany. The German authorities restricted what he could send by coded telegrams and he did not have enough money to make phone calls. Finally, two copies of Griebl's statement arrived in New York on the morning of 6 October. Turrou was at the pier when the ship arrived, according to the FBI's Dwight Brantley in 'frantic' mood. The plan was to restrict dissemination of the statement until the trial opened, so, as Turrou was no longer with the FBI, McLaughlin would not tell him what Griebl had said. McLaughlin also refused to speak to the press, who were there in force. Dix was at the pier. Griebl's confirmation of Hofmann's guilt must have been a blow to him, but he still fought for his client. He exchanged 'venomous glances' with Turrou before regaling the newspaper reporters with his conspiracy theory about Turrou helping Griebl to escape. Another FBI agent who observed that harangue reported that the press were just not interested in Dix's version of events.[15]

Just as George Dix sought to defend his client by seeking evidence in Germany, so Lamar Hardy sought foreign evidence that would bolster the government's case. His idea was to put Jessie Jordan on the witness stand. She had already confessed and had been convicted in Scotland, so her words would carry some authority in court. True, Jessie's knowledge about German espionage was limited. But she could testify about the Crown affair and about the Abwehr's poste restante system, and that would add credibility to the prosecution narrative.

American–British contacts over the spy case and its Jessie Jordan dimension are a chapter in the history of the developing special intelligence relationship between the two countries. Because of the news leaks at the time of Rumrich's arrest, the US authorities had been unable to keep their promise to keep the Jessie Jordan angle under wraps, yet the intelligence relationship continued to be important to both sides.

MI5's Guy Liddell kept a close eye on American developments. In March, he visited America and spoke to officials in the State Department, FBI and military intelligence. He noted a 'slight contretemps' between Hoover and the State Department over the handling of the spy case. More interested in arrests than in diplomacy, the FBI did not put the smoothing of American–German relations at the heart of its agenda. The State Department's James Dunn had a different approach. He said he was anxious to exchange information about the Nazi threat, *provided* it was kept secret to avoid the possibility of awkward questions being asked in Congress that would prejudice relations with Germany.

Over the next two months, Liddell liaised with US Army intelligence and the FBI over the case, and kept the anti-appeasement civil servant Sir Robert Vansittart abreast of events. He gave an undertaking that the Crown letters could be used in an American prosecution and advised that a qualified witness could be sent from the UK to testify at the trial, though he did not specify Jessie Jordan.

Colonel Lee, America's military attaché in London, was convinced of the need for US and UK cooperation to meet the German espionage threat. In October he would ask MI5 for advice on how a new US counter-espionage service might be constructed. MI5 responded by outlining how things were done in the UK. The FBI would take advantage of such thinking and J. Edgar Hoover was destined over the next two years to play a key role in boosting counter-intelligence and in US–UK intelligence cooperation. Meantime, in the summer of 1938, his special agent Sam Foxworth strove to promote cooperation over the approaching spy trial. In seeking British cooperation over the deployment of Jessie Jordan, Lamar Hardy had grounds to be optimistic.[16]

Through the summer, the American press reported on the progress of anticipated British cooperation. In mid-May, Hardy had spent two hours questioning Turrou before the Grand Jury and, although he refused to answer questions after the session, it was evident that he was looking across the

Atlantic for support. The *New York Times* sanguinely reported, 'British Evidence Made Available to US for Colleagues' Trial'.[17] In June, Britain's *Daily Herald* echoed the *New York Times* assumption that prosecution witnesses who had been lined up for the Jessie Jordan trial would cross the Atlantic and testify in New York.[18]

On 29 June, with the British press poised for a sensation, Hardy crossed the Atlantic. He sailed on the SS *Normandie*, the world's biggest liner and an even more luxurious ship than the *Champlain*. He took with him his daughter Micheline, whom he had long promised a trip to Paris to see her mother's relatives. On the eve of his departure he told the ever-attendant American press nothing about his objectives, other than saying he might look into 'angles' of the case in 'France and England'. A *Daily Mail* sleuth tracked him down on board the *Normandie* and conducted what he tried to pass off as an interview. He quoted the canny Texan as saying, 'I've got important clues.' The journalist injected an air of mystery into his revelation that Hardy was alighting in France as well as England (hardly news, as this was the *Normandie*'s usual route) and predicted that he would travel to Scotland. The district attorney having told him nothing, the journalist finished his story with speculative remarks about the dangers Hardy faced in travelling without a G-man bodyguard.[19]

The *Daily Express* considered Hardy to be America's 'spy-catcher No. 1'.[20] But if Hardy expected Jessie Jordan and possibly other witnesses to testify in New York, he did not understand MI5's mission to shield sensitive matters from prying eyes. In the event, that problem did not arise, for Hardy discovered to his cost that he had reckoned without Scottish legal scruples. Whatever the views of MI5 about Anglo-American intelligence cooperation, it could not deliver a result in the Scottish courts.

On 22 and then 23 July 1938, MI5 director Vernon Kell orally conveyed to P.J. Rose, assistant secretary of state for

Scotland, Hardy's request to interview Jessie in prison 'in the expectation of ascertaining from her that she is only a post box'. The word 'only' jumps off the page for its irrationality, as Jessie's post box function was potentially much more dangerous to all concerned than her amateur forays into direct espionage. But Hardy's seemingly illogical deployment of the word was calculated. It conveyed the message that the Americans would not come down too heavily on Jessie and that Scottish cooperation would not infringe her legal rights. Hardy was interested in documenting the links to the mastermind behind the Nazi spy ring. He diverted Jessie from that frightening thought by using the minimalist word 'only'.

Unfortunately for Hardy's plan, Rose had in conversation already explained to Kell that it would be contrary to Scottish legal practice to allow a foreign inquisitor to interrogate a prisoner. In the spirit of cooperation, Kell now tried to broker a compromise. If the Americans were to drop charges against Jordan, could they then interview her for informational purposes? Rose said yes, if she gave her consent, if her solicitor were present and (a special Scottish touch) if the Americans paid all expenses arising. He tartly added that the Lord Advocate had already told the 'American Authorities' that Jessie Jordan 'was just a post box'. The Scottish legal grandee and the New York lawyer were talking at cross purposes, for the Crown–Jordan correspondence was what interested Hardy most of all.

Rose concluded with a further note of caution, pointing out that Jessie was likely to be deported to Germany on the completion of her prison sentence. Her position there 'will be very difficult if she has given evidence [to Hardy or in New York] against her American associates'. In the event, Jordan played no direct part in the New York prosecution. As a setback for British–American cooperation, her non-appearance could be discounted as a blip and blamed on Scottish lawyers. As a setback for the trial prosecution in the USA, it was potentially more serious. It dictated a fallback to Plan A: relying on the testimony of Leon Turrou.[21]

Both Hardy's trip to Scotland in an effort to gain evidence from Jessie Jordan and his deputies' trip to Berlin to interview Griebl were official ventures, sanctioned by federal officials in Foley Square and reimbursed by the US taxpayer. In addition to these trips, there occurred, according to Erich Pfeiffer, two private American forays in search of evidence.

Towards the end of the summer, a person whom Pfeiffer identified as 'Lorenz of the *Bremen*' contacted him with a warning. When later under interrogation, Pfeiffer claimed that he knew little about Heinrich Lorenz, even being unaware of his first name. He did concede that Lorenz had worked for him from 1935. As the spymaster put it, Lorenz, as a captain with the North German Lloyd Line, 'gave permission for stewards on his ship who were working for us, to land'. If Pfeiffer suspected that Lorenz, the husband of an American woman, was playing both sides, he did not mention it.[22]

Lorenz's warning was about Leon Turrou. Earlier in the year, the FBI detective had been in hostile pursuit of German military personnel who were facilitating the spy ring. Now, though, he wanted to interview Pfeiffer 'on a friendly basis' to obtain copy for his intended book about the case. The following paraphrase of Pfeiffer's account indicates how the German intelligence officer took precautions: 'The naïveté of the suggestion amused [him], but he removed his nameplate from the door of the house in Misslerstrasse and warned his wife to stall off any callers.'

Pfeiffer continued by saying that Turrou's attempt at a visit was the first of two abortive approaches. The Misslerstrasse measures had been:

> ... a wise precaution, for shortly afterward another American, apparently Jenni Hofmann's lawyer, called at the house, to be told that Pfeiffer didn't live there any more. The

lawyer promptly had recourse to the Gestapo HQ, whence Haupt. Schultz phoned the news to Pfeiffer, who got him to sidetrack this very simple American.[23]

It was an unusual spectacle. The spymaster who normally lived a tranquil and sheltered life while he dispatched his agents to work at their peril suddenly had to behave like a fugitive in his home city, hiding from Turrou and then from the terrier-like George Dix. Pfeiffer's precautions were yet another signal that, from the German perspective, America with its tradition of free investigation would be a difficult country to deal with.

Of the two unwanted visitors, the former G-man would turn out to be the greater threat to the Abwehr. While Dix was nearing the end of the line, the forthcoming trial would show that Leon Turrou had been anything but naïve.

15

The Nazi Spy Trial

On 14 October 1938, a jury of ten men and two women filed into a federal courtroom in Foley Square. The accused, witnesses and other parties having also assembled, the spy trial was at last set to begin. John C. Knox, presiding, had been prosecution counsel in spy cases in the First World War and in 1918 President Woodrow Wilson appointed him one of the youngest ever federal judges. By 1938, he was thus an experienced member of the judiciary. He met with Leon Turrou's approval.[1]

Judge Knox opened proceedings in a trial that would have a political impact at home and abroad. At home, the view from the White House was distinctly unsettling. Mid-term elections loomed on 8 November. American internationalists might well exploit the case. Champions of American neutrality such as Senator Nye would then cause real trouble.

The significance of the event was apparent to commentators abroad. Describing the trial as the 'biggest show in town in twenty years', London's *Daily Express* reported that war ministries all over Europe and Asia were watching the case. In the Soviet Union, both *Pravda* and *Izvestia* devoted their front pages to coverage of the courtroom drama, which, they held, proved Stalin had been right to drive through the Moscow purges and spy trials of 1936–38. Only in Germany did the authorities discourage public interest in the Rumrich–Voss–Glaser–Hofmann case. *Völkischer Beobachter*, the Nazis' official organ, ignored it, as did other German newspapers.[2]

While the German press may have been silent, the diplomatic reaction was one of alarm. The German embassy in Washington saw a looming public relations disaster. Ambassador Hans Dieckhoff, a non-Nazi who had held the number two post in the German Foreign Ministry until the Hitler regime exiled him to the American mission, regarded the tussle unfolding on Foley Square with dismay. Following Wilhelm Drechsel's recommendation, he had been agitating for guilty pleas in order to shorten the trial and minimise German–American friction, but American defence lawyers were having none of it and now the eyes of his country's enemies would feast at length on the spectacle of Nazi malfeasance.[3]

These were jumpy times. Just before the trial began, Hitler's troops invaded Czechoslovakia. The dictator's action ended the illusions of those who still hoped that the carnage of 1914–18 had been the 'war to end war' and that the peace settlement of 1919 would hold.

Other nerve-jangling events occurred at the time of the trial. At 8 p.m. EST on 30 October, on the eve of Halloween, 23-year-old Orson Welles's radio broadcast of the novel *The War of the Worlds* was so realistic that it persuaded some Americans that a Martian (subconsciously, German) invasion was taking place. Just after the end of the trial, on 10 November, there was Kristallnacht in Germany, the smashing of Jewish business premises that signalled Berlin's anti-Semitic course and gave force to the message that Turrou and other anti-neutrality campaigners were trying to get across.

Because of recent events in America, 'spy' had become a dirty word at just the wrong moment from the German point of view. From 1936 to 1939, Robert M. La Follette (Republican, Wisconsin) chaired Senate Civil Liberties

Committee hearings that showed how corporation executives were systematically spying on American workers. People have always looked down on spies, but the La Follette hearings commanded a national audience and for a period made espionage especially repugnant, 'a veritable insecticide upon the Great-Man treatment of history', in the words of the contemporary writer Richard Wilmer Rowan.[4]

There was plenty in the spy trial proceedings to stimulate public interest. Notably, Mata Hari rose from the dead. According to the *Los Angeles Times*, Jenni Hofmann was a 'minor' Mata Hari. Minor, that is, compared with the star of the show, Kate Moog. When Kate testified about her rendezvous with Canaris on the banks of the Landwehr canal, the *New York Times* ran its account under the headline, 'Spy Witness Bares "Mata Hari" Offer'.

There was general agreement on the perfidiousness of Otto Hermann Voss, but some sympathy for Eric Glaser on the ground that he had been led astray by Rumrich and had ambiguous feelings about the United States having endured American bombing in the last war. The press took a wary interest in the FBI's use of wiretapping and noted the repeated (but unproven) charges that Germany was passing America's military secrets to Japan.[5]

While there was interest in such matters, one of the main features of the trial was the absence of fourteen fugitives who would not testify and who would not be held to account for their actions. Nobody had seriously expected senior Abwehr officers such as Udo von Bonin, Hermann Menzel and Erich Pfeiffer to make an appearance. The absence of Jessie Jordan was more frustrating. She was, of course, in prison in Scotland – and, in mid-trial, was under armed guard in the Edinburgh Royal Infirmary having a fibroid operation. MI5 had supplied information about her activities and the FBI and prosecution lawyers had a duplicate set of the 'Crown' correspondence. Assistant US Attorney Lester Dunigan was able to read out in court depositions on Jordan's correspondence and the circumstances of its interception – he did not mention MI5, and claimed his evidence had been prepared by the Dundee Post Office.[6] It was all damning evidence, but lacked the dramatic impact of a personal appearance by the Scottish spy.

Ignatz Griebl was the other notable absentee. In his absence, his wife Maria might have testified. Turrou at one point suggested she could have things to say, as, during her mission to Germany between 12 September 1937 and 21 April 1938 to leverage the expropriation of property from the Jewish Berliner family, she had frequently telephoned and corresponded with Erich Pfeiffer. After her husband absconded to Germany in May 1938, Maria planned to join him, but was taken into custody as a material witness. In prison, she loyally protested her husband's innocence and was not cowed by Hardy. She had already confronted his predecessor George Medalie a few years earlier, when Ignatz faced charges of Nazi subversion. On that occasion, she dismissed Medalie as a biased Jew. On 6 June 1938, she was placed on bail set at $5,000. It was too much for her to pay – her husband had transferred property to her to avoid car accident damages liability, but he had assumed power of attorney and was now missing. Seward B. Collins came to the rescue and paid the $5,000. The influential editor of the *American Review* was a stranger to Maria Griebl, but was developing fascist sympathies. He accused the government of holding his new protégé 'hostage'.

Maria Griebl testified to the Grand Jury on 28 July and on several other occasions. However, she sought to avoid a court appearance in the subsequent full trial saying she needed an operation in Germany (her physician said she had 'a fibroid tumour of the uterus approximately as large as an orange') and claimed she could not be a competent witness if required to testify against her husband.

In response, Lamar Hardy argued that her plea of ill health was opportunistic, that she would not be testifying against her husband as he was absent and that in any case her argument was outdated. He cited a recent Supreme Court case in support of his contention that 'recognition by the common law of a wife's privilege not to testify in a criminal case against her husband has become questionable as the cause for recognition of equal rights for women has triumphantly progressed'. The court denied Mrs Griebl's petition on 16 September.

However, the court released her from her bail conditions soon afterwards. It will be recalled that assistant district attorneys Dunigan and Burke, interrogating Ignatz Griebl in Berlin, had agreed to her release in return for Ignatz's provision of a statement. In November, Maria travelled to Vienna to join her husband. It was to be a reunion of partners in crime rather than a rekindling of conjugal bliss, for they would separate the following year, Ignatz having taken up with yet another woman.[7]

Maria Griebl would have contributed some detail, but not a great deal, at the autumn trial. Ignatz Griebl would have been a different proposition. If he had testified in person, he might have influenced the course of the trial. As things stood, the court had at its disposition Griebl's mutually contradictory evidential transcripts. First, there were the unsigned depositions and 'confessions' supplied to Turrou when under interrogation in New York. The FBI's Ed Tamm feared that their authenticity might be challenged as the stenographer had destroyed her original notes. Tamm disbelieved Turrou and Vetterli when they claimed they had instructed the stenographer to preserve them and saw the confessions as weak evidence.[8]

Second, there was the self-exculpatory transcript Griebl supplied to Dunigan and his colleague when questioned in the United States Consulate in Berlin. The exculpatory statement was potentially a damp squib, as Griebl had confessed to Dunigan privately he had made it under duress from the German authorities. The statement was nevertheless read into the court record on 9 November.

Dix exploited it. He said it proved that Turrou had 'coached' Griebl to make his earlier statements and that Hofmann was the victim of a 'frame-up'. But according to Turrou, the reading of Griebl's Berlin deposition provoked laughter among the jury. It lacked the credibility to be of use to Dix in conducting his client's defence. From the FBI's perspective, it had the effect of creating a double negative. Griebl's earlier narratives supplied to Turrou were, by implication, not incorrect. It was good news for the prosecution, even if Griebl's accounts were always questionable.[9]

Guenther Rumrich took the stand as a state's witness, testifying between 17 and 24 October against the other three accused who had all, regardless of any previous confessions, pleaded not guilty. With an eye on a lenient sentence, he tried to ingratiate himself with the court. Pretending to hold anti-Nazi views, he ventilated the rumour that Germany's winter relief funds had been diverted to pay for the programme of espionage against the United States. He had joined the United States Army because it gave him three meals a day at a time when he was starving. He had deserted the Army because his drinking had got the better of him and because his fellow soldiers mocked his German accent. He had spied for Germany and accepted payment for that, but his real motive was to find out all about Germany's spies so that he could reveal their identities to the American authorities. In that way, he told his incredulous listeners, he had planned to earn redemption for the sin of deserting the Army.[10]

In between his flights of fancy, Rumrich told what he knew about the workings of the Nazi spy ring. His words carried little weight. Defence attorneys dubbed him a 'beermug romancer'. The *Washington Post* poured scorn on his 'inexhaustible supply of spy-plot tales'.[11]

Jenni Hofmann, like the other two who pleaded not guilty, faced up to twenty years in prison. Her tactical predicament is summed up in the words of a later FBI report:

JOHANNA HOFMANN's cooperation with the Government ceased after she had furnished original statement and at the time of trial of this case, she recanted her former testimony not only to representatives of the Bureau, but also her testimony to the Grand Jury. During the course of the trial of this case she obviously perjured herself in attempting to avoid conviction.[12]

When she appeared in court on 20 October, the jury heard that in her confession to Turrou she said she had spied because 'I believed I was doing my duty to my fatherland'. At least she was unambiguous in her loyalty, which made her a more sympathetic figure than Rumrich. Being a 26-year-old redhead did her no harm and some members of the jury may have been swayed by the tears that she shed in court – though as there were to be repeat performances, the charm may over the course of the trial have worn thin. It is open to question whether Dix's shouted protests at the reading out loud of her confession helped her case in court.[13]

Dix was nevertheless doing the best he could for Jenni. He had, for example, prepared on her behalf a petition to the court, saying that when the FBI seized her locked case on Lorenz's vessel the *Europa*, it was a violation of her right to privacy under the Fourth Amendment. The incriminating letters found in the case should not therefore be used in court.[14] That attempt failed, as did the effort to obtain exoneration via Ignatz Griebl. Jenni Hofmann was an unlucky young woman. Her betraying lover, Karl Schlueter, had sent her to her fate in the first place and now Griebl wanted her to be convicted.

The Drechsel plan was being implemented. To have just a small number of spies convicted would under the circumstances be a reason-able outcome for Germany and would draw a line under an embarrassing affair. Hofmann was to be sold down the river.

The German authorities had reckoned without Dix, who would just not play ball. When, on 17 October, the spy trial court got down to serious business with opening statements by the prosecution and defence, the lawyers representing Glaser and Voss took a conservative approach, but Dix rose to deliver a fiery indictment of Leon Turrou. He told the jury that the special agent was interested solely in publicity and money. Turrou had told Griebl that he had an offer of $40,000 for his story and had attempted to groom the doctor in a series of out-of-office meetings. He wanted Griebl to flee the United States, because he feared that Dix would interview the alleged spy and obtain the truth from him.

To infuse his claim with credibility, Dix averred that Turrou had also tried to frame an unnamed government inspector at the Sperry Gyroscope Company by getting Griebl to approach him with an offer of recruitment as a German spy.[15] The inspector had complained via military channels about his rough treatment at the hands of the FBI. As we have seen, Turrou did interrogate an inspector named Johannes Karl Steuer about the Sperry Company's bombsight and perhaps Steuer was left with bruised feelings. However, Dix was plowing infertile soil, for the inspector had already signed a statement saying, 'Nobody ever contacted me representing any foreign power and I have no information that any of my men were contacted.'[16]

In the absence of reliable witnesses for the defence, Dix redoubled his attack on Turrou's credibility. He called J. David Stern to the stand. Under the compulsion of a subpoena the *New York Post*'s editor produced the contract he had agreed with Turrou. Contrary to earlier press speculation, this was dated 19 July, some time after Turrou's resignation from the FBI. Under cross-examination, though, Stern failed to remove the impression that he and the special agent had an understanding prior to that resignation, and perhaps earlier agreements had been torn up for convenience's sake. Dix did succeed in showing that Turrou was interested in publicity and money.[17]

He was less successful in his effort to show that Turrou was a 'crooked agent who embarrassed his government'.[18] He suffered one particularly embarrassing setback in his attempt to dishonour his opponent. Aware of Turrou's tendency to embroider the truth in discussing his past, Dix decided to take a chance. He called to the witness box Turrou's boss at the time of the 1921–23 American effort to relieve famine in Russia. William N. Haskell was by now a major general and commander of the New York National Guard. Dix had picked up from junior members of the American Relief Mission rumours about Turrou's unpopularity and unreliability. Griebl had assured him that Turrou was a communist Jew and he had high hopes of undermining the prosecution's case when he questioned the general:

> DIX: Didn't you receive reports from members of your staff that Turrou was suspected of being disloyal?
> HASKELL: Oh, I heard some gossip, but I paid no attention to it.
> DIX: Didn't you tell me last July that you used an interpreter named Lears whenever you could instead of Turrou?
> HASKELL: Yes, but I also told you why. I said Lears didn't have as much brains as Turrou, and anybody who has used interpreters a lot knows that the less brains they have the better they are apt to be, so long as they know the language.

Dix appears not to have picked up the point that Turrou hated the communists and for an excellent reason – they had, he thought at the time, wiped out his wife and children. That hatred must have contributed to his over-aggressive translation. The New York *Sun* summed up the impact of Haskell's testimony in one word, 'boomerang'.[19]

The poor relationship between J. Edgar Hoover and his former agent might have played into Dix's hands, had he known how to play the card. It was a clash of megalomaniacs.

One of Ed Tamm's reports gave an indication of the scale and nature of the problem, as well as of Turrou's sense of mission:

> I was advised that Assistant Dunigan, who is handling the trial; ... has agreed to use Turrou just as little as possible and Vetterli as well. [Special Agent Dwight] Brantley further stated that Turrou told McLaughlin, among other things, that he was working for a corporation receiving a salary of $10,000 a year; that he would be in a position soon to give other agents in the service jobs; ... that Turrou made statements to the effect that the President and Attorney General of the United States are behind him, Turrou, one hundred percent; that the only Government official who now is his enemy is the Director; ... that if it had not been for his, Turrou's work in uncovering spy activities in this country, the President would not have come out with his statement concerning his intention to coordinate the activities of the agencies investigating espionage; and that his, Turrou's work had made the public conscious of the spy conditions.[20]

Turrou had basked for so long in the rays of Hoover's approval that he had lost the ability to predict the director's behaviour. This came to light when he asked Assistant United States Attorney John Burke to subpoena the FBI director to appear in court to confirm that the former agent had served the Bureau faithfully and that he did not employ third-degree methods. Burke dismissed the request as a joke, but Hoover was duly informed, and wrote 'that if Burke mentions matter again he should be told my testimony would thoroughly discredit Turrou & that in turn might react unfavourably upon case of the government & wouldn't want to harm the case but I would have to tell the truth'. It was fortunate for the prosecution that Dix did not put Hoover on the witness stand.[21]

Turrou felt that the Bureau was withholding information that might have eased the prosecution case, but Hoover made the distinction between evidence that was strictly relevant to the court proceedings and 'general intelligence' that had 'no pertinence to the prosecutive action … but which may be of vital interest to the intelligence services'. If mistakes had been made, they were the fault of the New York office of the FBI and any embarrassment arising was attributable to 'the dishonest viewpoint of former Special Agent in Charge Vetterli and former Special Agent Turrou'.[22]

Ed Tamm saved the day. He was able to counterbalance Hoover's wrath because of his special standing within the Bureau. The organisation having gone through a number of name changes since its foundation in 1908, it was Tamm who in 1935 pressed for the adoption of its final label, the 'FBI'. Its newly coined motto, 'Fidelity, Bravery, and Integrity', similarly received his blessing. He was preeminent among those who invented an identity for the FBI. The FBI's number three man could see that the outcome of the trial was vital to the FBI as well as to national security, and that Turrou was vital to the trial.

Tamm turned to Special Agent Sam Foxworth for assistance in managing the event. With the help of New York Assistant SAC Dalton, Foxworth kept a close eye on the trial – and the two men guarded Turrou's credibility. Foxworth reminded Tamm that there had been an investigation into Turrou's alleged maltreatment of Steuer and Turrou had been exonerated – the relevant documents should now be placed in the hands of the United States Attorney.[23] Two weeks later – in a memorandum 'for the files' and not 'for the director' – Tamm noted with evident satisfaction Dalton's report 'that Turrou has been standing up under the cross-examination very well and has been making general denials of the accusations which Dix is insinuating in his questioning'.[24]

In an inspired move towards the end of the trial, Dix demanded to see Turrou's FBI file. He had already requested it at the time of the Berlin trip and McLaughlin had on that occasion told him to proceed through official channels. Dix's request, if granted, had the potential for explosive impact. This was because the FBI's personnel file for Turrou was being transformed into a file *on* Turrou, with derogatory information supplied especially by those agents who were sycophantic towards Hoover. With the file in hand, Dix might have delivered a killer blow in court, showing how unreliable Turrou was as an autobiographer and how much Hoover reviled him. But – and the director's minders may have played their part here – when Dix made his official request for the file, Hoover was 'out of the city'. There was no authorisation for release and Jenni Hofmann's counsel never received the smoking gun.[25]

When the trial drew to a close on 2 December, Turrou signed his contract with Warner Brothers and Stern planned to start the multi-part Turrou series three days later. But the United States Attorney's office announced that the restraining injunction was still in effect and they would be liable to contempt charges. Their action was based on the rather fanciful logic that the case was not yet closed, as fourteen defendants were still under indictment and might be tried one day. David Stern shot down to Washington, where he volubly demanded respect for the principle of a free press. Whether or not because of this, word reached the United States Attorney's office to 'lay off'.[26]

Now it was Lamar Hardy's turn to travel to Washington to meet 'the Great White Chief'. He was due to deliver to President Roosevelt a file on the Army's incompetence in dealing with the Lonkowski spy case. His plan was to take advantage of his brief meeting to protest against the dropping of contempt proceedings. By this time, though, wiser counsels had taken hold. Unlike President Richard Nixon at the time of the Pentagon Papers case, President Roosevelt did not risk incurring political fallout by challenging the First Amendment. Turrou escaped prosecution and was able to publish.[27]

The combined if fractious efforts of Tamm and Hardy were successful in the end. The jury believed Turrou. On 29 November, its members returned guilty verdicts in the cases of Voss and Johanna Hofmann. The next day, they convicted Glaser. Together with Guenther Gustave Rumrich, who had pleaded guilty, all four now awaited sentence. During the hiatus, the prosecution and defence gave their reactions. Hardy showed himself to be on the side of Turrou and his growing support when he pointed to the urgent need for stronger American counter-intelligence. George C. Dix said he would appeal, 'if Hitler would send us the money'.[28]

At 2 p.m. on Friday, 2 December, Judge John C. Knox began to sentence the four prisoners. Jenni Hofmann produced a handkerchief and sobbed into it. In her case, the judge showed leniency: 'She was thrilled to think that she served her government; but she has been abandoned.' Jenni's sentence was four years' imprisonment and a photographer caught her weeping again as she left in a police vehicle for the Federal Prison for Women at Alderson, West Virginia. Glaser and Rumrich each received two years. On Voss, Judge Knox imposed a six-year sentence, observing that he was 'inspired by a dream of *Deutschland über Alles*'.

Judge Knox backed up his sentences with a moral verdict: 'Had these defendants been apprehended within the confines of Germany, their fate would have been much more fearful ... we have no sawdust sprinkled on our prison yards.'[29]

Of Propaganda and Revenge

The conclusion of the spy trial released Leon Turrou to tell his story and to launch a propaganda campaign against the Nazis. He pursued no less a goal than to shift America from its position of neutrality. Ranged against Turrou and his allies were formidable figures who had hitherto commanded a majority of American opinion. In Congress, critics of a powerful pro-neutrality bloc stigmatised its members as 'isolationist' and backward-looking. But it contained progressives whose support was vital to the administration's New Deal legislative programme. Senators such as Gerald P. Nye and Hiram Johnson (Republican, California) brandished the anti-interventionist banner and held President Roosevelt over a foreign policy barrel. Turrou found himself politically opposed to Charles Lindbergh, whose son's killer he had helped convict. With Nye, Lindbergh in 1940 founded the totemic anti-interventionist movement, America First. Foreign atrocities by the Nazis were not enough to shift opinion against this charismatically led pro-neutrality bloc.

On 5 December 1938, the *New York Times* carried an advertisement in heavy bold that marked the start of Turrou's propaganda barrage. It appeared in every other metropolitan newspaper as well: 'Today It Can Be Told – Here are the articles, withheld until now by the New York Post at the request of the United States Government – Inside Story of the Spy Conspiracy in America – Revealed by Leon G. Turrou, former Ace G-Man, as told to David G. Wittels.'

Wittels was a journalist who had covered the spy case for the *Post*. In the course of the next year, he helped Turrou to write two books. *Nazi Spies in America* was published in London as *The Nazi Spy Conspiracy in America. How to be a G-Man* was aimed at a juvenile audience.

Turrou's writing activities did not stop there. Having contracted to write the *Post* articles for a set fee of $10,000, he promised twelve contributions to *Cosmopolitan Magazine* at $150 a piece, each to give the story of one of his earlier cases, thus being an advance serialisation of *Where My Shadow Falls*, a book that appeared in 1949. The money was clearly important to the former detective, but so was the message about anti-fascism and the need for better American security.

Reed Vetterli got in on the act. He accepted an offer from a newspaper syndicate of $100 per article for a series on the recent spy case. This annoyed both Turrou and Hoover, but the efforts of others in reality lent force to Turrou's campaign. Those efforts were becoming a contagion. The FBI's Ed Tamm wailed, 'the newspapers will all start running spy articles of one sort or another in an effort to compete with the articles in the New York Post'.[1]

Turrou's literary imitators multiplied. In a review for *The Nation*, Ludwig Lore deemed *Nazi Spies in America* to be different only in being 'less sensational' than two other books that had appeared by July 1939. One was by the veteran spy history writer Richard Rowan and the other by the communist John L. Spivak, who claimed (in Lore's paraphrase) that 'Americans without a drop of German blood in their veins are functioning as agents of the Nazi regime'. Spivak was especially critical of Henry Ford, postulating a link between the automobile

manufacturer's extensive espionage against his firm's workers
and the Nazi infiltration of America. Lore, a Jewish immigrant
from Silesia who edited the daily *New Yorker Volkszeitung* and
wrote a foreign affairs column for the *New York Post*, predicted that the three books' exposés about German spying in
America would be 'a shocking revelation to those who think
there is safety in isolation'.[2]

Nazi Spies in America remained the most important of all
the post-trial publications. That is to say, it was important in
America. Germany was a different matter. When the book
appeared early in 1939, Kate Moog mailed a copy to Erich
Pfeiffer. He would give the book his closest attention. Outside
the Abwehr, however, *Nazi Spies* had no impact in Germany.
Media censorship was now absolute and there were no reviews
or mentions in the press. Ordinary citizens in Germany had
no means of knowing how the reputation of their country was
crashing in the United States.[3]

Americans felt the impact of Turrou's message not just
through the printed word, but in other ways, too. For a man
who cited exhaustion as his reason for resigning from the FBI,
Turrou showed remarkable energy as a public speaker. As late
as February 1940, he was scheduled to give an additional fifty-
three lectures, each for a fee of $500, giving him a projected
total of $26,000. The proceeds had allowed him to buy a house
in Long Island and he was putting two sons through college.[4]

In his speeches, Turrou did not claim to have put an end to
the spy menace in the United States. In April 1939, he spoke
to the Baltimore and Washington Kiwanis Clubs. He warned
them that the Nazis were acting on the assumption that all
German–Americans were ready to betray the United States. A
'huge network' was 'systematically working from coast to coast,
rifling American files of military secrets', and his work in New
York the previous year had 'only scratched the surface'.[5] A few
days later, he gave a near-identical speech at a federated clubs'
luncheon in the world's second largest hotel, the William Penn

in Pittsburgh. A local newspaper reported his view that public indifference explained why America was 'swarming with Nazi spies'. In Pittsburgh as in addresses all over the nation, Turrou appealed for heightened public vigilance, stricter espionage laws and a boost to FBI finances and personnel.[6]

Towards the end of the year, Turrou told a gathering at the Chilton Club in Boston that Americans were at last becoming 'spy conscious', though there was still a need to increase the resources of the FBI, especially its counter-espionage branch. He praised J. Edgar Hoover for his determination in tackling the spy problem. For Hoover was engaged in more than administrative expansion. In 1938, he had escalated the efforts of the FBI's recently formed Crime Records Division, whose purpose, in spite of its name, was public relations.

Here, it should be noted that although Turrou and Hoover in one way sang the same tune, there were discordant notes. Hoover might well have preferred to continue with anti-communism as his dominant FBI-boosting tactic. There was a ready-made audience for anti-communist rhetoric and the newly formed House Un-American Activities Committee was strongly anti-communist, even if it also opposed the fascist version of totalitarianism. Turrou's campaign obliged Hoover to devote both resources and rhetoric to the anti-fascist cause, and Hoover hated being coerced. He wanted to be the sole owner and shaper of the FBI's image. When he received a press clipping about Turrou's praise for him in his Chilton Club address, he wrote in the margin, 'This is like a kiss of death.'[7]

Attempting to convert myth into reality through frequent repetition, Turrou continued to praise Hoover, and he recited an improved version of how their sweet relationship had originated. In a meeting at Indianapolis Town Hall on 3 February 1940, he omitted all references to the times when the FBI had turned him down. Instead, he said that he had come to the rescue of the Bureau. He reminisced that his early applications had not succeeded. But he went to Washington to meet Hoover:

> I then told him of my experiences, my knowledge of lan-
> guages, and he was somewhat impressed and gave me an
> application to fill out, and stated he would let me know
> later on. A week or so thereafter I received a wire to the
> effect I was appointed a special agent, to proceed immedi-
> ately to Washington to take the oath of office.[8]

Turrou modified his message according to his audience. For example, in early April 1939, he was returning to New York from Hollywood when a local journalist caught up with him. At the time, the train was approaching Kansas City, Missouri. Turrou had written about his work on the Kansas City Massacre case, but he now reassured the reporter that 'Kansas City is not to blame', and did not deserve the 'crime centre of America' label that out-of-state newspapermen attached to it.[9]

To please his audiences, Turrou varied his biography. In some places, he told his tales about his Polish birth and strug-gles as a boy and young man. In others, he became French. He gave one Midwestern journalist to understand that he 'was a native of France who came to America at the age of 16', which explained his 'broken accent'. Broadcaster Mac Parker intro-duced him on a Philadelphia radio station with the words, 'quiet looking, unassuming, a bit of the ancestral French accent'. There was never a hint of Turrou's Jewish identity.[10]

Turrou's literary and public speaking activities gave him a voice in what was a crucial American debate. In 1923, Italian Americans had formed the world's first anti-fascist organisa-tion, the Anti-Fascist Alliance of North America. Mistrust of fascism increased sharply in the Hitler years. There were wor-ries that the Nazi 'brown shirt' movement was taking root in the United States and fears of acts of espionage and sabotage perpetrated on American soil escalated.

Nazi atrocities in Europe may have seemed like faraway events, but they were brought home to the American public. World-famous anti-fascist exiles arriving from Germany – for example, Thomas Mann, Albert Einstein and, later, Hannah Arendt – contributed to the clamour. The novelist Ernest Hemingway was just one of a number of leading Americans who took up the cause in the 1930s. Hemingway had fought against the fascist insurrection in Spain and with fellow novelist John Dos Passos scripted the propaganda movie *The Spanish Earth*, narrated by Orson Welles and screened in the White House in July 1937 after Hemingway had dined privately with Franklin and Eleanor Roosevelt.

Hemingway also linked foreign events to domestic worries. His play *The Fifth Column* highlighted the danger posed by fascist 'fifth columnists' – traitors and spies who plotted to advance totalitarian objectives within free societies. It was published on 14 October 1938, the first day of the spy trial. Images created by such as Hemingway gelled with Turrou's depictions of Ignatz Griebl with his Brownshirt connections, and with fears of an *American* fifth column – William J. Donovan, who had sponsored Turrou for his FBI post in the 1920s, would write a booklet on the issue.[11]

The movie *Confessions of a Nazi Spy* ensured that Turrou's anti-neutrality campaign would have mass appeal. The impact of the movies had been huge ever since, in the silent era, they had reached out to all of America, regardless of literacy or a grasp of the English language. America's 16,500 cinemas could touch ordinary people's feelings in ways that the written word could not.

Turrou had had early dealings with Warner Brothers. The Warner studio dispatched screenwriter Milton Krims to be an observer at the spy trial and he came away impressed with the dramatic potential of the underlying story. But it was not a foregone conclusion that Hollywood would be ready for blockbuster investment in what would be a highly political, anti-Nazi movie.

Until very recently, the omens for such investment had been poor on both sides of the Atlantic. In 1930, Goebbels had led a riot at the Mozart Theatre, Berlin, to protest at a showing of *All Quiet on the Western Front*, a Universal Studios movie based on E.M. Remarque's anti-war novel of that title. In Hitler's Germany, there was blanket censorship and information control. The German government made it clear it would take offence at any film anywhere showing the Nazis in a bad light. When Universal Studios in 1937 produced *The Road Back*, based on Remarque's sequel novel, German officials complained and the critics panned it, and the same fate awaited Columbia Pictures' *The Spy Ring*, a 1938 film starring Jane Wyman, about the theft by agents with heavy German accents of a device to improve artillery accuracy.

Moving images that depicted the realities of life under the Nazis simply did not make it out of Germany. Prior to a main feature film, American cinemas in those days showed newsreels. They typically showed footage of an event two weeks after it occurred in Europe. However, US news cameramen were barred from filming in Germany. Hitler regime loyalists shot the one newsreel that did give American moviegoers a glimpse of Nazism in the 1930s and its adverse impact was unintended – it showed the book-burning event of 1933 that signalled the end of free speech on Germany.[12]

Against the background of political interference and earlier marketing flops, it would take courageous commitment to invest major funds in an anti-Nazi movie. Here, it was an apparent advantage to Turrou's campaign that Jews dominated the major studios in Hollywood. William Fox, for example, was a Hungarian Jew. In 1936, *Fortune* magazine estimated that 'of 85 names engaged in production, 53 are Jews'. However, these were not necessarily radical people. The author of a critical study of Hollywood's Jews once remarked that they aped the Eastern Establishment, voted Republican, and adhered to the maxim that 'Jews were to be seen and not heard'.[13] Leaders of the Jewish community faced a conundrum with which Turrou was all too familiar. If as a Jew one spoke out against the Nazis, one's argument might not be taken seriously, as it would appear to have come from a biased source.

The Hollywood moguls were, nevertheless, acutely aware of the threat Hitler's Germany posed not just to Europe, but to the United States as well. Secretly, they funded and encouraged propaganda and even espionage against the Bund and other fascist groups on the west coast. Neil Ness, for example, was a gentile anti-Nazi who penetrated the Bund on behalf of the Los Angeles Jewish Community Committee and exposed the role played by German ships in transporting to America anti-Semitic pamphlets falsely claiming to have originated in the USA.[14] Hollywood's studio bosses may have been social climbers, but they were ready to take on the Nazis when the time and opportunity arrived. *Confessions of a Nazi Spy* would be, in the words of one historian, 'Hollywood's first marquee posting of a four-letter word that had blackened newspaper headlines since 1933.'[15]

Like Turrou, the Warner brothers were of Polish Jewish heritage. Their 1936 movie *Black Legion* starring Humphrey Bogart had already pointed to the danger of American fascism. Jack Warner nevertheless remained wary right up to 1939 of making an explicitly political film: 'If I want to send a message, I'll use Western Union.'[16]

Now, they decided that the time had come to back a major anti-Nazi movie. On 30 January 1939, the Warner studio announced the start of production for *Confessions*. The film shoots would last fifty-five days and there were seventy-eight speaking roles including a Mata Hari part for Berlin-born actress Lya Lys. Eighty-three different sets would portray 'scenes in Germany, Scotland, Washington, DC, New York, aircraft factories and shipyards which figured in the international spy system'.

The movie's story was based on the revelations by Turrou, who appeared in a cameo role as an assistant to his celluloid self, special agent Ed Renard – *renard* being the French for 'fox'. The initial budget ran to a million dollars, and there was a 50 per cent overrun. In a perverse stroke of good fortune, a set of stage lights fell in unexplained circumstances on the actor who played Renard, Edward G. Robinson. His injuries did not render him unable to perform, but it was a golden opportunity for the studio to release stories about death threats sent to members of the cast. Adding to the air of mystery and intrigue, the film had to be shot in conditions of secrecy.[17]

Robinson's appearance in the leading role was in one way remarkable. He had become a Hollywood star by acting in gangster roles. He was everyman's underdog fighting the powers that·be, including the forces of law and order. Now, the man who had shot to fame in *Little Caesar*, about a small-time mobster, was all of a sudden an FBI agent. According to one journalist, there was a physical resemblance between Robinson and Turrou, but this was not the only factor. Like Turrou, Robinson was a cosmopolitan who spoke seven languages. His fans had not previously appreciated that Robinson had been born Emmanuel Goldenberg in Bucharest and had painful memories of anti-Semitism there. His attitude to Hitler was unambiguous. At the end of the 1938 spy trial, he had called for a boycott of German-made goods. Writing a piece called 'Little Caesar Joins G-Men', a Hollywood journalist concluded 'Mr. Robinson and Mr. Turrou have one thing in common: They just don't like Adolf.' A great film actor is always a story in himself and from Turrou's propagandist point of view, Robinson could not have been better cast.[18]

With the film in mid-production, Jack Warner and his wife Ann paid a visit to President Roosevelt in the White House. It cannot be confirmed, but the presidential diary indicates they were there long enough for FDR to see some rough cuts of *Confessions*. Certainly there must have been some discussion of the latest Warner movie.[19] The cause for which Turrou battled, if not the man himself, had come in from the cold.

Confessions opened at the Strand, New York, in late April 1939, with armed police theatrically posted on the roof of the great movie palace that was now part of the Warner Brothers' property empire. It was a direct piece of propaganda, with scenes straight out of Turrou's book and the Foley Square courtroom. It deployed a Voice of God voiceover and other state-of-the-art techniques. Its scenes depicted Jessie Jordan's treasonable actions, spies who desperately pleaded not to be sent back to Germany, Brownshirt summer camps in the United States and 'Trojan horse' references to the fifth column threat. The names were fictionalised, yet the film had a documentary character. The preliminaries dispensed with two conventions. There was no legal disclaimer such as 'all characters are fictional' and no initial credits – the cast list appeared at the end of the movie, sending the message that the stars were not the message even if Robinson was a box-office draw.

Turrou switched from promoting the book to promoting the movie of the book. Across the American continent, he followed a schedule so frantic that he once found himself stranded in Harrisburg, Pennsylvania, having lost his New York to Chicago train ticket.[20] In June, he turned up in Glasgow for the British launch of *Confessions*. He told a UK *Daily Worker* journalist that virtually the entire film was 'absolutely true' and expressed regret at having too little time to visit Dundee to meet the famous postie who had triggered the great tip-off. The English novelist and film critic Graham Greene welcomed *Confessions* as a movie that applied 'documentary technique … excitingly to fiction', and the British censors unusually allowed younger viewers to see the film in spite of its violent scenes.[21]

The $45,000 box office takings for *Confessions'* first American night were the highest so far recorded for 1939.

There was a critical reception to match. The *Nation* praised the excellence of the cast and the movie's verisimilitude, though it did hint that propaganda could not really be art. The *Los Angeles Examiner*'s Louella Parsons thought that Lya Lys was 'efficient' in her role, but the true message was the courageous statement by the Warner siblings. New Deal documentary filmmaker Pare Lorentz announced, 'The Warner brothers have declared war on Germany with this one ... Everybody duck.'[22]

There were limits to the impact of *Confessions*, especially in Hitler-controlled areas of Europe. The movie did make its way to the German military's high command bunkers at Zossen, 20 miles south of Berlin. According to Eric Pfeiffer, he and his colleagues enjoyed 'frequent showings' at that location.[23] But it was banned from general distribution, and, as in the case of Turrou's book, it had no impact on German public opinion.

Even in the case of America, one should keep in mind the fact that *Confessions* appeared in what was a bumper year in Hollywood's 1930s Golden Age. Other movies that appeared in 1939 were *The Wizard of Oz*, *Mr Smith Goes to Washington*, *Stagecoach* – and *Gone With the Wind*, with its record budget of $3 million. People still sought escape from the problems of a depressed decade and delighted in Scarlett O'Hara's waistline instead of worrying about Hitler. *Confessions* did not create spy neurosis overnight. In fact Greta Garbo, star of the 1931 movie *Mata Hari*, later in the year appeared in *Ninotchka*, a Metro-Goldwyn-Mayer film about Soviet spies. In one way it was a reminder of the problem of espionage, but it was mainly romantic comedy.

Yet *Confessions* did break the mould, and marked the moment when millions of moviegoers began to realise the full enormity of what was happening in Europe, and what that might mean for the United States. In the spring of 1940, another spy case broke that kept the issue of espionage in the forefront of public consciousness. Tyler Kent, a code clerk in the American Embassy in London, illegally secreted copies of confidential messages exchanged between President Roosevelt and British prime minister-in-waiting Winston Churchill. Kent was an anti-Semite and anti-interventionist, and his aim was to leak the messages to political opponents of the American president. On 20 May, MI5 secured his arrest in time to prevent a leak that might have affected the 1940 presidential election. Details of the Churchill–Roosevelt exchanges were kept under wraps. Anti-neutrality partisans including Bill Donovan stated that Kent had colluded with Germany. The FBI in later years suspected that Kent had Soviet connections. Whether 'isolationist' or totalitarian in motivation, Kent contributed to contemporary jitters about espionage.[24]

Turrou's propaganda campaign irritated J. Edgar Hoover. The FBI director did not object to what Turrou advocated. How could he, when his former favourite constantly boosted the FBI? But Hoover could not get over the fact that Turrou, if only briefly, had jilted him. Nor could he forgive him for a single instant for having become famous.

The Boss set out to besmirch Turrou's record. In June 1938, Reed Vetterli had turned over to the FBI boss the spy-hunter's personnel file.[25] Hoover instigated a fault-finding investigation of Turrou's past. FBI special agents gathered new evidence. For example, one morning in August, Louis Loebl interviewed Joseph Davidowsky, the long-term acquaintance of Turrou who had by now fallen on hard times and ran the Izba, a Russian-themed bar in Brooklyn. By 10 a.m., when Loebl turned up at the Izba, which he described as a 'dive' of ill repute, the 55-year-old had been drinking heavily. But in spite of downing 'numerous' further cocktails of indeterminate composition in the course of the five-hour interview, he spoke lucidly. He had taken against Turrou and obliged Loebl with a character assassination, branding his sister's former lover a liar, a cheat and a womaniser. All this went into Turrou's file.

The interview was to be part of Hoover's long-running campaign that eventually helped to drive his former agent into exile and contributed to the defamation and obscurity of one of the FBI's greatest detectives.[26]

Turrou campaigned publicly against the Nazis right up to the moment when the Japanese attack on Pearl Harbor brought the United States into the Second World War, even endorsing in July 1941 the kidnapping of Adolf Hitler.[27] By this time, however, he was thinking of a return to public service and Hoover did his utmost to prevent that from happening.

When Turrou asked Mayor La Guardia if New York City might have a job for him, Hoover sent a letter stating that the applicant was a disgraceful character. For a while, Turrou worked instead for a private philanthropy dedicated to the anti-fascist cause. Finally, in 1943 he lied about his age, enlisted in the Army and went though basic training. Hoover lobbied against his promotion to officer rank: 'Everything should be done to prevent this. It is an outrage.' When Bill Donovan established the Office of the Coordinator of Information, the precursor to the Office of Strategic Services (OSS), Hoover told him not to touch the man whose career he and Donovan had conspired to promote a decade earlier. When Turrou spun an improbable line, saying he saw signs of reconciliation with his former boss, Hoover scrawled another comment: 'The damned liar!'[28]

Mel Purvis, that other former FBI agent consigned to purgatory by the vengeful FBI director, sympathised with Turrou's predicament and helped him get a commission in the military police.[29] This launched Turrou on a significant new commitment. For when General Dwight D. Eisenhower learned of his talents, he assigned him to work with General Walter Bedell Smith in the Army's Criminal Investigation Commission. To the dismay of Hoover's office, Purvis and

Turrou began to recruit Americans for work in counter-espionage. Turrou worked closely with Bill Donovan, by now head of the OSS, established in June 1942, and in the Washington power games a rival to J. Edgar Hoover. With new patronage but also boasting first-rate credentials, Turrou became director of the Central Repository of War Criminals and Security Suspects (CROWCASS), headquartered in Paris after the war. This well-funded organisation hunted down Nazi war criminals, extraditing them to countries where harsh penalties awaited them, or, in some controversial cases, if they were potential 'assets', recruiting them to work for American intelligence.[30]

According to a 1949 article in *Der Spiegel*, it was Turrou's successful application of IBM computers to CROWCRASS work that brought him 'worldwide fame'. The German magazine credited his work against the Abwehr, but Turrou's success against Pfeiffer's spies did not really register in Germany and was everywhere fading from public consciousness.[31]

From Turrou's personal perspective, these later achievements were overshadowed by family tragedy. First of all, his wife died. On 1 May 1942 Teresa was buried in the Holy Rood Cemetery right across the railway line from the family home at 401 Union Avenue in Westbury (just 4 miles from the Lonkowskis' old haunts in Hempstead). Immediately afterwards, when notifying Hoover of Turrou's application to become an Army officer, Ed Tamm mentioned that Leon was 'extremely upset' about Teresa's demise. It was on this letter that the FBI director expressed his handwritten 'outrage' at the thought of Turrou's Army promotion.[32] Then on 16 August 1943, Leon's son Victor was killed in action flying in a bombing raid on the Ploesti oilfields in Romania. Both the United States and the city of Paris decorated Turrou for his war work. For their recipient, the plaudits must have had a hollow ring.

Turrou's decision to spend the rest of his life abroad contributed to the erasure of his American reputation. Two weeks after the Allies' victory against Germany, he remarried, and his new wife, Anna B. McLester from Atlanta, Georgia, was a frequent European traveller. In 1949 he settled in Paris, where he became billionaire J. Paul Getty's security man. He lived in France not because of Hoover's persecution, but because he loved the country: 'France is all the contrasts that one could wish for in life.' His profile has suggested to one historian that he continued to work for American intelligence through the period when his wartime boss General Bedell Smith was director of the CIA (1950–53). After he died in 1986 at the age of 91 and was interred at the Neuilly-sur-Seine cemetery outside Paris, his name was inscribed on the American Legion Memorial Mausoleum.[33]

In April 1965, Turrou wrote to Hoover saying that he was almost 70, that the removal of the dismissal with prejudice stain would be wonderful for his grandchildren and great grandchildren and that the exoneration could no longer be regarded as a move that might gain him federal employment. It was the latest of many such appeals and there had been a lobbying campaign on his behalf. One of Hoover's acolytes recommended that this appeal, like the previous ones, be ignored, but this time the Boss appended an initialled instruction: 'remove "with prejudice".'

On 21 June 1965, Hoover signed a Notification of Personnel Action form giving effect to his decision. Turrou had received a coldly worded advance notification from the director. Still cleaving to his supplicant stance, he had replied, 'Permit me once more to express to you my deep thanks and appreciation for your kindness and thoughtfulness in expunging the disgraceful blot from my service record which has tormented and haunted me since I left the Bureau.'[34]

Fifteen years earlier, the New York federal court had issued a *nolle prosequi* order, dropping charges against the spies Turrou had so effectively exposed, as well as against Jessie Jordan. The spies had been reprieved, while the detective who exposed their felonies remained under a cloud. The reprieved, though, had not shown repentance – as we shall see in the next chapter.

Spy Sequels

Leon Turrou blew his own trumpet, but did not blow it too hard. He did not want to give the impression that he had ended the German spy threat in the United States. This would have run contrary to his insistent campaign for more resources to be devoted to counter-intelligence.

The FBI took the same line, and ensured that its leaders across the nation remained alert to the spy ring's personnel and their possible successors. A few days after the spy trial's conclusion, New York's latest Special Agent in Charge, Dwight Brantley, sent a briefing to his corresponding SAC in Seattle, Washington, with notes on all those who had been indicted. There were clearly loose ends. There was 'little information' on the German War Ministry's Udo von Bonin, other than that supplied by Ignatz Griebl. The same could be said of Herman Menzel of the same Ministry. There was 'no information' about Erich Pfeiffer, although he was 'apparently' the head of the spy ring that had operated in America. Brantley speculated that 'Sanders' might be the same person as Pfeiffer.[1]

Thus a great deal remained unknown and there was no ground for believing that the named officials or their successors would refrain from future intelligence operations against the United States. The FBI knew it had a duty to be alert, but it lacked the resources to be fully effective and this was especially the case when it came to foreign counter-intelligence. Once America was in the war, the FBI dispatched personnel to foreign countries, especially in South and Central America. But in the 1930s, information about foreign intelligence agencies came only from indirect sources – US military attachés serving overseas, information from decoded international communications and liaison arrangements with friendly countries.

The latter arrangements were helpful in the case of Jessie Jordan. In that particular case, the FBI could be confident that there was no cause for concern. Although Jordan was technically a fugitive from American justice, she was safely incarcerated in the UK. In fact, she remained under lock and key until the end of the war and suffered from a number of problems that neutralised any espionage ambitions she may have continued to nurture.

Jordan's daughter Marga had in the meantime met a Glaswegian, Thomas J. Reid, and went through a marriage ceremony with him at Gretna Green, the Scottish border community famous for its accommodation of runaway brides. The suspicion was that she acted in order to obtain British residency rights – like her mother, she was a German citizen.

Marga, and possibly Tom as well, had neglected to enter into the formality of divorcing their previous spouses. When Marga visited her mother in prison, Jessie comforted her daughter with her view that she would not be prosecuted for bigamy in Germany, as the offence had been committed under Scots law.[2] The polygamous arrangement did not work out financially. Reid was not paid at a sufficient level to satisfy his partner and then he lost his job with little immediate prospect in those hard times of finding another. Marga appeared not to return his affections and she would sail for Germany on 25 October 1938. Photographers who pursued her onto the Hamburg-bound ferry at the port of Leith snapped a mischievous wee Jessie making faces at them around the corner of a cabin door. The photographers did not twig that Marga was by this time pregnant with another child.[3]

Meantime, the grandmother's health had declined. She began to complain of constant constipation, saying she was used to a fresh fruit diet that was not available in Saughton Prison. In late August, she was admitted to Edinburgh's Royal Infirmary under twenty-four-hour guard as MI5 wanted to shield her from the press 'in her own interest'. The gynaecologist W.F.T. Haultain performed what his junior described as 'a sub-total hysterectomy and bilateral salpingo-oophorectomy for a large fibroid'.[4]

Back in prison, the convalescent Jordan remained under round-the-clock surveillance. MI5's Hinchley Cooke felt sorry for her and relaxed the invigilation, but then Jordan suffered another blow. Late on the evening of 20 January 1939, Marga died at the Finkenau women's clinic in Hamburg. The death certificate stated, 'the deceased was not married, divorced'. Her unborn baby also died – Marga's death certificate appears to support Reid's contention that the catastrophe was the result of an 'illegal operation'.[5] Reid declared his intention to adopt his stepchild Jessie, but grandmother Jessie did not trust him. The paperwork formalities for such a procedure in Germany were formidable. Reid said it was beyond his capabilities and the following year he married a third wife.[6]

When the Second World War started, Jessie Jordan was evacuated to Aberdeen Prison. There, she suffered from further illnesses and complained about damp and cold conditions. The prison governor described her as 'insolent to all officials' and said she was stirring up discontent among the women prisoners. She had complained to him that laundry was hung to dry in the women's quarters – 'the whole place has never been without wet clothes' – whereas the men did not have to put up with such damp conditions. 'Why we women?' she asked, and it was not an isolated hint of feminism. Rumrich had criticised her for calling herself 'Mrs Jessie Jordan' and not, as was the custom in 1930s Scotland, after her first husband's full name, giving 'Mrs. Frederick Jordan'. It was poor tradecraft, he thought, as she was drawing attention to herself. But there may well have been a reason for it; Jessie's desire for independence.[7]

Like Mata Hari, who had complained about prison conditions for women as she awaited her execution, Jessie Jordan had a penchant for resistance.[8] To male officials, Jordan seemed difficult. P.J. Rose, Assistant Secretary of State at the Scottish Office, referred to her as 'a woman of tortuous mentality and of a designing nature'.[9] In contrasting vein, Jordan's conduct reports categorised her as a model prisoner who worked hard and broke no rules – her recommendation for release on licence summed up her conduct as 'excellent'. She is reputed to have converted to Christian Science when in prison.[10]

Jessie Jordan's good behaviour qualified her for early release on 14 January 1941. It was to no avail. The moment she set foot outside Aberdeen Prison, she was rearrested as an enemy alien and interned for the duration of the war. At the war's end, the British authorities deported her to Germany. Her granddaughter Jessie Wobruck, who had spent the war in an orphanage, was able to join her. Jessie Jordan became a missionary for the Christian Scientists. She fell ill in 1954, and, in accordance with the precepts of her adopted religion, she refused medical treatment. She died in Hanover without having given the FBI a moment's serious concern since her arrest in 1938.[11]

A little more disturbingly, the FBI lacked information on Dr Ignatz Griebl. He appears to have enjoyed the fruits of his misdemeanours, owning property in Germany and Austria, and practising gynaecology in Vienna. He and the long-suffering

Maria divorced, but he appears to have made no attempt to take up with Kate Moog. At the end of the war, he applied to the Allied Military Government for a travel permit. The military authorities were forewarned and arrested him in Salzburg. They did not, however, remove him to the United States for trial. He remained a fugitive from US justice until the *nolle prosequi* order of 1951, as much a mystery to the FBI as he ever had been.[12]

The FBI had been unable to touch Udo von Bonin. When the British interrogated the senior Abwehr official in Denmark at the end of the war, he claimed he only became involved in American work because he spoke English and the responsible official was away from his desk when Griebl and Moog presented themselves in 1937.[13] Bonin's interest in America was not, however, transient. For example, in 1942 he sent a Dutch-born agent to the United States. A terrified Alfred Meiler was trying to keep his Jewish identity secret. He was an easy recruit for Bonin, who promised to protect his brothers from persecution in the German-occupied Netherlands. Issued with a forged US passport in the name of Arthur Koehler, Meiler was initially tasked with finding out about the US nuclear weapons programme. Then, right up to the end of the war, 'Uncle' (as Hamburg now called itself) gave him a whole variety of other missions. The evidence indicates that the FBI had Meiler under surveillance and used him to send disinformation to Uncle. He may well have been complicit in this procedure, making him a double agent. But the FBI did not have a rounded knowledge of Bonin until the British interrogated him and passed what they knew to J.A. Cimperman, the FBI's representative in the American Embassy in London.[14]

Turrou and his colleagues had glimpsed the fish, but Bonin swam nowhere near the FBI's net. The same could be said of Herman Menzel. According to Bonin, Menzel was his immediate superior in the mid-1930s Berlin headquarters of the

Abwehr. These senior intelligence bosses were well outside the FBI's control.

Nikolaus Ritter, who, as we have seen, pulled off the Norden bombsight coup, eluded the FBI's grasp. He managed to remain an unknown entity until he became a focus of FBI interest in 1941. His former wife Aurora helped the FBI with its inquiries once she had shaken off the Bureau's suspicion that she was herself a German agent. But it was not until September 1945 that the FBI finally interviewed him, finding out about his childhood, his training to be a textile engineer, his unemployment in the 1920s, his services as a spy in the years 1918–33 and his subsequent operations against both the UK and the USA.[15]

We shall revisit Ritter in the next chapter, while noting here that he became a spy of note in the Second World War because of his dealings with Arthur Owens, code-named SNOW. Owens was a double-double agent, working for both the Abwehr and MI5 and betraying both sides. For example, he promised the Abwehr he could deliver a Plaid Cymru (Welsh Nationalist) saboteur. Such persons were to be found – Saunders Lewis is an example – but 'SNOW' was in no position to deliver. MI5 were on to him and from Wandsworth Prison under the tuition of British intelligence he transmitted carefully crafted misinformation to Uncle, the beginning of the famed 'Double Cross' system.[16]

Many years later, when Ritter learned from the American journalist Ladislas Farago that some wartime intelligence documents had survived and would be released, he wrote a memoir in which he was to a certain degree forthcoming. In 1945 he had told British interrogators he had never joined the National Socialist Party and in his book he reiterated his claim to have been an apolitical patriot: 'I was a soldier and served my fatherland under the Emperor in the First World War and under Adolf Hitler in the second, and would, God forbid, serve under the leader of my fatherland should there be a third.' He revealed how much he admired tall, blond and blue-eyed people like himself, how he scorned American women with their 'regal' expectations, how he shamelessly abused his American wife – and how he worked with Canaris and with Dierks, the inventor of 'Sanders'. Such personal details would have been of great interest to Turrou and his collaborators, but, until the 1940s, Ritter's was largely a blank page in the FBI's inventory of spies.[17]

How much did all this ignorance matter? While every piece in a jigsaw is significant, what really concerned the FBI was its performance against spies who tried to operate within the United States. Here, the Bureau built on what Turrou had started and operated with determination and effectiveness. The New York trial marked the end of one FBI operation, but also spurred an expansion of counter-espionage surveillance. Special agents pursued all kinds of leads, responded to tip-offs from members of the public and kept an eye on the four convicted spies.

Guenther Rumrich attracted continuing attention. On 10 July 1940, he was released on probation from the federal prison in Milan, Michigan. The FBI placed him under surveillance. It emerged that the former agent was interested solely in the exploitation of women and in petty crime.

Rumrich returned to New York City, working for short spells as a doorman. He took up with a new mistress, Lottie Einsele, who dumped him when she discovered he had been a spy. After a short visit to see his children in Montana, he got a job in the Portland, Oregon, shipyards.[18] Production was already booming because of wartime demand and Rumrich worked as a timekeeper, then an apprentice welder. Meantime, he engaged in criminal behaviour to an almost compulsive degree. He deceptively signed onto the crew of a merchant ship under the assumed name of Joseph de Bors – de Bors was his mother's maiden name. He fraudulently tried to join the US Coast Guard in Seattle, giving a false name and address and denying his criminal record. He cashed three bogus cheques in Seattle and temporarily gave his FBI watchers the slip.[19]

By now, his wife had divorced him and remarried. An FBI report filed in October 1943 told a sad story. The released prisoner had issued four more dud cheques in the name of Joseph Rumridge. He preyed on the kindness of others and had defrauded an old lady. Rumrich used the Ramapo Hotel in Portland as a place of sexual convenience. The report listed eight women he had dated there. He did not make a good impression on them. One of his lovers was Mrs Juanita Carol Raney, a 'full-blooded Indian', who was prepared to turn him in.

His sons, now aged 6 and 7, visited him, and perhaps this inspired their father to try to reform. Rumrich explored ways to find a way out of his fix, even if he did not follow them through. An FBI search of his travel trunk uncovered, interleaved with love letters from yet another woman in the Bronx, New York, the drafts of several short stories. The serial Army deserter also tried to re-enlist in the military, which would have been a potential cause for concern had he succeeded. But he had ceased to be a threat to US national security and that was what mattered most of all to the FBI.[20]

The FBI watched the spy case witnesses, as well as those who had been indicted. Kate Moog had escaped prosecution, but was of interest because of her former association with Ignatz Griebl. She promised to keep the Bureau informed of her whereabouts and in January 1939 told the New York office she had moved into a new apartment in the city and was moving to Florida for a number of weeks. She promised to contact the New York office immediately, should she receive any communication from Griebl.[21]

The Bureau focused mainly, however, on those who had received prison sentences. It maintained a watch on post-trial legal moves. The Rumrich conviction had been cut and dried, but there were judicial developments in the cases of his three co-defendants. The FBI followed the proceedings on 16 December 1938 when counsel representing Erich Glaser called for the verdict in his case to be set aside on the ground that Juror Number 4 should have been barred from serving because he had concealed his Jewish identity.

Judge Knox slapped this down and refused to pass the request to the Circuit Court of Appeals: 'So far as this Court is concerned, the record made at the trial will stand.'[22] The Circuit Court of Appeals did hear a plea from Glaser to be allowed to appeal *in forma pauperis*, meaning that he had no money and wanted court expenses to be waived. The Court of Appeals dismissed the motion. In a 'comprehensive' FBI review of the spy convicts in 1943, the FBI intimated that Glaser, having completed his term in prison, was working as a caretaker on a farm in Vermont and recommended that he should be stripped of his US citizenship.[23]

An FBI parole report on Johanna Hofmann two weeks into her prison sentence took an unsympathetic line. She had initially admitted to her work as a spy courier under the instruction of Karl Schlueter, as well as to her trip to Czechoslovakia to recruit Gustav Rumrich. But in the course of her trial, she had ceased to cooperate with the government. She recanted her testimony and 'obviously perjured herself in attempting to avoid conviction'. Hofmann remained in the Federal Reformatory for Women, Alderson, West Virginia, until her conditional release on 30 December 1941. By this time, the United States was at war. Attitudes towards spies and traitors harden under such circumstances and like Glaser she could expect little leniency. Immigration and Naturalisation officials immediately rearrested her upon her release and removed her to Ellis Island, where she awaited deportation. There, she was rearrested yet again, under a Presidential Warrant, as a dangerous enemy alien.

The Alien Enemy Hearing Board for the Southern District of New York examined her in March 1942 and recommended to the US Attorney General that she should be interned. Confronted with this probability, Hofmann chose to be repatriated, under the terms of the original deportation order, before the Attorney General handed down his decision. On 7 May, having plucked her eyebrows for the last time on American soil, the beautician departed on the SS *Drottingholm*. The Swedish American Line's ship had once transported Greta Garbo to America, en route to ultimate stardom in the movie *Mata Hari*. By arrangement with the Axis powers, the US State Department had recently chartered the passenger liner to repatriate civilian internees and diplomats from both sides. The deportation option would prove to be a short-lived arrangement, but Hofmann had availed herself of the window of opportunity. When the vessel arrived in the neutral port of Lisbon, she disembarked a lucky woman.[24]

The FBI's parole report on Otto Hermann Voss was never going to be exculpatory. It observed that Voss had perjured himself in an effort to avoid conviction. It opined that 'the information furnished by Voss to agents in Germany was by far the most damaging' as he had divulged the latest design details of the Army's fighter planes. It noted that 'during the trial of this case Voss was asked whether he believed in the principles of the National Socialistic Party in Germany and he stated he could not answer the question'. Voss appealed his sentence, but pragmatically 'elected to serve the sentence imposed upon him during the pendency of his appeal'. Still under observation by the FBI, he served his term in the high-security Federal Penitentiary in Lewisburg, Pennsylvania.[25]

In the aftermath of the 1938 spy case, the FBI received increasing support from the administration of Franklin D. Roosevelt. Over the next year or two, there was little sign that this would boost its *foreign* counter-intelligence aptitude. Even if this aptitude had increased to the degree that persuasive evidence could have been produced, Germany would have refused to extradite senior officials such as von Bonin, Menzel and Pfeiffer, and in all probability would have protected lower-rank intelligence officers as well. When it came to protecting the continental United States, it was another matter. The Bureau watched the captured spies of 1938 very closely and events would show that the FBI remained vigilant when it came to future German spy ventures on American soil.

The Case Named for Duquesne

In June 1941, Americans woke to the fact that Germany was once again spying on their nation, and on a considerable scale.

The Duquesne spy ring, the cause of the new alarm, was named for a man with a lurid image. Frederick Joubert 'Fritz' Duquesne was a South African of Dutch and Huguenot heritage. Fond of embroidering his life story, he told the tale that, as a pre-teenager, he fought the 'Kaffirs'. He applied the derogatory term to the Zulus, whose lands the Dutch settlers aimed to appropriate as if by Divine Right.

In the second Boer War, Fritz Duquesne fought against the British. When the might of the Empire prevailed, they took him prisoner and exiled him, somewhat benevolently, to the island of Bermuda. He escaped that paradise to enter America illegally. Some years later, he boasted of having achieved his revenge by killing the British general who had crushed the Boers. The official version of Lord Kitchener's death holds that he died when the armoured cruiser that was taking him on a diplomatic mission to Russia struck a mine off the coast of Orkney on 5 June 1916. Duquesne, however, asserted that he was with Kitchener aboard the HMS *Hampshire* as it left Scapa Flow for Archangel and that he signalled a German submarine.

The U-boat torpedoed the warship and Kitchener perished along with 736 others. The signaller escaped by swimming to the submarine through the cold North Atlantic waters.

Subsequently, Duquesne said that he was glad to spy for Germany because he hated the British. The Nazis' racism in any case appealed to him. Their money was a further attraction for a man who bore the twin burdens of low income and expensive women.[1]

It was in 1931 that Duquesne first met Nikolaus Ritter. Billing himself as 'the man who killed Kitchener', he had by this time made up a whole inventory of heroic exploits and had promoted himself to the rank of colonel. He told Ritter that as a boy he had watched his mother die in a British concentration camp. His tales impressed the German agent and the two men became drinking friends, meeting in a private New York university club where they were able to quench their thirst in the dry decade. Ritter left for Germany. By the time he returned Prohibition had ended, but old habits die hard. One day in November 1937, as he was waiting to hear that the Norden bombsight plans passed on by Hermann Lang had been safely smuggled out of the country, Ritter again visited Duquesne at his apartment on West 57th Street. They once again drank whisky.

The time had come to recruit Duquesne. The 60-year-old 'colonel' had the qualification of speaking several languages. Ritter also recalled that while his host 'never had money', he had 'excellent social connections'. He gave him the code name Oskar, the code number A.3518 and a cheque for $100. The South African celebrated what was to be his new income stream by moving to more upscale accommodation with his wife Evelyn – a Southern belle who was twenty-six years his junior and a fashionable sculptress.

Ritter saw Duquesne as 'a daredevil with nerves of steel and whatever he aspired to, he succeeded in'. He claimed that when Duquesne brazenly asked for secret information from official sources 'he was rarely rejected and all his information was immediately transferred to Germany'. The reality is that, compared with Lang's espionage, Duquesne's activities were trivial. Fritz gave his Abwehr controllers information about the design of a new US gas mask, but the source of his data could not have been more open – it was the *New York Times*. He did have credentials as an investigating journalist and he did obtain other information simply by writing to people and requesting it, but it is doubtful that the intelligence was at all important. As in the earlier instance of Rumrich, Duquesne was not entrusted with any of the Abwehr's inner secrets. FBI files on the 1938 and 1941 spy rings were named for Rumrich and Duquesne respectively, but that was deceptive. Like Rumrich, Duquesne gave his name to a spy ring, but was not a productive member of it.[2]

By virtue of his seniority, Ritter was in a position to achieve more. The architect of the Lang coup became the principal spymaster operating against the United States. He operated from Hamburg, which had always been a larger Abwehr station than Bremen. Pfeiffer left Bremen following the 1938 debacle and Hamburg from then on directed espionage against the United States. In 1946, London's Counter-Intelligence War Room produced a 'liquidation report' on the activities of the Hamburg station. It noted that its headquarters from 1937 were at 14, Knochenhauerstrasse. 'Very few records were left undestroyed' after the war, but it was clear that operations against the UK and USA were 'practically unrestricted'. The report noted there was a sharp increase in Hamburg's activity in 1938, with some thirty agents dispatched to the United States and more to Latin America. Pfeiffer having relinquished his American responsibilities in that year, Canaris was thought to have given Hamburg the kind of pep talk that cannot be ignored.

The liquidation reporters observed that Ritter showed poor judgment and tradecraft, and tended to 'cross swords with his superior officers over policy'. They belittled the performance

of his American agents: 'None … can be considered successful.' In 1940, Ritter's unit in Hamburg redoubled its efforts,
instigating extensive technical training for its agents, but the
commanding officers lacked the skills to orchestrate major
results: 'It was probably for this reason that the successes they
achieved were very few.' The liquidation reporters' conclusion
that Hamburg's overall performance was poor was not entirely
objective. Reflecting British victory hubris and ignorance of
Abwehr successes elsewhere, they claimed that the German
intelligence organisation failed everywhere. They added that
it made no difference with Germany's democracy in a strait-
jacket, for fascism's leaders were able to ignore intelligence that
might have suggested a different course and would not have
listened even if their spies had delivered accurate findings.[3]

The tone of the liquidation report contrasted with the FBI's
caution in an earlier, 1941 assessment. This FBI review of the
'Duquesne' case saw ominous signs. Looked at together, the
Rumrich and Duquesne files indicated 'that the conspiracy of
the German Government to engage in espionage activities in
the United States existed continuously from 1935 to date'. In
harmony with its exiled prodigy, Leon Turrou, the FBI was by
the date of this review a firm believer in the continuous existence of the German spy menace.

The FBI review dwelled on links between the Lonkowski,
Pfeiffer and Ritter phases in German espionage. There was
evidence on the courier connection. The FBI had a note from
'Sex' (Lonkowski), apparently addressed to Pfeiffer, saying
he proposed to use the courier Eitel. Lonkowski had used
another courier, Schlueter, who was connected with Hofmann
and thus Griebl and Moog. And there was another connection. Duquesne had been active in the now-defunct German
Aviation Club, located near Roosevelt Field, Long Island. The
Club had National Socialist leanings and one of its members,
Ulrich Hausmann, had helped Lonkowski to flee the country
in 1935.[4]

The FBI's report did not fully credit the damage Turrou's detective work caused the Abwehr operation in 1938. In their anxiety to point to a national security threat, its review's authors undervalued their own organisation's efficacy. Unlike the authors of the 1946 British report, they did not have the comfort of having just won a war.

If the Abwehr threat to American security was low, this was in no small measure the result of the FBI's improving skills. Like a hitherto overlooked younger sibling, the Bureau was catching up with its peers. British counter-intelligence had a longer tradition than its American counterpart, and British entry into the Second World War accelerated MI5's expertise at a time when the United States was still neutral and unengaged. But America would pull abreast and then ahead in some intelligence domains. Military code-breaking was a notable example, but the FBI, too, improved its performance. It began to impress MI5 with its expertise in particular areas.

One of those areas of expertise was the Hamburg spy station and its director of American espionage, Niki Ritter. In its assessments of Hamburg, the FBI was edging ahead of MI5. An MI5–MI6 exchange in March 1942 revealed that the British knew two of Ritter's code names, Rantzau and Renken, but not all of them, and that the security service had no reliable photograph of the Abwehr spy. The FBI had both a list of code names and photographs. Noting that 'the FBI has quite a quantity of information about the Hamburg Stelle [office] which is new to us', an MI5 official wondered whether the Bureau might agree to send a report, 'as we still have several cases on our hands which originated from Hamburg'.[5]

The FBI was developing more than regional expertise. Hoover had always been keen for the FBI to keep up with technological change and such change was occurring in the spy profession. Gone, for example, was the reliance on rolled umbrellas as the means of transporting secret documents onto ocean liners plying between New York and German ports. In

1928, a professor at Dresden Technical University had developed microphotography and a decade later Germany's spies began to take notice. Big documents were out and the microdot was in. Nor would Germany be so reliant on transatlantic telegraph cables as it had been, to its cost, on the eve of the First World War. The coded telegram was giving way to the coded radio transmission.

The FBI kept up with these changes and exploited them – with the assistance of what every successful intelligence operation needs, a stroke of luck. That stroke of luck came in the shape of a walk-in spy.

The spy who walked in was Wilhelm Gottlieb Sebold. Born in 1899 in the city of Mülheim in Germany's industrial Ruhr area and named, like so many German children of the era, after the reigning monarch, Wilhelm trained as a mechanic. In the First World War, he joined the Imperial Army as a machine gunner. He spent months in the Somme area of the Western Front and inhaled mustard gas, an experience that affected his health for the rest of his life. The experience of war left him in a troubled state. In a hot-headed moment in the post-war days, he struck a police officer and served a short prison sentence.

Life was grim in his part of Germany after the war and in 1922 he emigrated to the United States. Wilhelm became William, and then just Bill. He moved around, served as a merchant sailor and worked in South America, where he developed his knowledge of diesel technology. In 1931 he married Helen Büchner, an American of Bavarian stock. They settled in San Diego, where he worked at the Consolidated Aircraft Company.

They did not stay long. Moving east for medical reasons, Sebold settled into greater New York City's Yorktown suburbia (not to be confused with Manhattan's Yorkville neighbourhood) and applied himself to working at any jobs he could find in the Depression-torn 1930s. In 1936, he became a United States citizen. He encountered pro-Hitler militants in

Yorktown's German–American community, but, unlike some of his fellow veterans who were embittered by the First World War experience, he took away from the Somme the lesson that peace should be cherished. In the wake of the rise of Hitler, he was convinced that American democratic values were superior to those of Nazi Germany.[6]

In the winter of 1937, surgeons at Bellevue Hospital removed half of Sebold's stomach after diagnosing an ulcer problem. His recuperation was slow and at the same time he experienced marital problems, resulting in a temporary separation from Helen in 1938. He decided to return to his mother's house in Mülheim, where he arrived early in 1939. He recovered sufficiently to work for a local manufacturing company.

One day, the Gestapo arrived on his doorstep. They had heard about his employment in the aircraft manufacturing industry and considered him to be a potential asset. They said they knew he was part Jewish and reminded him of his brush with the law in 1918. Had the American authorities known about his criminal record, he would not have obtained US citizenship. The Gestapo took away Sebold's American passport and threatened to inform American officials of his past misdemeanour if he applied for a replacement without agreeing to cooperate. In a finishing touch, they referred to the funeral clothes that lay in wait for him if he did not comply.

Sebold travelled to Hamburg to meet a 'Dr Renken', who was really Nikolaus Ritter. As in the case of Jessie Jordan's recruitment, the Abwehr took up where the Gestapo had left off. Sebold underwent training as a spy, learning about microphotography, encryption and radio technology. He expressed enthusiasm for his role and presented himself to the credulous Ritter as a German nationalist.[7]

In January 1940, the Germans issued Sebold with a new American passport in the name of 'Harry Sawyer' and with $1,000 in cash, of which $500 was to be delivered to Everett Roeder, an Abwehr agent who had worked at the Sperry bombsight plant. They gave him five microphotographs of documents containing espionage instructions, each the size of a postage stamp. Two carried encryption and password information for his own use and were for his retention. All five fitted into a pocket watch that the Abwehr also supplied. Ritter told him his task was to establish a shortwave radio transmission facility and use it to relay communications between Hamburg and its agents on the United States. He was to make contact with Hermann Lang. The three remaining micro documents were to be delivered to Roeder, Lilly Stein (a model whose chief role in the spy ring was that of *femme fatale*) and Colonel Frederick Duquesne.

These arrangements having been made, Ritter accompanied 'Sawyer' to Genoa, in Italy, for embarkation on the crack US liner, the SS *Washington*. War having broken out four months earlier, the voyage across the Atlantic was potentially hazardous, even if the United States was not yet a belligerent. The *Washington* had to protect itself from accidental attacks by belligerent warships, so on each side were painted US flags and the words 'United States Line'. On 8 February 1940, the vessel arrived safely in New York. There, special agents of the FBI greeted Sebold/Sawyer in a discreet manner. Sam Foxworth, veteran of the 1938 spy trial and now special agent in charge, New York, had arranged the reception committee and already had more than fifty agents working on the case. For prior to his departure from Germany, Sebold had given the Gestapo the slip for long enough to confide his story to US consular officials in Cologne. One of them, it is unclear who, advised him secretly to play along with the Abwehr's designs. The FBI duly received notification. If Sawyer was to be trusted, he could be a double agent.[8]

The FBI allocated Special Agent James C. Ellsworth to work with Sebold: at first he established the double agent's bona fides and then he helped him to achieve his goals. To oversee the case, Hoover parachuted in one of his trusted colleagues.

This was Earl Connelley, Turrou's former boss in Chicago who now carried the rank of Inspector. Connelley moved to New York from Washington and Foxworth returned to his original duties of running the FBI's New York office.

The Bureau refrained from making immediate arrests. It put Sebold on a monthly retainer and let the spies run so that they could be followed, watched and identified. It supervised and assisted Sebold in his work of tracking down spies and finding evidence that could be used to prosecute them. It secretly took over the Abwehr's banking arrangements.

The Bureau also turned to the businessman and philanthropist W. Vincent Astor for help. In his private life, Astor was a neighbour of Franklin Roosevelt in Hyde Park, upstate New York. They had been close friends ever since the 1920s when the future president had comforted his polio-afflicted legs in the Astors' heated swimming pool. Astor had conducted informal intelligence tasks for the president and as managing director of the Western Union Telegraph Company had a feel for technology. He helped the Bureau set up an office on the sixth floor of the *Newsweek* building at 152 West 42nd Street. This was an FBI facility masquerading as an Abwehr office masquerading as a research centre, and the Bureau's technicians had bugged it. At this special facility, hidden film cameras and microphones recorded eighty-one spy meetings in all.

The FBI helped Sebold set up the shortwave broadcasting facility the Abwehr had requested. As information came in from spies, it was encoded and then transmitted in messages to Hamburg. Following standard practice, encryption followed keywords selected from a literary work, in this case Rachel Field's novel (later a movie) *All This, and Heaven Too*, a breathless best-seller: "'Paris – Paris – Paris," her pulse beat over and over.'[9]

As an additional security measure, the Abwehr had familiarised itself with Sebold's 'fisting' signature. Like every code operator, Sebold had individual idiosyncrasies in tapping out messages. The FBI realised this and had its own man, Morris H. Price, learn how to mimic Sebold's fisting style. Thus it was able to send out disinformation. By April 1941, Friedrich Busch (not to be confused with Canaris's alias) was in charge of American espionage in Berlin, where he received spy reports forwarded from Hamburg. He was convinced that Sebold was 'controlled', noticing, for example, that Sebold sent across a report on US aircraft engine production based on 1939 figures, when output was one-twentieth what had been achieved by 1941. But, he claimed, nobody listened to him and both the case officers and the air force hierarchy insisted on taking American disinformation at face value. Though America was still at peace, the FBI was successfully using deception techniques that mirrored those being used by the warring British and Germans.[10]

By the end of June 1941, there were fears that members of the spy ring would resort to sabotage. For example, Fritz Duquesne proposed to Sebold the bombing of President Roosevelt's Episcopalian church in Hyde Park, New York. While the policy of watch and deceive had much to commend it, acts of terrorism could not be tolerated and the FBI prepared to pounce. Its agents arrested thirty-three spies and this time there would be no escapes – they were kept in custody until the trial.

Compared with the 1938 case, the result at first sight looked good. This was partly because of a more prudent indictment policy. There were no indictments of untouchable members of the German spy hierarchy, neither were there indictments of lesser agents who could not be arrested as they lived abroad. According to one tabulation, there were, in addition to the thirty-three arrestees, a further thirty-seven 'unindicted Duquesne ring coconspirators', making seventy spies in all. The extra thirty-seven ranged from Nikolaus Ritter to minor field agents across the globe. Had all thirty-seven of these extras been indicted, the FBI's arrest rate would have been a more modest thirty-three detained out of a total of seventy.

Disregarding such niceties, Hoover announced that the FBI had achieved the 'greatest round-up of its kind in the nation's history', adding that 'this is one of the most active, extensive, and vicious groups we have ever had to deal with'. Officials made an effort to paint Duquesne as a dangerous spymaster. The media dutifully made various references to the betrayal of military secrets to Germany. The greatest news story was, however, a delayed revelation. It was about Lang's theft of the Norden bombsight. This event had occurred four years earlier, before the engagement of Duquesne and prior to the 1938 fiasco that had prompted a renewal of the Abwehr's efforts in America.[11]

The Pearl Harbor attack of 7 December 1941 was significant for the Duquesne case in two ways. First, as it occurred before sentencing, it may have affected the punishments meted out. Lilly Stein, a minor figure and little more than a 'Viennese prostitute' according to Hoover, received a sentence of ten years, a much harsher punishment than that handed to Johanna Hofmann in the 1938 trial.[12] Nations at war do not treat espionage lightly. Everett Roeder's sentence was sixteen years. Lang received eighteen years and so did Duquesne.

Second, Pearl Harbor and the outbreak of war stripped the case of its potential significance as an opinion shaper. The spy ring of 1938 had helped to galvanise American opinion on Nazi Germany. The spy ring of 1941 did not, for Pearl Harbor and Hitler's declaration of war in its wake had a definitive impact and no spy case could make Americans angrier than they already were.

The political impact of the so-called Duquesne case was one of history's what-might-have-beens. But there is another question to be asked. What made a few dozen German–Americans betray the United States? In a way, that is the wrong question. For in spite of the high profile of the German spies, of the German Bund activities and of the alleged German 'Fifth Column' in the United States, the great majority of German–Americans were loyal United States citizens. *Confessions of a Nazi Spy* had made this point. In one of the movie's opening scenes, Dr Karl Kassel (a fictionalised Dr Ignatz Griebl) harangues an American Nazi meeting. He is in military uniform, most of the men wear Nazi headgear and swastikas adorn the room. Kassel rants against 'racial equality', demanding that this must be 'our America'. A member of the audience rises to interrupt the proceedings. It is one of the movie's powerful moments. The man is hatless and dressed in ordinary best clothes. He protests, 'but we German Americans are not like that'.

This became evident once America entered the war. A short list of US military and naval leaders of German heritage – Eisenhower, Spaatz, Nimitz – makes the point in one way. To offer another perspective, 33,000 men who fought in the US Army were born in Germany, of whom 14,000 were not yet American citizens. German exiles fought in the American armed forces and served in the OSS.[13]

In Germany itself, opposition was extremely risky, yet Allen Dulles of the OSS, who had the job of cultivating the opposition, estimated that around 10 per cent of the Abwehr was hostile to Hitler.[14] The Bendlerblock, the building complex on Berlin's Landwehr canal that housed the German military command, supplies a mini-illustration of how resistance and repression occurred. The 20 July 1944 plot to assassinate Hitler was hatched in the building and its perpetrators were executed in one of its courtyards. Admiral Canaris, whose office remained in the Bendlerblock's Abwehr suite until bomb damage prompted a move to the Zossen bunkers, was later executed for shielding the 20 July plotters.

Today, the Bendlerblock (controversially) houses a section of the Ministry of Defence, but it also accommodates the German Resistance Memorial Centre. Even in repressive Germany, some brave Germans resisted Hitler. On the other side of the Atlantic, that resistance was the norm.

Looking at why certain individuals spied, it is true that German–Americans often felt uncomfortable in the land of their adoption. In both the 1938 and the 1941 episodes, the spies were predominantly first-generation immigrants to the United States – twenty-eight of the thirty-three arrestees of 1941 were US citizens, but twenty-seven of them were born in Germany. A decade later, Oscar Handlin (a historian of Russian Jewish heritage) wrote of the alienation that first-generation immigrants suffered. With their different ways and manner of speaking, they met with hostility. While some American racist theorists postulated the superiority of 'Teutonic' nations that included Germany, others narrowed their preference to the English-speaking nations, which made outsiders of German immigrants.[15]

The vast majority of German–Americans overcame these difficulties. The tiny minority of German–Americans who did succumb to their feelings of alienation and spied tended to be bitter about the 1919 peace settlement, with its imposition of humiliating terms on Germany. Typically they had fought in the 1914–18 war, felt robbed of both victory and justice and found inspiration in the rhetoric of Hitler, who promised to restore German pride.

A good number of them had experienced identity confusion not just in America, but also before they left Germany. Secret agents, of whatever nationality, tend to act out a process of 'splitting'. They can live double lives, just like a man who is unfaithful to his wife (as many of the spies were).[16] Several of the spies discussed in foregoing pages came from borderlands such as East Prussia and Alsace, where identity confusion and split loyalties were endemic.

It is notable, too, that the Abwehr's agents who operated in America were lower middle class in background. The prize catch for the Abwehr was a machinist who understood military technology. As for the couriers, they were hairdressers or ship stewards. All this was evident not only in 1938, but also in 1941 – six of the arrestees were mechanical engineers and eleven of them worked on ships. While the role of social status has been a matter for debate, the weight of historical evidence supports the popular view that Hitler typically drew his followers from the lower middle classes. The typical Hitlerites belonged to a condition in society that made them resent both the working class with its socialist tendency and the traditional ruling elite. The agents who served in America had a social status that made them just such Hitler supporters – unlike the officers who controlled them and unlike the better-educated German émigrés who hated the Führer.[17]

Loyal to America though the great majority of German immigrants were, the presence amongst them of potential traitors offered a special opportunity to the Abwehr. Against this background, it was a credit to the FBI that its special agents succeeded in neutralising both the 1938 and the 1941 spy rings. The occasional potent microdot must have got through, but the FBI appears to have effectively snuffed out the Abwehr's operations against the United States post-1938.

The Bureau continued to reap the reward of fame, for example through a new movie. *The House on 92nd Street* (1945) was to the 1941 episode what *Confessions of a Nazi Spy* has been to its 1938 precursor. Its plot was about the 1941 unravelling of the Ritter–Lang story of 1937. It was recognisably about the Norden bombsight leak, updated to appeal to end-of-war concerns about the potential theft by spies of America's atomic bomb secrets. The substitution of the bomb for the bombsight reflected the realities of 1945. As we saw in the last chapter, Ugo von Bonin did dispatch an agent, Alfred Meiler, to Manhattan with a view to obtaining information on US nuclear physics.[18]

The 1941 arrests may not have been significant politically, but Berlin still reacted angrily to them. The German authorities dismissed the architect of the ring, Major Ritter, and dissolved his section of the Hamburg branch of Abwehr.[19]

Ritter subsequently served in ground-to-air flak artillery units in Sicily and mainland Italy, and in April 1945 surrendered to Allied troops in the Harz Mountains in northern Germany, his days in intelligence a fading memory.[20]

MI5's Special Guest

It was 21 April 1945, a spring day in the Aegean. An 11,000-tonne steamship eased its way out of the Dardanelles and headed for the wider reaches of the Mediterranean. Captain Nordlander did not want to be mistaken for a combatant. '*Drottningholm*' appeared in very large letters on its white-painted hull, along with the words 'Sveridge' (Sweden) and 'Diplomat'.

It does not take too much imagination to picture a cluster of individuals who gazed at the receding Turkish coastline and engaged in desultory talk. A casual observer might have noted among them a hulking figure of military bearing. We know that Erich Pfeiffer was over 6ft tall and weighed 210lb. His head was large, even for one who was so strongly built. A crop of fair, greying hair surmounted his small mouth and jutting chin. A scar ran down his left cheek to the nostril of his long, straight nose. He had the disconcerting habit of standing on one foot while talking, then swinging away and gazing into space when someone tried to reply.[1]

Down below, Pfeiffer's copious luggage pointed to a person of substance and to a man who was unusually well prepared for travel. It consisted of three suitcases, a kit bag and a briefcase.

Pearl cufflinks, grey kid gloves, silk shorts and a bottle of scent hinted at the voyager's extracurricular interests. There was a white metal star with a swastika in the middle. And money. Pfeiffer had US dollars, Swiss francs, Swedish kronor, Turkish lira and smaller amounts of currency from the Netherlands, Denmark, Portugal, France, Greece and Yugoslavia.[2]

The voyager's luggage had not travelled for a while. Pfeiffer had spent the last few months confined to the German consulate's compound in Istanbul. His cover job had been Deputy Naval Attaché until August 1944, when Turkey broke off diplomatic relations with Germany and interned that nation's diplomatic staff. Unable to leave the compound, he whiled away the time learning to play bridge and – he was an ambitious man – waited for word from Berlin about the promotion he felt was his due. By this stage in the war, Berlin had other matters to consider and Pfeiffer waited in vain.

Having left Turkey behind, Pfeiffer hoped the quiet hum of the *Drottningholm*'s steam turbine engines would serenade his return home. On 1 May, the steamer berthed at Lisbon, where Pfeiffer made two trips ashore. Portugal was a conservative dictatorship, although it had been neutral in the war, and he remembered the days when there had been German intelligence assets on the banks of the Tagus. His agent Karl Eitel, formerly of the American run, had operated there during the war until recalled to Bremen in May 1944. Perhaps Pfeiffer did not realise that early in 1944 Eitel's Lisbon landlord had informed on him to the OSS. The American secret service recruited him as a 'diver', or double agent. Thereafter, Eitel fed British and American 'chicken feed' and disinformation to his Abwehr spy bosses.

Lisbon was no longer a reliable outpost of German intelligence. Nevertheless, our voyager requested orders from Berlin. None was forthcoming. Hitler had just killed himself and his capital city was about to fall. Resigned to his fate and suspecting, as he put it, that 'the British would pick [him] up', Pfeiffer continued his voyage on the *Drottningholm*. A few days later, the ship docked on Merseyside for 'control'.[3]

As he must have foreseen, Pfeiffer was at this juncture 're-routed'. He travelled from Liverpool to an establishment called Camp 020. Situated in Latchmere House, a barbed-wire-surrounded Victorian mansion near Richmond on the outskirts of London, this was a secret interrogation centre run by the Security Service, MI5. It came to be celebrated for its recruitment of double agents, perhaps most famously Eddie Chapman, known to the Abwehr as Fritzchen and to his British controllers as Zigzag. A monocled half-German colonel, Robin 'Tin Eye' Stephens, presided over an outfit that had quizzed 480 spies and other prisoners in the course of the war. Stephens later survived a court martial having been charged over the brutality of his interrogation techniques. He banned the use of violence, but his interrogators did use psychological techniques such as silence, head-bagging, bright lights and sleep deprivation.

Tin Eye also had at his disposal another way of concentrating prisoners' minds. It was a consequence of wartime legislation. Early in the conflict, Parliament had passed the Treachery Act. The law on treason had hitherto applied to British citizens and was medieval – its 1351 enactment prescribed death for whomsoever warred or plotted against the King. Revised in 1534, it targeted religious dissenters.

One of its victims was the Catholic Guy Fawkes, condemned to be hanged in 1606 for plotting to blow up the House of Lords. The 1940 revision, a reaction to the Tyler Kent affair, had stimulated a debate in the House of Commons with members questioning the efficacy of the death penalty and expressing doubt about enemy military personnel being 'handed over and shot' whether or not they were in uniform.[4] For the Bill that received royal assent on 23 May 1940 enabled the trial for 'treason', resulting in possible execution, of non-British as well as British 'traitors'. In the course of the war, the

British authorities executed sixteen persons convicted under the new Treachery Act. For example, Charles Albert van der Kieboom, a Dutchman who spied for Germany, was hanged in Pentonville Prison on 17 December 1940 after he had resisted efforts to force him to become a double agent.

Camp 020 produced fourteen of the unfortunates known as 'the unlucky sixteen' who were executed for infringement of the Treason Act. Three of them were Germans, men who were still deemed 'treasonous' in spite of the fact that their country was at war with Britain. There was uncertainty about who was to be executed and why. The uncertainty must have been terrifying for the inmates of Camp 020, who can only have thought of themselves as subject to the whim of Tin Eye and his fellow MI5 officers.[5]

By the time Pfeiffer arrived in 020 the war in Europe was over, but British and American interrogators were still at work. They were turning their minds to the prosecution of Nazis for war crimes. There were other reasons, too, why they continued. Though currently allied to America and Britain, the Soviet Union with its new-found military might was emerging as a potent threat to democracy, and Germans with knowledge about the Soviet military could be helpful – indeed the Americans recruited and made an ally of Reinhard Gehlen, who had been the Reich's senior intelligence official regarding the Eastern Front. From 1956 Gehlen would head the BND, the Abwehr's peacetime successor. Camp 020 interrogators anticipated that there would be such a revival of German intelligence activity after the war. They wanted to know about the Abwehr not just out of curiosity about a former foe, but also because it would be good to know about one's future friends.

How did Pfeiffer come to be an inmate of Camp 020? There is a discrepancy between 020's accounts of how this happened. One version holds that Pfeiffer was loyal to his country to the last. The officer who wrote up a conclusion after Pfeiffer's

interrogation saw him as a 'good and loyal German', while
Pfeiffer's own account suggests he waited passively in captivity
until the arrival of the *Drottningholm*.[6] Quite another version
appears in 020 correspondence. It indicates that the extermi-
nator sent to deal with the 'rats leaving the sinking ship' joined
them.[7] As soon as Turkey broke off diplomatic relations with
Germany, Pfeiffer approached an OSS intermediary with a
view to going over to the Americans.[8]

The British objected to the proposal that Pfeiffer should
become an OSS asset. They felt that Turkey fell within their
sphere of influence. They furthermore charged that the
Americans were less well equipped to interrogate Pfeiffer.
Some Americans did feel that they could learn from the interrogation techniques used in 020. General Bedell Smith of US
Army intelligence, the former employer of Leon Turrou who
would serve as a future director of the CIA, had visited the
camp and arranged for US personnel to study its methods.
When people show a willingness to learn from you, it is all too
tempting to believe that they know less than you do.[9]

Pressing the British case, an MI5 representative wrote to
MI6's Aubrey Jones insisting that Pfeiffer's fount of knowledge
could 'be more suitably tapped by interrogation at 020'. He
stressed the urgency of a proper resolution and added: 'If they
wish him sent to the United States, he should be routed via
the United Kingdom.' Jones accordingly got in touch with
Robert D. Murphy, a career diplomat who had worked closely
with the late President Franklin D. Roosevelt and for General
Dwight D. Eisenhower. At this time, US forces were being
swamped by offers of surrender by Germans who wanted at
all costs to avoid falling into the hands of vengeful Russians,
Czechs and others. From the US viewpoint, handing over
some cases to the British must have seemed an attractive proposition. Murphy acceded to the British request for jurisdiction
in Pfeiffer's case and lobbied OSS director William J. Donovan.
So 020 got its man.[10]

That did not spell the end of American interest. Back in 1942, the British had agreed with the OSS's Whitney Shepardson to share the benefits of interrogation.[11] Liaison took place in 1945 as in the preceding three years. The FBI sent 020 their own report on Pfeiffer and a list of questions he should be asked. The 020 interim report on Pfeiffer went to the American Embassy. A copy of the report found its way back to 020 bearing notations in US diction (for example, 'fall' as opposed to 'autumn'), indicating that an American official had taken the trouble to read it carefully.

Appendix III to 020's Pfeiffer report was of special interest to the FBI. This was the German spymaster's detailed, page-by-page commentary titled 'Observations by PHEIFFER on "THE NAZI SPY CONSPIRACY IN AMERICA" by Leon G. Turrou, London Edition (George G. Harrop & Co., 1939).' In this commentary, Pfeiffer gave his interpretation of how his spy ring had operated in the United States. He rejected the account rendered in *The Nazi Spy Conspiracy in America* by the FBI's crack detective. He objected to Turrou's use of the term 'Nazi' to describe the German spy 'conspiracy' of the 1930s. He accused Ignatz Griebl of issuing 'wild fabrications', and Turrou of being 'absolutely rotten' in testifying to the veracity of Griebl's comments on 'high-placed German personalities'. He denied helping the Griebls to sequester Jewish property. Pfeiffer's commentary found its way into the FBI's counter-intelligence files.[12]

MI5 may have had to share its secrets, but Pfeiffer was still a prize catch as he knew the Abwehr inside out. Yet what about his character and reliability? His reputation had preceded him in a dubious manner, for Karl Eitel had expressed opinions on his former boss. In September 1944, with the American invasion in full swing, the Free French had detained Eitel just outside Nancy and handed him over to the US Army's Counter-Intelligence Corps (CIC) for questioning. CIC interrogator Oliver Burglund noted that Eitel had been born in the Alsatian community of Mulhouse (in German, Mulhausen). Mulhouse had witnessed heroic scenes of French resistance and its inhabitants insisted that they spoke an *autonomous* version of the German language.[13] But it was also an area of disputed loyalties that were replicated in the personal life of Karl Eitel. His mother was French, his father German. His mistress in Brest, Marie Cann, had been French, but his wife Magda was German. Burgland concluded that Eitel's story, about being a French patriot who worked against Germany at every opportunity, had 'several outstanding weaknesses'. He should be sent to London for further investigation and if his 'story is not proved, he should be executed'.[14]

Alerted, yet taking heed of his claim to have worked with OSS Portugal, MI5 decided to treat Eitel 'with a velvet glove'. Facing death, the double agent decided to distance himself from his espionage escapades on behalf of Pfeiffer, whom he described as a 'complete egotist, ambitious, unscrupulous'.[15]

Transferred to 020 custody, he continued in that vein, but also made some remarks that were indirectly helpful to Pfeiffer. For example, he inadvertently assisted what would be Pfeiffer's defence, that he had not been in control of what Hamburg got up to, when he said that Pfeiffer had been furious with him for dealing with Lonkowski, insisting that Lonkowski was being run from Hamburg and he should deal only with his own agents – it was a cardinal principle of good intelligence. Another of his remarks potentially helped Pfeiffer at a time when captured German officers were desperately trying to establish that they had never been Nazis. Contrasting his former employer with Griebl, who was 'a fanatical Nazi', Eitel said that Pfeiffer was 'too much of an egotist to be interested in politics'.[16]

When Pfeiffer arrived from Istanbul five months later, 020's interrogators at last had the opportunity of assessing the master spy who had been Leon Turrou's principal opponent. They were in awe of him. They reported that he had the 'doubtful distinction of world-wide notoriety as a spy master'. They realised that Pfeiffer had a deep fund of knowledge about secret intelligence. 020 further noted that Pfeiffer was a 'superior' type and a 'snob', a personality trait that helped to explain his deep resentment of the disdain with which the German hierarchy had over the past decade treated the Abwehr – for Pfeiffer, 020 concluded, was 'never a nazi'.[17]

When Col Stephens wrote up a final report on his unit's activities, his prejudices were evident. He admired Pfeiffer and despised his manservant in equal measure. The manservant Pfeiffer had been allowed in captivity was none other than Karl Eitel. He may have chosen him on grounds of familiarity or, very possibly, to save him from the gallows. A prosecutor might have taken the line that Eitel was a Frenchman who had spied for Germany. Stephens had an ominously low estimation of a person who was short, fat and of indifferent social standing. In a potentially lethal opinion, he judged Eitel to be 'a bad spy, a bad German and a bad man' who had enjoyed 'a long run for his unearned Abwehr money'. Tin Eye fondly recalled the occasion when Eitel ventured an opinion and Pfeiffer told him to stick to the things he was good at, 'cooking and scrounging'. To Tin Eye's evident delight, Eitel 'winced and wept and whimpered a sycophantic "*Ja mein Kapitän*".' The class-conscious Stephens made no attempt to disguise the fact that he saw superior qualities in his prize captive: 'PHEIFFER could never be wrong.'[18]

Pfeiffer took a line and got away with it. He denied he was a Nazi, denied that those who spied on America under his aegis were a Nazi spy ring and rejected Turrou's idea that he was a master spy who pulled all the strings regarding the espionage effort against the United States. Yes, he had administered Lonkowski, but Lonkowski was 'an agent of Berlin'.[19] He did not originate the Kate Moog/Mata Hari plan, nor did he connive in the expropriation of Jewish property. His close associate Eitel never had any Gestapo connections. He disclaimed responsibility for the Crown correspondence and thus for both the McAlpin kidnapping/murder plot and the passport application forms scam, instead laying these escapades at the door of rogue fanatics who were out to please the Party hierarchy and who answered not to Bremen, but to Hamburg or to Berlin directly.

According to Pfeiffer, the villain of the piece was Karl Schlueter. Though admittedly one of Pfeiffer's agents, Schlueter was a maverick with Gestapo connections. In plotting extreme endeavours to ingratiate himself with the Party and Abwehr hierarchies, he had committed a breach of security in using one of Pfeiffer's own code names, 'Spielman'. The mysterious Spielman who had briefed Rumrich and Hofmann was then Schlueter and not Pfeiffer as Turrou had supposed. Schlueter, as a Bremen agent, had poached Rumrich from the Hamburg Abwehr station, whose asset, so Pfeiffer claimed, he was supposed to be. By contravening the Abwehr's security procedures in these ways, Schlueter had contributed to the 1938 debacle and had given Pfeiffer's spy programme a bad name that it did not deserve.[20]

In spite of his self-exculpations, it must have been clear to at least some of his interlocutors that Pfeiffer was an opportunist and a fellow traveller with the Nazis. But the interrogators were dazzled by the information he chose to divulge. So well informed was he, that, in the words of his interrogators, the 'exhaustion of PHEIFFER's encyclopedic knowledge of the Abwehr and its personalities defies the very attempt'. He passed on his knowledge in large, if not exhaustive, quantities. For example, he supplied mini biographies of 438 German spies with whom he had been in contact. His interrogators did realise that Pfeiffer held some things back, sometimes 'by design', but they concluded that he talked well, perhaps because his country was no longer at war.[21]

020 were able to piece together, for the first time, the story of Pfeiffer's life and espionage activities. The narrative illustrated that,

by and large, Pfeiffer succeeded in his spying efforts. His successes elsewhere threw his American failures into relief and underlined the impressiveness of Leon Turrou's achievement in combating his German rival. Some of his successes pre-dated the American disaster of 1938 and others occurred through the period of the Second World War. Pfeiffer claimed that his methods improved because of his tussle with the FBI:'It was his principle that neither agents nor officers should know more of each others' activities and interests than was necessary for the execution of their assignments; the American lesson had not been lost on him.'[22]

Pfeiffer's European operations were successful. In 1936, he took on Marc Aubert, a French naval officer who had offered his services to the German attaché in Paris. At their first meeting, Aubert was indiscreet. He turned up with a woman he introduced as his wife – 'she was the type of wife to whom the French refer between quotes'. But Pfeiffer was in no position to preach on such matters and when Aubert delivered a package of secret documents that weighed fully 95lb, he became an enthusiast in spite of his contemptuous view that Aubert was a 'born traitor' and in it for the money.

The traitor continued to be a 'gold mine' until 1938. In that 'calamitous' year for Pfeiffer, the French and British services tracked spy correspondence that was going through a poste restante address in Dublin. They identified Aubert and although they played him back as a double agent, the traitor's fate was not in doubt. Pfeiffer saw through the play-back. He told his interrogators he was so upset about Albert's likely fate that he told his wife Lotte to cancel the family's 1939 New Year party. He was also fearful of Berlin's reaction to Aubert's demise. In the event, Canaris received the news with his usual aplomb, saying that two undetected years was a good run for a spy in Aubert's risky position. For all his professions of grief, Pfeiffer basked in the rays of Canaris's approval. The venal Aubert was less fortunate. In March 1939, he met his death in front of a Toulon firing squad.[23]

After the outbreak of the war, Canaris entrusted Pfeiffer with intelligence and counter-intelligence responsibilities in France. The former Bremen station chief found himself in charge of the Abwehr station in Brest, the seaport in the Celtic province of Brittany, with the mission of gathering intelligence on Britain and France. A few of his Bremen staff had travelled with him, including his mistress-secretary and another familiar culprit, Karl Eitel.

Eitel did not contribute to Pfeiffer's success story. In the summer of 1940, Pfeiffer learned that Breton fishermen were sailing beyond the limit prescribed for them by the German authorities and communicating with the British. He turned for help to Eitel, who spoke French, and, as a former wine steward on a German ship, claimed he knew how to handle sailors. Pfeiffer requisitioned the 45-tonne *Breiza Isel Arvor* and gave the boat and a scratch crew to Eitel, who was to patrol the Atlantic approaches. This and similar missions met with indifferent success. Eitel's crew, as the name of their boat suggests (it is Breton for 'lower Brittany shore') may well have spoken their own language and the Breton workers had no time for the Alsatian-accented Karl Eitel. They engaged in the theft of maritime equipment, 'go-slow' working and the concealment of Allied agents.

In 1940, Pfeiffer played a more constructive role when he took part in preliminary planning for the invasion of Britain dubbed Operation Sealion. Ever since his days in Wilhemshaven, he had been an authority on maritime logistics. Now, he concluded that the invasion scheme was impractical. He believed that the Germans simply did not have enough ships and troop barges to do the job. His findings were among those that percolated upwards and on 20 June Navy chief Admiral Erich Raeder informed Hitler that Germany lacked the maritime capacity to transport an army across the English Channel. The Luftwaffe nevertheless attempted to prepare the way by asserting air supremacy in what came to be known as the Battle of

Britain (July–August 1940), but lost. The survival of the Royal
Air Force's fighter defences meant it would have been hazardous to invade even with an adequate fleet. If in a minor way,
Pfeiffer, by pointing to the armada's inadequacy, contributed to
the wise German decision to cancel Operation Sealion.[24]

In March 1942, Pfeiffer moved to Paris and undertook work
against the French Resistance. This time, only one survivor
of his Bremen staff accompanied him, Hilde Gersdorf. They
lived together at rue St James in Neuilly, using the surname
Kross. 020 staff noted that when an Allied bomb hit his home
in Bremen, causing Lotte to lose one eye, Pfeiffer managed
only a five-day visit to comfort her and his children, and to
move the family to a safer location in Siegen, Westphalia. His
interests lay elsewhere. Paperwork consumed more and more
of his time and, he told 020, he pined for command of a fighting ship.

Pfeiffer at this time worried about the penetration of the
Abwehr by Heydrich's Sicherheitsdienst (SD), or Security
Service, an outfit with a terrifying reputation. Perhaps with his
own safety in mind, he told his 020 interrogators that he had
scruples about interrogation methods. His role model, Max
Ronge, had interrogated prisoners of war without 'invasive
methods', arguing that the offer of a cigarette or glass of wine
at the right psychological moment could produce miracles,
especially when combined with *rumours* of torture. Ronge's
disciple told his Camp 020 questioners that he had resisted
political pressure to employ 'special methods to make a man
talk … drugs, rays or hypnotists'.[25]

Not long after taking over in Paris, Pfeiffer said, he 'was
summoned to Berlin to meet "The Knights of the Green
Table" – the supreme chiefs at HQ'.[26] The reference calls to
mind the ideal of medieval chivalry as conveyed, for example, in the anonymous poem *Sir Gawain and the Green Knight*
(*c.*1400). More recently, Kurt Jooss had in 1932 developed a
macabre theme in his ballet *The Green Table: A Dance of Death*

in Eight Scenes. The Essen-based choreographer depicted the futility of peace negotiations with diplomats seated around regulation green-baize tables and pointed to the inevitability of militarism and death – but without endorsing the philosophy of Nazism.

Whatever one makes of the image, the skies were closing in on those who struggled to keep the Abwehr professional and military in purpose. The Nazi political squeeze continued until, in February 1944, Himmler persuaded Hitler to abolish the agency and give its functions over to the Ausland-SD, the Party's foreign security wing. Canaris went on trial on a charge of having plotted against the Führer. A few weeks before the war's end, he was stripped naked in Flossenbürg concentration camp and, within earshot of approaching Allied artillery, hanged.

Pfeiffer had operated out of Berlin since mid-May 1943. His desk diary reveals that over the next twelve months he travelled all over Europe in pursuit of his new supervisory duties. In May 1944, four months after the axing of Abwehr, the same source indicates that he awaited the urgent delivery of a Turkish entry visa. Berlin had ordered Pfeiffer to restore German intelligence in Turkey, where three agents had defected to the Allies. At this point, Pfeiffer welcomed the prospect of a break. His health was deteriorating, his mentor was under suspicion, what remained of his cherished Abwehr had been rehoused in a section of the Reich's politicised bureaucracy and the war was going badly. He told his mistress to pack her bags, for the ever-obliging Fraulein Gersdorf would accompany him. She could not have foreseen that, within a year, her lover would desert her for the bachelor confinements of Camp 020.[27]

On 9 October 1945, after he had spent four months in Camp 020, the British authorities allowed Pfeiffer to leave. Under escort and in company with eight other recent inmates of 020, he travelled to Croydon Airport.[28] Their aircraft took off for Germany. As it soared to cruising altitude, Pfeiffer no doubt turned his mind to a coming reunification with his family, or what remained of it. At least he had remembered to repack his bottle of scent.[29]

Perhaps as he stared into space, as was his wont, or gazed down at the receding mists of London and then at the infernal English Channel that had not since the sixth century yielded to German invaders, his recollections flickered for a moment over the time when he was in charge of great ventures in Abwehr Bremen. Yes, there had been setbacks in the course of his work there. But, according to what he told the British, his failures had sprung from political interference by zealots on his own side. He held firmly to his delusions that Leon Turrou was a naïf, and that America had never outwitted him.[30]

Diplomatic Consequences

Foreign attempts to infiltrate or manipulate the United States have always run the risk of counterproductive consequences. Thus it was in the 1790s, when Citizen Genêt plotted to entangle America in revolutionary France's war with England. Edmond Genêt succeeded only in provoking a distinct antipathy towards the French, an antipathy that later governed the actions of President John Adams' Federalist administration. Thus it was also in the 1940s, when Soviet espionage produced a hostile reaction. So did the spying efforts of Wen Ho Lee on behalf of China in the 1990s. All these cases helped to turn American opinion and American policy against the perpetrators. Just so, the 1938 revelation that Germany was stealing America's military secrets helped to recast opinion in the United States and to reshape the nation's foreign relations.

For the shift in opinion affected not just US policy, but also the attitude of Germany's diplomats. If America's champions of neutrality were wrong-footed by the 1938 spy revelations, Berlin's emissaries were just as dismayed. It was not like the period of American neutrality in the First World War, when the Washington embassy had run Germany's spies.

No, the agents of the Hitler regime had reported directly to their homeland controllers and, until trouble brewed, the denizens of the embassy on Massachusetts Avenue remained blissfully ignorant.

The spy revelations were a shock because a misleading impression had gained ground in the embassy and beyond. The notion had taken root that Germany, America's enemy in 1917–18, had since that war won a measure of sympathy and even affection. With Wall Street in bad odour following the 1929 Crash and ensuing Depression, opinion turned against financiers and arms manufacturers, whom 'isolationists' now accused of having dragged America into the First World War. Historians and others further argued that Germany had been badly treated in the post-war settlement, the punitive terms of which imposed the payment of reparations that had the effect of stimulating hyperinflation in the new German republic, causing a loss of faith in democracy and the rise of Hitler. There was a concomitant feeling that the whole issue of German war guilt should be revisited. All this looked good for German–American relations, but then came the spy scandal that threatened to reverse the trend.[1]

The perceived impact of the revelations on domestic opinion rocked the complacency of Germany's diplomats. In January 1938, when new in his post, Ambassador Dieckhoff had warned that the activities of the Bund were causing a decline in American regard for Germany.[2] Just after that, the first spy arrests occurred. By the time autumn came around, the ambassador's months-long efforts to limit the fallout from the arrests seemed doomed to failure. Under-Secretary of State Sumner Welles remarked, in the wake of a conversation, that the envoy was 'in a distinctly emotional and nervous condition'.

The meeting between Dieckhoff and Welles was tense. The ambassador tried for a whole hour to justify Germany's policies of expansion and he complained about criticisms of his country in the American press. Welles replied that the American press was critical because Germany's treatment of Jews was intolerable. He added that the German press was just as hostile to the United States, with the difference that it was ordered to take this line, whereas the American press was free.

'Finally,' Welles recorded, 'I said the trial of alleged German spies now going on in New York ... had deeply incensed public opinion in the United States and would continue to arouse the deepest indignation.' This worried Dieckhoff. He knew that Welles was a confidant of the President. He felt personally vulnerable, as the press had linked his name to Theo Schuetz, the spy who escaped via Havana. He told Welles he had nothing to do with the spy ring and that the German War Department, Foreign Office and intelligence service 'had all been completely ignorant of any activities of this kind'. He admitted the spies were likely to be found guilty, but asserted they had received their orders 'from persons of lesser authority in Germany who were acting on their own initiative without orders from the top'.[3]

Dieckhoff's remarks could be regarded as a common diplomatic response to a situation where one's country's spies have been exposed. To explain away one's secret agents as rogue elements is a standard cover-up. In this particular case, though, there is a hint of tragedy. It seems likely that Germany's envoys had not been briefed, but were aware that covert operations were under way. This made them uncomfortable, yet the best they could do was to speak in a coded language. Dieckhoff's 'persons of lesser authority' may be a reference to Nazi party functionaries. As has so often been the case, the prudent course of action is to blame a ruler's advisers, in this case Hitler's Party officials, not the ruler himself.

Soon after his meeting with Welles, Dieckhoff was summoned to Germany. The abrupt termination of his mission was only indirectly connected with the spy case. It was Berlin's response to President Roosevelt's recall for 'consultation' of Hugh R. Wilson, the US ambassador to Germany. Wilson had made the mistake of expressing admiration for Hitler at an unfortunate moment. At the time, the Kristallnacht anti-Semitic atrocity was occurring in Germany and the spy scandal was in full spate in America. Dieckhoff's recall, then, was for a number of reasons. But the fact that he was never replaced by a person with ambassadorial rank reflected a chill that emanated at least in part from the spy scandal and its continuing reverberations.

A month after his return to Germany, Dieckhoff warned his government that Wilson's recall might well herald a complete break-off of diplomatic relations. He said this would be a disaster, as it would give President Roosevelt a reason for spending 'billions' on the US military on the pretext that a German attack was imminent. Given what he described as the subjective approach of American judges, the 'political trials' taking place in New York were going to result in convictions. The American press was already anti-German and the American Government would seize the opportunity for further propaganda in the wake of the inevitable guilty verdicts.[4]

With Dieckhoff detained in Europe, the embassy's Counsellor, Hans Thomsen, took over as Germany's representative, with the lower rank of Chargé d'Affaires. One of his first actions was to arrange for more security in the delivery of confidential letters, telegraphs and 'secret political files' – the US Postal Service was no longer to be trusted. It was a response to fears that America would tighten its counter-intelligence measures.[5]

In May 1940, Thomsen found a new reason to complain to the Foreign Office in Berlin. He asserted that Germany's secret agents were still at large and a real problem. They were using methods that might be justified in times of war, but could not be defended in peacetime – and while Europe was by this time at war, America was not. He said that the source of his information about German undercover activities was a one-legged agent called Bergmann, who reported that a Major Osten was directing him to conduct sabotage operations in the United States. He had obeyed orders and had already caused an explosion in a munitions factory and sunk a ship at a Baltimore pier. In spite of his complicity therein, Bergmann believed these operations to be counterproductive: 'It was his opinion that when his activities were discovered, America's entry into the war would be inevitable.'[6]

Foreign Affairs State Secretary Ernst von Weizsäcker later confirmed that an agent with the alias 'Bergmann' existed. He claimed that the agent worked only in counter-intelligence, but, as a precaution, ordered his repatriation. However, Thomsen had insisted that he and his military attachés agreed with Bergmann's view. He declared that his main task was to keep America out of the war, but the reckless deeds of secret agents 'are the surest way of bringing America into action on the side of our enemies and of destroying the last vestiges of sympathy for Germany'.[7]

Thomsen was not entirely out of step with Berlin. For although Hitler regarded America as a potentially inconvenient obstacle, he was biding his time. He knew he would have to force Western Europe into submission before turning his attention elsewhere. This meant keeping America out of the war until such time as he was ready, with Europe prostrate at his feet and perhaps Japan ready to strike America from the rear. His diplomats continued their efforts to keep America friendly and no doubt some of them harboured genuinely good feelings towards the United States.

So the diplomatic assessment and stance towards risky espionage enterprises persisted into 1941. When German Foreign Minister Joachim von Ribbentrop heard of the 'Duquesne' ring arrests, he told Admiral Canaris he would hold him personally responsible if the latest spy scandal caused the United States to declare war on Germany.[8]

In spite of the ready availability of such evidence, historians have paid scant attention to the impact of the Nazi spy case on America's relationship with Germany in the run-up to US entry into the war.[9] Diplomatic historians have credited the influence of other spy cases at other times.[10] However, in part because of Hoover's obliteration of Turrou from the historical record, the 1938 spy case has not yet featured in discourse on foreign relations.

The omission is all the more striking because there is a growing recognition of the case's impact in other spheres. Indeed, that diversity of impact needs to be acknowledged. First of all, historians have shown how the affair spurred the growth of American counter-espionage.[11] It is worth noting that such growth had its own, distinctive impact on foreign relations. Boosting intelligence and counter-intelligence resources was a way of preparing for future conflicts and, especially when done in collaboration with the British, it was a departure from neutrality.

There was contemporary recognition of the spy scandal's likely impact on security policy. MI5's Guy Liddell noted in a report dated March–April 1938 that Turrou's 'enquiries have been very much of an eye-opener to the State Department, War Department and FBI'. He foresaw that the last two in particular would exploit the situation politically by bidding for more power and resources.[12]

Percy Hoskins, the crime correspondent for Britain's *Daily Express*, thought the scandal would accelerate what was an international trend. 'War ministries all over Europe and Asia,' he claimed, 'are watching New York's spy trial, where espionage is having the biggest show-down in twenty years.' France was saturated with spies, and in 1938 Britain was spending £550,000 on espionage and counter-espionage, compared with just £180,000 four years earlier.[13] American journalists agreed that spying was an international threat that called for action and plucked figures out of the air to prove their point. The *New York Times* reported in June 1938 that the 'European nations alone are now estimated to be spending between $50,000,000 and $80,000,000 annually on spying.' The *Los Angeles Times* claimed a year later that there were 10,000 Nazi spies at large in Europe and America, and cited a *Paris-soir* report that there existed in Germany ten training schools for spies.[14]

In May 1938, as the Nazi spy case gained momentum, the FBI had announced that because of budgetary pressures it would reduce its force of special agents. In response, President Roosevelt asked Congress to appropriate $106,000 as an emergency measure to allow the Bureau to conduct 'important investigations' over and above the 'regular work of the bureau'. In the event, the number of special agents did not decrease in 1937–38, instead rising from 623 to 658. There were 896 by 1940.[15]

At the time of the Grand Jury's indictment of eighteen spies in the summer of 1938, Roosevelt backed an increase in Army, Navy and FBI intelligence. American expenditure on military intelligence had declined since the end of the First World War and had reached a low in 1937. There were dwindling numbers of US military attachés in foreign capitals and F.H. Lincoln, a G-2 general staff officer, estimated that in that year the US government spent only $1.5 million on all its intelligence activities – compare this, for example, with the UK's £550,000, which translated as $2.7 million. All this was consistent with America's policy of demobilisation in the 1920s, then neutrality in the 1930s. Lincoln pointed at the higher expenditure levels in other countries. He did not mention Germany, but reckoned that Japan spent $12 million and the Soviet Union $10 million on internal security alone.[16]

Alert to the developing danger, President Roosevelt gradually increased expenditure while seeking to avoid confrontation with Germany and his own country's opponents of militarism. He placed his faith in Hoover. The FBI director drew on his celebrated administrative skills to centralise and coordinate, and his Bureau looked abroad for help. The tip-off for the McAlpin plot had, of course, come from a British agency. In the summer of 1939, there was a Franco–British–American agreement to share data concerning the activities of German and Italian agents. In the following year, with the war under way in Europe, two FBI special agents, Hugh Clegg and Lawrence Hince, travelled to London to study British intelligence arrangements with a view to learning lessons and future cooperation. It would be a stretch to argue that all these counter-intelligence developments stemmed from the 1938 spy case, but it was the initial spur.[17]

Like the growth of counter-intelligence, the issue of civil liberties arising from that growth has commanded the attention of historians and has diverted attention from the spy case's erosion of American neutrality. The issue of civil liberties does, of course, merit scrutiny.

According to a widely credited proposition, the FBI's counter-intelligence effort promoted the development of an American surveillance state. Through its over-zealousness in protecting freedom, so the indictment goes, the FBI was in danger of becoming just like its foe, the Nazi-ridden Abwehr with its Gestapo ally. The charge gained traction at the time of the 1975–76 US Senate's inquiry into intelligence abuses, following revelations about illegal domestic activities by the CIA and other agencies. Testifying to the Senate inquiry, William C. Sullivan, number three in the FBI hierarchy in the 1960s, asserted that the techniques of the 'Nazi intelligence services' had been 'brought home' in the 1930s and were still evident in the Bureau's programmes.[18] Thirty years after FDR's death, the idea that he had set in motion the machinery of an incipient police state threatened to dent his image as a liberal icon.

At the time, there were significant expressions of concern. An editorial in the *New York Times* complained in December 1938 that the American people were being subjected to a confidence trick. Anticipating the neglect of the spy case in future years, the editorial poured scorn on the 'petty' proceedings of the recent trial. In an age of transparency there were no real secrets any more and the German spies had been engaged in a pointless exercise. Building them up into a serious menace was absurd. The *Times* accepted there might be a need for modest FBI enhancement, but warned that a 'super-espionage' agency or 'secret police' was not 'wanted or needed here'.

In the ensuing months, there were further complaints that the FBI was becoming a menace to civil liberties. When the FBI raided a group of Spanish Loyalist sympathisers in Detroit there was a perception that the Bureau was targeting left-leaning anti-fascists. In liberal circles, there was uproar. The *New Republic* was appalled at the FBI's admission that in the pre-dawn operation its agents smashed doors, illegally seized papers and refused arrestees access to telephones and to counsel.[19]

Preparing Roosevelt for a press conference in the wake of the 1938 trial, his speechwriters wrote briefing notes that were defensive on the civil liberties issue. He would find a way of saying that the nation needed to boost its counter-intelligence capability and that he would give the matter his 'personal attention'. He would add, however, 'I don't believe for one moment that we need an OGPU [Soviet political police to 1934, when it was incorporated into the NKVD] or Gestapo, or any other form of secret police organisation.' Even as he pressed ahead, the president recognised there was real concern about the possibility of an American Gestapo. At the same time, he tolerated and benefited from political surveillance. For example, his FBI made an unsuccessful attempt to collect dirt on that prominent champion of neutrality, Senator Gerald P. Nye.[20]

Resentment against the expanding remit of the FBI would be a powerful force in politics, especially when the Bureau expanded into South America during the Second World War, raising the possibility that in the post-war world there would be just one, all-powerful intelligence agency responsible for both domestic and foreign security. Upon the establishment of the CIA in 1947, Hoover's organisation was required to pull out of foreign engagements because of 'super-Gestapo' fears.[21]

The argument that America was becoming a police state was, however, overstated. By the end of the war, the FBI had 4,370 special agents, one for every 32,037 citizens. This compared with the Gestapo's one for every 2,000 – and, in later years, East Germany's Stasi had one officer for every 175 citizens.[22]

Nor can it be argued that the 1938 spy scandal inspired an *exceptional* swing against civil liberties. Private surveillance, for example by private detective agencies, was a long-established practice. Questionable government surveillance had already occurred on several previous occasions, for example when J. Edgar Hoover orchestrated the activities of the FBI's anti-radical division during the Red Scare of 1919–20. It would be fallacious to argue that there occurred overreactions to the Nazi spy ring that triggered a loss of American freedom. Such ideas have diverted attention from the more important foreign relations repercussions of the case.

Just as fallacious would be the idea that the spy ring affair inspired an increase in American belligerency, as distinct from an erosion of neutrality. From 1936 to the outbreak of war in Europe, the American Institute of Public Opinion periodically released poll data in response to the question, 'Will America be drawn into a European war?' In September 1938 – in between the Grand Jury indictments and the start of the spy trial and with Hitler threatening Czechoslovakia – the composite poll indicated that 68 per cent of those asked believed America would be plunged into another conflict. This was a peak and a sharp rise from the previous year, when the figure was 46 per cent. However, fear does not always result in anger and can trigger caution rather than aggression. Sir Ronald Lindsay, British Ambassador to the United States, recognised this when he cabled Foreign Secretary Lord Halifax claiming that Roosevelt was willing to help Britain withstand the Nazi tide, but was being held back by public opinion.[23]

In the spring of 1939, a Gallup poll indicated that the American public's fears of war in Europe had eased. One iconic study of the period concluded that there was at that point 'almost unanimous opposition to any involvement in another war'. Another study summarising the scholarship on the issue gives it as the 'conventional wisdom' that it was not until the bombs dropped on Pearl Harbor on 7 December 1941 that Americans favoured intervention.[24] The spy events had failed to convert Americans into a nation of aggressors.

Nor had the events converted the German public. There had been worldwide press coverage of the spy trial, for example it had been front-page news in the Soviet Union, where the authorities promoted fears of Nazi spy penetration.[25] But in Germany, there was no coverage at all. Minister of Propaganda Joseph Goebbels had told Ambassador Wilson earlier in the year that he personally ensured that adverse American commentary on Germany did not get into the German press. It was to prevent war fever, he said.[26] Even senior officials had to read the foreign press to find out what was going on. Udo von Bonin, for example, read nothing in the German press about Ignatz Griebl's charge that he planned to deploy Kate Moog as a 'Mata Hari' mantrap in America's capital. He learned only in the overseas media of derogatory references to him in the New York trial.[27]

Because Germany was a totalitarian state, German public opinion did not in any case affect Berlin's policies. *American* public opinion did, however, influence Berlin. As we have seen, the German diplomatic interpretation of the 1938 spy trial and its media aftermath was that Hitler's regime had lost its hold on American sympathy and failed in the propaganda war. America, by then increasingly favouring France and Britain, was an obstacle to Hitler's long-harboured designs, and thus became a more likely target. So, in contemplating its attack on Pearl Harbor, Japan proceeded in the understandable expectation that Germany would also wage war against America.[28] Hitler very quickly satisfied this expectation with his war declaration of 11 December 1941. In the critical realm of expectation, the spy scandal played its part.

Though the spy scandal did not persuade the American public or government to support aggression, it did, as Germany's diplomats rightly noted, move American opinion and policy away from the neutrality that had held the nation in its grip in the mid-1930s. There was no getting away from the Nazi spy story. As soon as the trial ended, Turrou prepared to launch his publishing career. Before a single word appeared, every New York newspaper had published a full-page spread telling the story of the story about to be told. Thereafter, Turrou's propaganda wagon with its anti-Nazi theme rolled on and on.[29]

Poll data indicated that the public's support for the Neutrality Acts only recently adopted began to collapse in September 1938. Arguably, contemporary foreign events, such as the Munich conference's cession of Sudetenland to Germany, swayed opinion.[30] Such events did worry America's educated élite. However, in peacetime it has been rare for such foreign events to influence general opinion – people have been more concerned with domestic matters, such as westward expansion, race issues and the economy.[31] In fact, as we know from research conducted by Samuel Stouffer in 1954, people have worried most of all about personal matters such as family income, health and errant daughters, and have troubled themselves little about politics.[32]

The American politicians of 1938 had no means of knowing that. In supporting preparedness, they heeded the signs
of opinion at their disposal. Historians agree that President
Roosevelt did study and heed public opinion. Sometimes he
was swayed by it, at other times he utilised it to justify policies
he already had in mind.[33]

With anti-interventionists in control in Congress, the president's freedom to respond to shifting opinion was apparently
limited. However, Congress, too, was taking heed of the spy
problem. An indication of this is the frequency with which
members of Congress referred to espionage in debates. Taking
the period from the mid-1920s to the outbreak of war in 1939,
the highest frequency (at forty-five occurrences) was in 1937,
when there were protracted exchanges in the Senate over the
La Follette Committee's exposure of labour espionage, a sure-
fire domestic issue. The next highest frequency was in 1938
(thirty occurrences). Congress, as well as the White House,
gave serious attention to the Nazi spy activities exposed in
that year, and by 1939 the proponents of neutrality were losing
their grip on the Hill.[34]

Just as Chargé d'Affaires Thomsen feared, the spy case's
impact on opinion injured Germany's image and its ability to defend its national security interests. Gallup came up
with a concrete example of the injury in a February 1939 poll.
Some 65 per cent of those polled favoured the sale of aircraft
to Britain and France in contravention of the neutrality laws,
while 44 per cent wanted a ban on such sales to Germany.
The message was clear, even if it took the outbreak of war in
September to persuade a special session of Congress to revoke
the 1936 Neutrality Act in favour of a 'cash and carry' provision allowing exports to the European belligerents, which
effectively meant Britain and France. By this time, only 2
per cent of the public supported Germany, with 84 per cent
favouring the Allies.[35]

Chicago's liberal-Protestant *Christian Century* deplored the 'campaign' based on the activities of 'alleged' spies. It had 'far too much the flavor of an effort to arouse a popular anti-Nazi furor. For one thing, it is a little too timely.'[36] Its argument was that anti-Nazis had invented the spy menace to assist their propaganda against Hitler's pogroms and aggression. The campaign may indeed have been 'timely' in the sense of being opportunistic. But it drew further strength from wider contemporary perceptions of espionage. Perhaps one can set aside the contemporaneous Moscow spy trials on the grounds that American opinion reacts to stimuli closer to home. But spies were very much in the public eye and had a dubious reputation.

The La Follette inquiry in the US Senate had dragged labour spies through the mud. Spy movies magnified the profile of undercover agents, adding glamour but not sanctity. This is just a short spy filmography: Fritz Lang's *Spies* (1928); Greta Garbo in *Mata Hari* (1932); and Alfred Hitchcock's *The 39 Steps* (1935), *The Secret Agent* (1936) and *The Lady Vanishes* (1938). Though *The 39 Steps* was hardly pro-German, these films were not anti-Nazi. But they did alert millions of moviegoers, many of whom may not have ordinarily followed foreign affairs, to the phenomenon of espionage. When *Confessions of a Nazi Spy* came along in 1939, with its powerful indictment of fascism, it addressed those millions in a medium that had already made them empathetic and ready to be sympathetic.

There were other factors that made so many Americans change their view on the subject of neutrality. Nazi misbehaviour in Europe was one of them, but foreign events do not in peacetime shape public opinion as much as domestic considerations. It is reasonable to suppose that the 1938 spy exposure and its long-running after-effects rank as one of those formative domestic considerations. The spy affair with its floods of anti-Nazi newspaper coverage undermined Americans' sympathy for neutrality. The associated ebbing in the public respect for Germany caused Hitler's servants to despair of America and this helped to open the door for Japan's attack on Pearl Harbor. The scandal was in these ways a discernible eddy in the stream of international history.

Notes

Chapter 1

1 Louis A. Langille report, 'Guenther Gustav Maria Rumrich', 5 April 1943, pp. 72–3, FNAZ 38/1664; *New York Times*, 26 June 1938.
2 A.H. Leviero, *New York Times*, 21 June 1938; J.E. Lawler, Memorandum for E.A.Tamm, 6 December 1939, FNAZ 26/1229. So little was known about Lonkowski in the United States that there were doubts as to his real name. His official record dismisses any such doubt, confirming that he was born on 20 January 1896 in Worleinen, East Prussia: *Personalnachweis*, Wilhelm Lonkowski's air force personnel file, PERS 6/154245, BArch.
3 Langille report, pp. 65, 68, 75; Turrou, *Nazi Spy*, pp. 135, 140.
4 Reile, *Die Geheime Westfront*, p. 301; quotation and numbers from Adams, *Dictionary*, pp. 3, 111. Article 160 of the Treaty of Peace with Germany (Treaty of Versailles), agreed to by Germany on 10 January 1920, stated that the 'maintenance or formation of forces differently grouped … is forbidden'.
5 Ahlström, *Engineers*, p. 95; Anderson, *European Universities*, p. 158.
6 Lonkovski's signed entry into a technical personnel questionnaire, 28 July 1937, in PERS 6/154245, BArch.
7 Langille report, p. 61.
8 Bailey, *Kid from Hoboken*, p. 260; Huchthausen, *Shadow Voyage*, p. 19; *Forward*, 28 July 1935; Whitman, *Hitler's American Model*, p. 18.
9 Eitel paraphrased in Camp 020, 'Interim Report in the Case of Carl Eitel', 9 November 1944, p. 10, KV2/384-2; Langille report, p. 62.

10 Lonkowski's $30,000 claim to Ignatz Griebl recorded in Turrou, *Nazi Spy*, p. 223; Guy Liddell, 'German Espionage in the United States' (March–April 1938), p. 12, KV2/3533. Liddell was an MI5 officer who gleaned his information from the FBI, Bureau interrogations passed on to him and from MI5's own sources. According to Liddell, Steuer delivered the bombsight secrets to the Abwehr, but (see later chapters) the FBI gave Steuer the benefit of the doubt.

11 Turrou, *Nazi Spy*, pp. 137–8; Langille report, p. 103.

12 The FBI became aware of the Abwehr's activities in Los Angeles and San Francisco in mid-1937, but was unable to foil a botched Abwehr effort to extort Atlas Powder Company secrets that resulted in the murder of the wife and daughter of industrialist Weston G. Frome in the Chihuahuan Desert east of El Paso, Texas. See Richmond, *Fetch the Devil*, p. 185, and Chapter 9.

13 E.A. Tamm, Memorandum for the Director, 5 April 1938, FNAZ 7/320. Tamm's sources indicated the Driscoll invention was passed to Japan as well.

14 FBI memorandum, 'NIKOLAUS FRITZ ADOLPH RITTER,' 22 May 1944, KV2/87. Here and in the rest of the book, capitalisation in both notes and text follows the original.

15 FBI memorandum, 'NIKOLAUS FRITZ ADOLPH RITTER,' 2 September 1945, based on an interrogation of Ritter on 26 July 1944 in Hamburg, KV2/87-1; Ritter, *Deckname*, pp. 15–20, 27.

16 Josef Starziczny, chief of an Abwehr-related spy ring in Brazil, quoted in FBI memorandum, 'NIKOLAUS FRITZ ADOLPH RITTER,' 22 May 1944, and FBI memorandum, 'NIKOLAUS FRITZ ADOLPH RITTER,' 2 September 1944, both in KV2/87-1.

17 Ritter, *Deckname*, pp. 51–2, 72–9.

18 FBI memorandum, 'NIKOLAUS FRITZ ADOLPH RITTER,' 22 May 1944, KV2/87-1.

19 Career summary in Preliminary Interrogation Report on Obstlt Nikolaus Fritz Adolf Ritter, 14 December 1945, KV2/88; 020R, p. 14. Ritter's brother Hans operated on behalf of the Abwehr in California. Thus, one might discern a multi-tentacled reach of the Lonkowski/Gudenberg ring, even if it maintained its cellular structure.

20 Ritter, *Deckname*, pp. 83–92; Ronnie, *Counterfeit Hero*, p. 208.

21 Kahn, *Hitler's Spies*, pp. 328–30; Duffy, *Double Agent*, p. 319n225; Ritter interview with Ladislas Farago quoted in Farago, *Game of the Foxes*, p. 41; Andrew Jeffrey email to author, 14 December 2017.

22 Statement of Senta de Wanger to Special Agents George A. Callaghan and J.T. McLaughlin of the FBI, 31 March 1938, in Turrou, report, 2 April 1938, pp. 75–6, FNAZ 5/213; Turrou, *Nazi Spy*, pp. 147–8.

23 Leon G. Turrou, Rumrich et al. espionage report, 2 April 1938, p. 82, FNAZ 5/213.

24 Statement of Senta de Wanger in Turrou espionage report, pp. 76, 79.

25 Data from Historical branch, G-2, 'Materials on the History of Military Intelligence in the United States, 1885–1944' (unpublished document, 1944), Part I, Exhibit B: 'Headquarters Personnel and Funds Military Intelligence Activities', MHFB; Langille report, p. 72. The quotation is Langille's paraphrase.

26 Translation from German of a letter from Wilhelm Lonkowski to 'my dear sister-in-law and brother-in-law', postmarked Montreal, 17 October 1935, reproduced in Langille report, p. 74.

27 As of 1 October 1935, Lonkowski was a member of the Nationalsozialistische Volkwohlfaht (NSV or People's Welfare Organisation), the Party's attempt to nationalise and politicise social welfare. A record of his political loyalties dated 22 January 1942 is in the Lonkowski personnel file PERS 6/154245, BArch, as are various documents indicating his employment status between 1935 and 1942.

28 Transcript of an order implementing Lonkowski's dismissal of two employees, 31 March 1938; transcript of Lonkowski's agreement to take a pay cut on his transfer to the Air Force's engineering corps, 20 April 1938; telegram to the Minister for the Air Force noting Lonkowski's failure to complete further military training, 19 October 1938; Geheime Staatspolzei Stettin (Gestapo, Stettin branch), report on Lonkowski, 8 June 1940; Lonkowski's defence quoted in a report by the Air Force's engineering department, 17 September 1940, all in Lonkowski personnel file PERS 6/154245, BArch.

29 Interim report on Eitel, p. 10.

30 Turrou, *Nazi Spy*, p. 157; Statement of Senta de Wanger, p. 78.

31 The US Secret Service (not the FBI) had taken the lead in combating German agents in the First World War, and it had neutralised a Spanish spy network in the War of 1898. However, by the 1920s it concentrated on the protection of the President and his entourage and devoted no resources to counter-espionage: Jeffreys-Jones, *American Espionage*, chapters 3, 5, and 8; Jeffreys-Jones, 'United States Secret Service'; Philip A. Melanson, *Secret Service*, pp. 36–9.

Chapter 2

1 *Daily Express*, 17 May 1938.

2 Jordan 'My Amazing Life' serialised memoir (henceforth 'Jordan memoir'), *Sunday Mail*, 5 June 1938.

3   Extract of entry in register of births, Edinburgh, 1 December 1937, KV2/193; statement of Sergeant Sutherland of Glasgow Police Alien Registration Department concerning Jordan's visit to the department on 1 July 1937, 11 March 1938, KV2/3534; Jordan memoir, *Sunday Mail*, 12 June 1938. For the construction of Jessie Jordan's family tree, thanks go to Ross Nisbet, a great grandson of Lizzie Wallace (later Haddow), and to Pat Storey, who very kindly put at the author's disposal her genealogical skills using Family Search, UK censuses, births, deaths and marriages registers and Old Parochial Registers.

4   Karl Wilhelm Friedrich Jordan death certificate, Hamburg, 9 August 1918, kindly supplied by Jessie Jordan's kinsman Donald Haddow; Marga quoted in *Daily Express*, 17 May 1938. The *Express* correspondent interviewed Marga.

5   Jordan memoir, *Sunday Mail*, 29 May 1938.

6   Jordan memoir, *Sunday Mail*, 5 June 1938; *Daily Express*, 17 May 1938.

7   Ferguson, *Paper and Iron*, pp. 31–9, 199.

8   Marga quoted in *Sunday Mail*, 12 June 1938.

9   Jordan quoted in the *Daily Express*, 17 May 1938. For elaboration on Jessie Jordan's spying motives, see Rhodri Jeffreys-Jones, 'Jessie Jordan', pp. 769–72.

10 Liquidation Report No. 206 KDM Hamburg, 28 March 1946, p. 3 and Situation Report KDM Hamburg, 1 August 1946, both in KV3/204; Preliminary Interrogation Report on Obstlt Nikolaus Fritz Adolf Ritter, 5 December 1945, p. 4, KV2/88; Kluiters and Verhoeyen, 'International Spymaster', p. 2.

11 *Empire News*, 22 May 1938; Andrew, *Defence of the Realm*, p. 210; Lieutenant Colonel William Edward Hinchley Cooke statement addition, Precognition of Witnesses against Jessie Wallace or Jordan (for proposed High Court trial in Edinburgh), Dundee, 22 March 1938, p. 1, KV/3534; Kluiters and Verhoeyen, 'International Spymaster', p. 8.

12 *Brecon Country Times*, 30 July 1925. Pat Storey's research indicates that in 1911, Mary Wallace was working as a qualified sick nurse in the home of a widow in Bath. She is in the telephone directories with Felin Newydd as her address, 1926–56. Huw Evans-Bevan, the manager of Felin Newydd, told the author in 2013 that his great grandfather owned the house in the 1940s and that records confirm that Mary Jean Mackay Wallace was the owner in 1930: email, Evans-Bevan to author, 23 February 2013.

13 Report by Lieut Col Cooke on Jordan's espionage activities, 29 March 1938, KV2/3534.

14 Letter postmarked 'Brecon' purporting to be from Mary Wallace to her niece Jessie Jordan in Perth and offering money, 12 September 1937,

and undated report by MI5 handwriting analyst, concluding that the
foregoing letter was written in the same hand as another letter written by Jessie Jordan, making the Mary Wallace epistle a forgery, both in
KV2/3534. See also Jeffrey, *Dangerous Menace*, p. 16.

15 Letter translated from German and narrative in report by Lieut Col
Cooke on Jordan's espionage activities, 29 March 1938, pp. 5–7, KV2/3534.

16 Guy Liddell (of MI5), 'German Espionage Case in the United
States', 28 April 1938, p. 16b, KV2/3533; *Daily Express*, 17 May 1938;
Oppenheim, *Evil Shepherd*, pp. 11, 21, 21, 28, 29.

17 Boghart, *Spies of the Kaiser*, p. 62; Sir John Lavery's painting titled 'The
American Battle Squadron in the Firth of Forth, 1918: "New York" (flag-
ship), "Texas", "Florida", "Wyoming", "Delaware"' is in the Imperial War
Museum, London: Art.IWM ART 1250. The canvas depicts nine ships in
a row, not five as stated in the artwork's title.

18 Draft deposition by Alexander Jack dated September 1938, KV2/194.

19 Detective Lieutenant J. Carstairs, report to Chief Constable, Dundee
City Police, 29 November 1937, KV2/193; John Curran and Mary
Curran statements, 10 March 1938, Precognition of Witnesses, pp. 101,
105, KV2/3534; the Currans' narrative of events as related by J.W. Fraser,
staff reporter, in *Daily Record*, 23, 24 May 1938.

20 Chief Constable Joseph Neilans to Colonel Sir Vernon Kell, 8 December
1937, KV2/193.

21 'They Unmasked Spy Mrs Jordan', banner headline front page story in
Daily Record, 24 May 1938, the first in a series; Dingle Foot, MP, to Sir
Victor Warrender, MP, 23 November 1938, KV2/194. Acting on behalf
of the Currans, Foot was the Liberal Member of Parliament for Dundee
and a barrister. He argued that the *Daily Record* payment should not
be regarded as an obstacle to further government recompense for his
clients, who had acted from patriotic motives. Warrender was Financial
Secretary for the War Office with authority to make compensation pay-
ments in relation to MI5 matters.

22 Signed copy of Kell statement, 5 December 1938, KV2/194.

23 The historian Andrew Jeffrey states that MI5 obtained an additional
HOW on 1 Kinloch Street as the result of Mrs Curran's discoveries:
Jeffrey's written commentary on the author's article 'Jessie Jordan', kindly
supplied in November 2017. As will be seen in the next chapter, a crucial
letter intercepted on 29 January 1938 was addressed to 1 Kinloch Street.

Chapter 3

1 Jones, *German Spy in America*, p. 292.
2 Jeffreys-Jones, 'Montreal Spy Ring', pp. 119–34.

3 Text of message in Louis A. Langille report, 'Guenther Gustav Maria
   Rumrich', 5 April 1943, p. 107, FNAZ 38/1664.
4 Guy Liddell, 'Liaison with the United States Intelligence organisations
   arising from the German Espionage Case' (March–April 1938), p. 5.
   Copies of this report are in KV2/3533 and VNST II 2/21.
5 'Rt.' to 'Mr. S.', 1 December 1937, enclosed in an envelope addressed to
   Jessie Jordan at 1 Kinloch Street, KV2/3534.
6 Crown letters in envelopes addressed to Jessie Jordan, 19, 31 January and
   15 February 1938, KV2/3421.
7 Crown letters in KV2/3421. Copies of some of the Crown letters are
   to be found in FBI files. They are redacted in order to disguise MI5's
   involvement in the tip-off, but the McAlpin plot letter of 17 January
   1938 is there in its entirety, for example in Langille report, pp. 94–5.
8 Crown letter dated 17 January 1938 in KV2/3421.
9 Re Mrs. J. JORDAN formerly WALLACE', undated typed memorandum bearing the handwritten note 'shown to PUS [Permanent
   Under-Secretary of State] and HO [Home Office]', KV2/193.
10 President Roosevelt quotations in Swift, *Kennedys Amidst Gathering
   Storm*, pp. 3, 6; Whalen, *Founding Father*, pp. 213–14.
11 House of Lords debate reported in *The Times*, 17 February 1938.
12 Robert Allen, 'Behind the Scenes at Whitehall', *Evening Standard*,
   21 October 1938, clipping in CAD.
13 Cadogan Diary, 18, 26 January, 1 March, 1938, CAD, and copy of
   17 January 1938 Crown/McAlpin letter in VNST II 2/21.
14 [MI5] 'Memorandum for US Military Attaché [Lt Col Raymond E.
   Lee]', 29 January 1938, KV2/193.
15 Guy Liddell, 'German Espionage in the United States' (March–April
   1938), pp. 2–3, VNST; Batvinis, Origins, p. 10.
16 J.E. Lawler, Memorandum for Edward A. Tamm, 5 January 1939, p. 2,
   FNAZ 28/1281; Batvinis, Origins, p. 10. *The New York Times* first mentioned Colonel Eglin by name on 27 February 1938.
17 [MI5] 'Memorandum for US Military Attaché [Lt Col Raymond E.
   Lee]', 29 January 1938, KV/193.

Chapter 4

1 Memorandum (probably by E.A. Tamm), 5 April 1938, p. 1, FNAZ
   7/320.
2 Turrou claimed fluency in French, German, Russian, Polish, Ukrainian,
   Malay and English, and when Hoover had him tested on these languages
   he proved his linguistic ability. Turrou application to the Department

of Justice, 24 June 1928, and Hoover, 'Memorandum for Mr [Lewis J.] Baley [chief of the Bureau of Investigation]', 19 March 1921, both in FBIT 1/1/1; also Tolson, 'L.G. Turrou … remarks', 6 November 1935, and D. Milton Ladd, Inspector Report on Turrou, 1 April 1929, both in FBIT 1/2/1.

3 Tolson, 'L.G. Turrou … remarks', 6 November 1935 in FBIT 1/2/1; J.M. Keith, Inspector, Memorandum for the Director on Turrou, 22 April 1929, in FBIT 1/1/1; Anon. (indecipherable signature), Memorandum for the Director re Leon G. Turrou, applicant for appointment as special agent, 17 December 1928, FBIT 1/1/1; Turrou, *Nazi*, p. 268; Turrou, *Shadow*, p. 70.

4 Walter F. Stillger to Department of Justice, 8 March 1929, in FBIT 1/1/1.

5 Loebl, Memorandum for the Director re Leon G. Turrou, formerly Leon George Turovsky, 22 July 1938, in FBIT 1/3/1.

6 Transcript of Turrou's address to the Breakfast Club of Los Angeles broadcast over local radio, 7 March 1939, in FBIT 1/3/1.

7 Leon Turrou's grandson Bob Turrou gave this reaction: 'Kind of funny, but my father never mentioned that his father was an orphan. He [Leon Turrou] had two brothers, Rudolph and Joseph (I think it was). I think they were actual brothers, but not sure. Joseph never came to the US. Rudolph was the father of Sandy and David. He died in [approximately] 1938': Bob Turrou email to author, 6 May 2017. Rebecca settled in Brooklyn with her son Rudolph, who registered for the draft on 12 September 1918. This and further details from shipping records and marriage registers in Richard Bareford, comments sent to the author, 5 March 2019.

8 Communication from Bob Turrou's sister, Teresa Turrou-Bressert, to Bertrand Vilain, kindly forwarded to the author in email of 28 October 2019. Vilain is a French journalist and author who has researched Leon Turrou's background in connection with his investigation of the alleged murder of Pierre Quéméneur in May 1923. See Vilain, *L'affaire Seznec: nouvelles révélations* (Cesson-Sévigné: Coetquen, 2011), and the same author's forthcoming volume, *L'affaire Seznec: les archives du FBI ont parlé*.

9 Turrou, text of radio broadcast in California, 7 March 1939 in FBIT 1/3/1; Turrou application form to join the Bureau of Investigation, 1921, indicated by Bareford, above.

10 'I did the DNA 23 and Me thing and I'm not 25 per cent Jewish like I should be if Granddad was 100 per cent Jewish, I'm only about 3/16, which would have made my dad 3/8 and his dad 3/4, which would have meant that one of his parents was 100 per cent Jewish and the other 1/2 Jewish, unless both of them were 3/4 Jewish': Bob Turrou email to author, 6 May 2016.

11 Turrou, *Nazi,* p. 268 (emphasis in the original).

12 Except for the maxim, the quotations are from Turrou, text of radio broadcast in California, 7 March 1939 in FBIT 1/3/1.

13 Information from Thomas Shoemaker, assistant commissioner of immigration and naturalisation, given to Louis Loebl, and cited in Loebl, Memorandum for the Director re Leon G. Turrou, formerly Leon George Turovsky, 22 July 1938, and Turrou, text of radio broadcast in California, 7 March 1939 in FBIT 1/3/1.

14 Louis Loebl to Director FBI, re Leon George Turrou, 24 August 1938, in FBIT 1/3/1.

15 Louis Loebl to Director FBI, re Leon George Turrou, 24 August 1938, in FBIT 1/3/1.

16 Loebl, Memorandum for the Director re Leon G. Turrou, formerly Leon George Turovsky, 22 July 1938, in FBIT 1/3/1.

17 Kusielewicz, 'Paderewski and Wilson's Speech', 66ff.

18 Robert M. Turrou, supplement to 'Leon G. Turrou: Biography', www. imdb.com/name/nm0878103/bio (accessed 26 June 2017).

19 Turrou, text of radio broadcast in California, 7 March 1939, in FBIT 1/3/1.

20 Turrou, 'An Unwritten Chapter', a typescript that Turrou offered to 'the next edition of the ARA "Review"', enclosed with Turrou to Brooks, 12 September 1926, in Collection no.YY545, HILS, supplied by kind courtesy of Richard Bareford; Patenaude, *Big Show,* p. 685.

21 Turrou, 'An Unwritten Chapter'.

22 Patenaude, *Big Show,* p. 685; Bob Turrou, supplement to 'Leon G. Turrou: Biography'.

23 Louis Loebl to Director FBI, re Leon George Turrou, 24 August 1938, in FBIT 1/3/1. Davidovksy may have confused Turrou's Catholic mother-in-law with his Jewish mother.

24 Hoover to Turrou, 29 March 1921, FBIT 1/1/1.

25 Thomas C. Desmond (New York Young Republican Club) to Donovan, 10 December 1928, Alan Fox to Donovan, 31 January 1929, Donovan to Turrou and Hoover to Turrou, 16 March 1929, Turrou's oath of allegiance, 1 April 1929, all in FBIT 1/1/1.

26 Turrou, *Shadow,* pp. 20–1.

27 Rosendahl, 'Loss of Akron', 928; *New York Post,* 20, 21, 22, 24, 25 July 1941; *Pittsburgh Press,* 23, 24 July 1941.

28 Ladd to Hoover, 17 November 1933, in FBIT 1/1/1. Further details in Special Agent F.S. Smith Memorandum for SAC Oklahoma City R.H. Colvin, 14 November 1933, also in FBIT 1/1/1.

29 *Jonesboro Daily Tribune,* 15 November 1933; *Memphis Press-Scimitar,* 15 November 1933.

30 R.H. Colvin to Hoover, 21 November 1933, in FBIT 1/1/1.

31 Turrou, *Shadow*, pp. 107, 122.

32 Hoover to Francis X. Fay, scientific evidence expert, 5 January 1935, in FBIT 1/2/1.

Chapter 5

1 Turrou, *Nazi*, p. 31.

2 E.A. Tamm, Memorandum for the Director, 5 April 1938, p. 4, FNAZ 7/320; text of message in Louis A. Langille report, 'Guenther Gustav Maria Rumrich', 5 April 1943, p. 107, FNAZ 38/1664.

3 Tamm memorandum, p. 14.

4 Turrou, *Nazi*, p. 52; Rumrich's protest paraphrased in Tamm memorandum, p. 23; Turrou, Report on Rumrich/Espionage, 27 February 1938, p. 3, FNAZ EBF 74.

5 *New York Times*, 27 February 1938; *Hamburger Nachrichten*, 28 February 1938; *Washington Post*, 20, 27, 28 February 1938; Welles paraphrased in R.C. Lindsay to UK Foreign Secretary Lord Halifax, 1 March 1938, KV2/3533.

6 Turrou, *Nazi*, pp. 63–4.

7 Batvinis, *Origins*, p. 21.

8 Turrou, *Nazi*, p. 56.

9 Jones, *German Spy*, pp. 24, 74, 97, 205, 231.

10 Turrou, *Nazi*, p. 64.

11 Later on, Rumrich would say that 'furs' referred to passports: L.A. Langille, report on Hofmann/Internal Security, 19 February 1942, p. 5, FNAZ 26/1651.

12 Turrou, *Nazi*, pp. 53–7.

13 Rumrich confession, 21 February 1938, p. 3, in Turrou, Report on Rumrich/Espionage, 27 February 1938.

14 *Washington Post*, 28 February 1938.

15 Rumrich confession above; Langille Rumrich report above; J.T. McLaughlin Parole Report, Rumrich/Espionage, 14 December 1938, p. 8, FNAZ 27/1258.

16 Photocopy of the advertisement placement in Leon G. Turrou, Report on Rumrich/Espionage, 2 April 1938, p. 153, FNAZ 5/213.

17 Rumrich's paraphrase in his confession, p. 9.

18 Statement by Mrs. Juanita Carol Raney, in Julius S. Rice report, Rumrich/Espionage, 21 October 1943, p. 10, FNAZ 42/1988.

19 On splitting: 'Spies, Guerrillas & Violent Fanatics' (London, *c.*1971–72), an analysis by psychologists at the Tavistock Institute of Human Relations, London, supplied to the author by Lily Pincus.

20 Rumrich confession, p. 12.

21 Rumrich confession, p. 11.

22 Tamm memorandum, p. 11. Earlier speculation about the Soviet penetration plan, based on 'cable dispatches from Moscow', appeared in the *Washington Post*, 28 February 1938.

23 'H. Spielman' to 'Dear Friend', 1 January 1938, reproduced in Langille Hofmann report, above, pp. 4–5.

24 See Chapter 19 on Schlueter's alleged agency on the plot. Schlueter frequented New York bars using the name 'Schmidt': Farago, *Game of Foxes*, p. 55.

25 Turrou, *Nazi*, p. 89; Erich Glaser confession, 21 February 1938, p. 3, in Leon G. Turrou, Report on Rumrich/Espionage, 27 February 1938.

26 Turrou, *Nazi*, p. 20; Rumrich confession, p. 14.

27 Turrou, *Nazi*, pp. 57–8.

Chapter 6

1 All quotations from Turrou, *Nazi*, pp. 64–8.

2 Hofmann's version of the event reflected coaching by her defence counsel and there are minor discrepancies as to dates and words spoken compared with Turrou's account. United States District Court, Southern District of New York, USA vs. Johanna Hofmann et al., Johanna Hofmann petition, 16 September 1938, p. 2, NANY.

3 Ferguson, *Paper and Iron*, p. 31.

4 Lorenz, *Spy Who Loved Castro*, pp. 5, 7, 8, 11, 31, 36.

5 Turrou, *Nazi*, p. 73; Hofmann petition, pp. 1, 3; Leon G. Turrou, Report on Rumrich/Espionage, 27 February 1938, p. 3, FNAZ EBF/74. Hofmann's confession of 25 February 1938 is included at pages 43–6 of Turrou's report.

6 Confession of William Drechsel, 28 March 1938, in Turrou Rumrich/Espionage report, 2 April 1938, pp. 18–22 at p.18, FNAZ 5/213; Turrou, *Nazi*, pp. 91–3.

7 Drechsel follow-up interview, 29 March 1938, in Turrou Rumrich/Espionage report, 2 April 1938, p. 27, FNAZ 5/213.

8 Drechsel follow-up interview, pp. 28–9.

9 Hoover paraphrased in a Reuter report in an unidentified clipping from a British newspaper, in KV2/193 TNA; *Daily Mirror*, 28 February 1938; *Time*, 7 March 1938.

10 Farago, *Game of Foxes*, p. 56.

11 C.E. Lee, Parole Report, Johanna Hofmann/Rumrich/Espionage, 14 December 1938, FNAZ 27/1255; Stephenson, *Nazi Organisation of Women*, pp. 11–12.

12 Summary of Hofmann trial testimony and Schlueter biographic details in Louis A. Langille report, 'Guenther Gustav Maria Rumrich', 5 April 1943, pp. 85, 87, FNAZ 38/1664.

13 Hofmann confession, p. 45; Langille report, 'Guenther Gustav Maria Rumrich', pp. 84–5.

14 Turrou, *Nazi*, p. 87.

15 All quotations from memorandum, 'GERMANY: Cover Addresses in Dublin and Dundee for German Espionage', 3 May 1938, KV2/3421; Hofmann's account in Langille report, 'Guenther Gustav Maria Rumrich', p. 17.

Chapter 7

1 *Daily Express*, 22 June 1938.

2 Andrew, *Defence of the Realm*, pp. 56, 78, 143.

3 Joseph Neilans statement, 10 March 1938 in High Court case file on Jessie Jordan, pp. 73–82, KV2/3534; *Daily Express,* 3 March 1938.

4 Author's conversation with Dr Andrew Jeffrey, 24 October 2017; Neilans statement (KV2/3534) listing items corresponding to evidential productions 19, 21–31(a), 32–34 and 46 (b) in *Indictment against Jessie Jordan or Wallace Con. Official Secrets Act, 1911 and 1920, Sec. 1 (1)*, Edinburgh, High Court, May 1938, in JC 26/1938/46, SSC. The indictment cited here and in further notes is the original text that pre-dated alterations following legal manoeuvres.

5 *Daily Express*, 4 March, 30 September 1938; Neilans statement; Christiansen, *Headlines*, p. 171; Allen, *Voice of Britain*, pp. 64–6.

6 *Courier*, 4 March 1938.

7 *Courier*, 11 March 1938.

8 Report by Lieut Col Cooke on Jordan's espionage activities, 29 March 1938, p. 63, KV2/3534.

9 *Evening Standard*, 3 March 1938.

10 *Courier*, 6 May 1938.

11 Nigel West remark to the author in conversation, Gregynog, 24 May 2013.

12 *Empire News*, undated clipping, KV2/194.

13 Quoted in Jeffreys-Jones, *FBI*, p. 100.

14 Statement by William George Quinlan, Chief Inspector in Charge, Royal Marine Police, Scottish Area, in Cooke report, p. 114, KV2/3534.

15 Cooke report, p. 63, KV2/3534.

16 Cooke report, p. 2, KV2/3534.

17 *Daily Herald*, 4 March 1938.

18 *Washington Post*, 4 March 1938; *Daily Express*, 22 June 1938.

19 Jordan to 'Dear Sir', 19 March 1938, Scottish Office File, Criminal Case
    File: Jessie Jordan, 1938–1952, HH 16/212/1597/1, SNA.

20 J. Mayo, governor of Perth Prison, to Secretary of State for Scotland,
    22 March 1938, and W. Steele Nicoll, solicitor of 3 Great King Street,
    Edinburgh, to Under-Secretary of State for Scotland, 27 April 1938, HH
    16/212/1597/1, SNA.

21 According to Andrew Jeffrey, conversation with author, 24 October
    2017.

22 Instructions approved by The Lord Justice Clerk re Trial on 16 May
    1938, in JC26/1938/46, SSC.

23 Note of Objections to Relevancy of Indictment in H.M. Advocate
    v. Mrs Jessie Wallace or Jordan, stamped 10 May 1938, and undated
    note indicating defence counsel's acceptance of 'relevancy' objection,
    accused's intention now to plead guilty, and agreement over procedure
    whereby there would be a speech in mitigation followed by sentencing,
    both in JC26/1938/46, SSC.

24 Handwritten deletions, *Indictment against Jessie Jordan*, 1, JC26/1938/46,
    SSC.

25 New indictment reproduced in *Empire News*, 22 May 1938; *New York
    Times*, 17 May 1938.

26 *Scotsman*, 10 May 1948.

27 Duffes quoted in *Empire News*, 22 May 1938.

Chapter 8

1 Louis A. Langille report, 'Guenther Gustav Maria Rumrich', 5 April
   1943, pp. 27–8, FNAZ 38/1664.

2 Turrou, *Nazi*, p. 104.

3 'William Hamilton', *Salute the Jew!* (privately printed, 1935; reprinted by
   'Sons of Liberty', 1978); Langille report, p. 39; E.A. Tamm Memorandum
   for the Director, 're Contemplated Prosecution in connection with
   the GUENTHER GUSTAVE RUMRICH ESPIONAGE CASE
   on October 14, 1938', 10 October 1838, p. 5, FNAZ 23/1043.

4 Quotation from Turrou, *Nazi*, p. 108.

5 Turrou, *Nazi*, pp. 106–7; quotation from Turrou, *Shadow Falls*, p. 150.

6 Langille report, p. 26; Maria Griebl quoted in Turrou, *Nazi*, p. 212.

7 Benjamin Lichtman, attorney-at-law, Brooklyn, action of 7 November 1933,
   quoted in report by J.T. McLaughlin on Rumrich and aliases, enclosed with
   R.E. Vetterli to Director FBI, 21 July 1938, FNAZ 15/696, p. 20.

8 Turrou, *Nazi*, pp. 99–100, 218; *New York Times*, 29 March 1935.

9   McLaughlin report, p. 18; Langille report, p. 44.

10 Diamond, *Nazi Movement*, p. 132.

11 Turrou, *My Shadow Falls*, p. 151.

12 Turrou, Report, 13 March 1938, p. 2, FNAZ 4/141.

13 E.A.Tamm, Memorandum for the Director re Rumrich/Espionage, 5
    April 1938, p. 4, FNAZ 7/320.

14 'Camp 020 Report on the Case of Erich Pheiffer' (September 1945),
    KV2/267, p. 58. According to the historian Andrew Jeffrey, Herbert
    Wichmann of the Hamburg office of the Abwehr recruited Griebl and
    then allocated him to Pfeiffer, who would be his case officer. Jeffrey adds
    that Griebl worked up contacts in the United States and passed these on
    to Lonkowski: Jeffrey, *Dangerous Menace*, p. 14.

15 Pfeiffer's account in 020 Pheiffer Report, p. 62; Guy Liddell, 'German
    Espionage Case in the United States', 28 April 1938, KV2/3533, p. 12.

16 Langille report, p. 75.

17 Perlman, *Theory*, p. 123.

18 '020 Pheiffer Report', p. 13.

19 '020 Pheiffer Report', p. 27.

20 Carl Eitel seems to have believed Pfeiffer's Kronprinzenstrasse house
    was his family home, possibly mistaking his mistress for his wife: 'Interim
    Report in the Case of Carl Eitel', 28 October 1944, p. 8, KV2/384. A
    municipal change of address entry from 1951 retrospectively records
    Pfeiffer's quitting of the Misselstrasse address on 13 July 1941 and gives
    his family's period of residence there as starting on 1 October 1935:
    SB. Comments on the Misslestrasse neighbourhood kindly supplied by
    Marion Alpert of Staatsarchiv Bremen.

21 Ronge, *Kreigs*, pp. 5, 10, 364–5.

22 Weinberg, 'Hitler's Image of US', 1009; Heinemann, 'Abwehr', p. 1;
    Simms, *Hitler*, pp. 119 ff., 331; Hitler quoted in Compton, *Swastika and
    Eagle*, p. 17.

23 Canaris talk in Bremerhaven, 2 February 1935, quoted in Breuer, *Spy in
    Bed*, p. 5.

24 Pfeiffer quoted in '020 Pheiffer Report', p. 21.

Chapter 9

1   Louis A. Langille report, 'Guenther Gustav Maria Rumrich', 5 April
    1943, p. 56, FNAZ 38/1664.

2   Maria Griebl quoted in Turrou, *Nazi*, p. 216; J.T. McLaughlin report,
    'Guenther Gustav Maria Rumrich/Espionage', 20 July 1938, p. 8, FNAZ
    15/676.

3 Turrou, *Nazi*, p. 218; E.A. Tamm, 'Memorandum: The Inception of the Rumrich Espionage Case', 5 April 1938, p. 32, FNAZ 7/320; Flint–Larsen personnel summary, 4 September 1945, KV2/1973.

4 A search of six collection indices and lists in the Franklin D. Roosevelt Library, for which thanks are due to archivist Virginia Lewick, revealed no reference to Kate Moog/Bush/Busch by either her family or married name. For example, there is no mention of the future spy in the 'Cumulative List of Employees, Roosevelt Estate, 1867–1970' compiled for the *Roosevelt Estate Historic Resource Study* (National Park Service, 2004). The Roosevelt family may have employed her in a casual, short-term capacity, but Moog and her lover Griebl exaggerated, if they did not invent, her role in this phase in her past. There is no mention of Moog in one book that describes in some detail nursing arrangements made for FDR in Campobello, New Brunswick, Canada, and the Presbyterian Hospital in New York City: Cook, *Eleanor Roosevelt*, pp. 308–14.

5 Moog paraphrased in E.A. Tamm, Memorandum for the Director, 5 April 1938, p. 2, FNAZ 7/320.

6 J.T. McLaughlin report, 'Guenther Gustave Rumrich with aliases', 20 July 1938, p. 3, FNAZ 15/696. Kate Moog's married name appears as 'Bush' in this report, but was elsewhere given as 'Busch'.

7 Langille report, p. 56; Pfeiffer quoted in Turrou, *Nazi*, p. 222.

8 Pfeiffer's account of the meeting in 'Camp 020 Report on the Case of Erich Pheiffer' (September 1945), p. 21, KV2/267.

9 Pfeiffer quoting Griebl in 'Camp 020 Pheiffer Report', p. 21.

10 Pfeiffer paraphrased and quoted in 'Camp 020 Pheiffer Report', p. 21.

11 Pfeiffer paraphrased in Langille report, p. 54.

12 Griebl gave two versions of how he achieved contact with the Abwehr hierarchy. In one version, he said that Schlueter introduced him and Moog to Canaris's deputies Menzel and Bonin on the *Europa* on the way to his meeting with Pfeiffer: Batvinis, *Origins*, p. 20. In another version, he said that his brother, who held (in the FBI's paraphrase) 'a responsible position with the German Labor Ministry', introduced him to 'Colonel Busch' (Canaris) once Griebl and Moog had travelled on to Berlin, and that Canaris had then 'summoned his chief assistants' Menzel and Bonin to meet him: Langille report, p. 29, FNAZ 38/1664.

13 Pfeiffer quoted in 'Camp 020 Pheiffer Report', p. 22.

14 Kahn, *Hitler's Spies*, p. 92.

15 Promotions data related to a military pension claim, 16 November 1978, in Udo von Bonin Personnel file, no. 6/12477, BArch; biographic summary, Udo Wilhelm Bogislav von Bonin, Civilian Interrogation Centre, Civilian Military Mission Denmark, 31 August 1945, KV2/1973; Farago, *Game of Foxes*, p. 143.

16 Ashdown, *Nein!*, pp. 79.8, 139.8 (DV); quotation in Langille report, p. 29. According to one of Griebl's accounts, von Bonin first proposed the idea that Moog should perform Washington services when he met her and Griebl on the *Europa* as they travelled to the Pfeiffer rendezvous in Bremen: Batvinis, *Origins*, p. 20.

17 Langille report, p. 29; Guy Liddell, 'German Espionage in the United States' (March–April 1938), VNST, p. 5; Turrou, *Nazi Spy*, pp. 8–12.

18 Bonin biographical summary, p. 7.

19 Statement of Katherina Moog Busch, 24 March 1938, pp. 2–3, FNAZ 5/213.

20 Moog statement, p. 4.

21 020 Memo, R.G. Fletcher to D.M. Ladd, being observations by Dr Erich Pheiffer, 'head of Nest Bremen from 1934 to 1941', on the London edition of Turrou's *Nazi Spy Conspiracy in America* (1939), 16 January 1946, p. 7 (commenting on p. 120), FNAZ 45/1875.

22 Langille report, p. 43. Turrou put the values at $100,000 and $20,000: Turrou, *Nazi Spy*, pp. 217–18.

23 Gempp in *Köilnische Zeitung*, 31 January 1929, quoted in Craig, *Tangled Web*, p. 256. Craig suggests that, at a time when France was pressing for the payment of war reparations, Gempp was trying to defame the French by inferring that they had executed an innocent woman.

24 Reile, *Frauen*, pp. 43, 44, 92. Reile may have been influenced by the more feminist temper of the 1970s, the decade in which he wrote his book.

25 *New York Times*, 15 June 1938.

26 Langille report, p. 38.

27 Extract from FBI Report on Hans Ritter, 21 May 1942, KV2/2130.

28 Richmond, *Fetch the Devil*, p. 277.

Chapter 10

1 *Washington Post*, 26 June 1938.

2 E.A. Tamm, Memorandum for the Director, 3 April 1938, pp. 43–4, FNAZ 7/320.

3 Turrou Rumrich/Espionage report, 2 April 1938, pp. 4–5, FNAZ 5/213.

4 *Washington Post*, 28 February 1938. Vetterli worked on the tragic Charles Mattson case of 1936–37.

5 Statement of William Drechsel, 28 March 1938, in Turrou Rumrich/Espionage report, pp. 16–20, 34.

6 Paraphrase of Drechsel statement, Turrou Rumrich/Espionage report, pp. 26, 42. Because of declining passenger numbers, the two firms were

placed in administration and their management fell under the control of the National Socialist Party.

7   Statements of Drechsel and of Wilhelm Boehnke, political officer on the SS *Bremen*, 3 June 1938, in J.T. McLaughlin report, Guenther Gustave Rumrich with aliases, 20 July 1938, pp. 6–11, FNAZ 15/696.

8   Turrou Rumrich/Espionage report, p. 28.

9   Tamm memorandum, 5 April 1938, p. 7. On the seizure of phone records: Report of Special Agent Leon G. Turrou on von Bonin and others, 13 March 1938, pp. 69–72, FNAZ 4/141; on the polygraphic testing of Drechsel, Moog, Griebl and others: R.E. Vetterli to Director FBI, 30 April 1938, p. 2, FNAZ 9/335.

10 C.K. Lee, Parole Report on Voss, 14 December 1938, p. 2, FNAZ 27/1254.

11 Turrou report on von Bonin and others, p. 35; Tamm memorandum, 5 April 1938, pp. 56–7; Turrou, *Nazi*, pp. 140–3.

12 Turrou Rumrich/Espionage report, 2 April 1938, p. 106.

13 Turrou Rumrich/Espionage report, pp. 83–90.

14 Turrou Rumrich/Espionage report, pp. 79–81.

15 Tamm memorandum, p. 49.

16 Herrmann statement, in Turrou Rumrich/Espionage report, pp. 48–55.

17 Rossberg statement, 29 March 1938, in Turrou Rumrich/Espionage report, pp. 59–62.

18 *Daily Telegraph*, 6 June 1938.

Chapter 11

1   Turrou, *Nazi*, p. 165.

2   Kruse statement, 25 March 1938, in Turrou Rumrich/Espionage report, 2 April 1938, p. 9, FNAZ 5/213; Turrou, *Nazi*, p. 167. Often accidentally but sometimes reflecting Abwehr deception, spellings varied considerably in FBI, MI5 and German documents. Theodore Schuetz may have been identical to an agent called Schultz, who, according to Pfeiffer, was Schlueter's replacement on the *Europa*: F.G. Beith, 'Interim Report in the Case of Erich Pheiffer' (September 1945), p. 13, KV2/267.

3   Paraphrase of Drechsel's statement to the FBI, 31 March 1938, in Turrou Rumrich/Espionage report, p. 32; Janichen identified in Beith Report, p. 13.

4   Turrou, *Nazi*, p. 130.

5   Turrou, *Nazi*, p. 235; Louis A. Langille report, 'Guenther Gustav Maria Rumrich', 5 April 1943, pp. 27–8, FNAZ 38/1664.

6 Statement of Harry Grundling, Room and Table Steward, SS *Bremen*, 19 July 1938, FNAZ 15/696; Griebl to Vetterli cable, 16 May 1938, reproduced in Langille report, p. 39.

7 Grundling statement, p. 22; Pfeiffer paraphrased and Griebl quoted in translation, in Beith Report, p. 31. MI5 personnel habitually used the spelling 'Pheiffer' as they saw it as the phonetic rendering of 'Pfeiffer'. Wurzburg is in Bavaria, where Griebl must by this time have taken possession of the house the Abwehr had promised him for his services.

8 Turrou, *Nazi*, p. 259; Pfeiffer evidence recounted in Beith Report, p. 15; Preliminary Interrogation Report on Obstlt Nikolaus Fritz Adolf Ritter, 14 December 1945, p. 3, KV2/88; Langille report, pp. 103–5.

9 Turrou, Rumrich/Espionage report, 20 June 1938, enclosed with J. Edgar Hoover to Rear Admiral R.S. Holmes, Director of Naval Intelligence, 8 July 1938, and quoting German communications, pp. 1–4, FNAZ 12/546; Turrou, *Nazi*, p. 263.

10 Hinsley, *British Intelligence*, pp. 11–12; Andrew, *Defence of the Realm*, p. 209.

11 Weiner, *Enemies*, p. 79.

12 Batvinis, *Origins FBI*, p. 25; *New York Times*, 4 June 1938.

13 Abortive inquiry into Dr Karl Otto reported in 'Blamierte Spionjäger', *Hamburger Nachrichten*, 19 June 1938, p. 1; *Los Angeles Times*, 21 June 1938. On behalf of the author, Leonie Werle perused the files of the *Völkischer Beobachter* for selected dates, finding no references to the American spy affair: Werle to author email, 15 October 2018. Another newspaper, the *Frankfurter Zeitung*, reported sympathetically on American politics and covered the contemporary Moscow spy trials, but steered clear of the Abwehr spy scandal in the United States.

14 Crawford in *Congressional Record*, 75 Cong., 2 sess., Senate Proceedings 83/6, 3 May 1938, 6186; Ashurst in *Congressional Record*, 75 Cong., 3 sess., House Proceedings 83/8, 10 June 1938, 8672–3; Dickstein in *Congressional Record*, 75 Cong., 3 sess., Appendix 83/10, 31 May 1938, pp. 2303–4; Duffy, *Double Agent*, p. 308n54.

15 Both quotations from Turrou, *Nazi*, p. 264.

16 Jeffreys-Jones, *FBI*, p. 91.

17 E.A. Tamm, Memorandum for the Director, 5 April 1938, p. 1, FNAZ 7/320; Hardy and others paraphrased in *New York Times*, 20 February 1938.

18 *New York Times*, 27 February 1938.

19 Lamar Hardy obituary, *New York Times*, 19 August 1950.

20 Both quotations from *New York Times*, 2 June 1938.

Chapter 12

1　Theoharis, *Chasing Spies*, p. 35; Lokhova, *Spy Who Changed History*, ff nn 2, 7 (DV); Haynes and Klehr, *Venona*, pp. 50, 174; Christopher Andrew quoting Hoover from MI5 files in Andrew, *Defence of the Realm*, p. 388.

2　Erickson, 'Soviet Losses', pp. 256–8.

3　Pfeiffer's quotations, and Pfeiffer quoting Canaris, from F.G. Beith, 'Interim Report in the Case of Erich Pheiffer' (September 1945), pp. 29–30, KV2/267.

4　Turrou article in *New York Post*, 3 January 1939. According to Turrou, the promotion was from Kapitan-Leutnant to full Kapitan, the US equivalents being lieut commander to full commander.

5　Hoare, *Camp 020*, p. 361.

6　[MI5] Counter-Intelligence War Room, London, Liquidation Report No. 206, KDM Hamburg, 28 March 1946, KV3/204.

7　Pfeiffer's naval-design assertion could well have related more to his espionage activities, extensive from 1937 on, against the UK, activities that gave MI5 great concern: Andrew, *Defence of the Realm*, p. 211.

8　Undated 'Report from FBI re Dr Eric Pfeiffer, with aliases', p. 2, KV2/267.

9　Turrou quoting Griebl quoting Pfeiffer in Turrou, *Nazi*, p. 15.

10　Turrou, *Nazi*, p. 15.

11　Turrou, *Shadow Falls*, p. 143.

12　Memorandum (probably by E.A. Tamm), 5 April 1938, pp. 45–7, FNAZ 7/320.

13　Turrou Rumrich/Espionage report, 2 April 1938, pp. 99–118, FNAZ 5/213. The Burgess aluminium design was tried out, but abandoned when cracks appeared in the destroyers' hulls.

14　Report of Special Agent Leon G. Turrou on von Bonin and others, 13 March 1938, p. 58, FNAZ 4/141.

15　Turrou Rumrich/Espionage report, pp. 140–2.

16　Turrou report on von Bonin and others, p. 65; Turrou Rumrich/Espionage report, p. 140.

17　Editorial, *New York Times*, 1 December 1938.

18　Liddell, 'German Espionage Case in the United States', 28 April 1938, p. 15, KV2/3533.

19　J.T. McLaughlin report, 'Guenther Gustave Rumrich with aliases', 20 July 1938, p. 2, FNAZ 15/696; Turrou, Rumrich/Espionage report, 20 June 1938, enclosed with J. Edgar Hoover to Rear Admiral R.S. Holmes, Director of Naval Intelligence, 8 July 1938, and quoting German communications, p. 11, FNAZ 12/546; Dix quoted in *New York Times*, 23 June 1938.

20 *New York Times*, 23 June 1938.

21 Press release, 20 June 1938, 'Statement of Lamar Hardy, United States Attorney. Re: Spy Investigation', pp. 2, 5–6, FNAZ 14/661.

Chapter 13

1 Turrou to Hoover, 20 June 1938, FBIT 1/2/1.

2 *Washington Post*, 23 June 1938.

3 *New York Post*, 22 June 1938.

4 *Washington Post*, 23 June 1938; 'G-Men and Publicity', *Newsweek*, 11 July 1938; *New York World*, 9 July 1938. These reports indicated that the contract was signed fifteen minutes after Turrou's resignation. There was no doubt agreement in principle, but the operative contract was signed on 19 July. See chapter 16 for the actual amounts paid.

5 Turrou to Tamm, 11 August 1938, FBIT 1/2/1.

6 Hoover, memo for Tolson, 14 May 1938, Vetterli to Hoover, 1 June 1938, Hoover to Vetterli, 6 June 1938, Tamm, memo for files, 10 June 1938, all in FBIT 1/2/1.

7 Stern quoted in *Washington Post*, 23 June 1938.

8 P.E. Foxworth, Memorandum for Mr Tamm re Rumrich Case, 23 June 1938, FBIT 1/2/1.

9 *New York Times*, 24 June 1938.

10 Rifkind quoted in Foxworth memo.

11 *New York Times*, 25 June 1938.

12 Hoover to Rear Admiral R.S. Holmes, 8 July 1938, enclosing two reports by Leon G. Turrou dated 14 and 20 June 1938, in FNAZ 12/546.

13 Alston Purvis, *Vendetta*, pp. 11, 182.

14 Hoover, Memorandum for Mr Tamm, reciting a briefing Hoover had given to a journalist from the *Buffalo Evening News*, in FBIT 1/3/1; *New York Times*, 20 July 1938.

15 Critique of Hoover's 13 August 1938 *Collier's* article by John D. Pennekamp, managing editor of the *Miami Herald*, reported in *Newsweek*, 22 August 1938.

16 Hoover, two separate memoranda to Assistant Attorney General Joseph B. Keenan, both dated 24 June 1938 and in FBIT 1/2/1.

17 Denniston, 'Yardley's Diplomatic Secrets', pp. 81, 122–3.

18 Percy E. Foxworth headed the FBI's Special Intelligence Service in South America, created in 1941, until killed in a plane crash in Dutch Guiana (later Suriname) in January 1943.

19 Text of *New York Times* editorial reproduced in P.E. Foxworth, Memorandum for Mr Tamm, 22 June 1938, and Foxworth, Memorandum for the Director, 24 June 1938, both in FBIT 1/2/1; facsimile of the text of the 1933 'Yardley Act' in Kahn, *Reader*, p. 170.

20 The full text of *Totten v. United States*, 92 US 105 (1875) is at https://supreme.justia.com/cases/federal/us/92/105/case.html.

21 Turrou, sworn statement, FBIT 1/2/1, emphasis added.

22 Cummings to Turrou, '20' June 1938, Hoover dismissal recommendation, 25 June 1938, Hoover to all Special Agents in Charge, 27 June 1938, all in FBIT 1/2/1; *New York Times*, 1, 2 July 1938.

23 Hoover, Memorandum for Mr Tolson, 30 June 1938, in FBIT 1/2/1.

24 Turrou quoted in the *Washington Post*, 24 June 1938.

25 Turrou quoted in 'G-men and Publicity', *Newsweek*, 11 July 1938.

26 Turrou quoted in *New York Sun*, 1 July 1938.

27 *Washington News*, 1 July 1938; *Washington Post*, 24 June 1938.

28 Undated clipping from New York's *Daily Mirror*, in FBIT 1/2/1.

29 George C. Dix, Supplementary Affidavits in Support of Motion for Commission, US District Court, Southern District of New York, 2 July 1938, NANY.

Chapter 14

1 Turrou to Hoover, 30 September 1937, FBIT 1/2/1; E.A. Tamm, Memorandum for the File re Turrou, 1 December 1938, FBIT 1/3/1; Hoover memorandum for Tolson, 25 August 1938, FBIT 1/3/1; *New York Times*, 23 August 1938.

2 Motion for Bill of Particulars and Affidavit, 18 July 1938, US District Court, Southern District of New York, NANY.

3 Barnes, *Life of Wasemann*, p. 170, n. 8; Christgau, *Enemies*, p. 172.

4 Dix quoted in *New York Times*, 30 June 1938.

5 George C. Dix affidavit, 2 July 1938, NANY.

6 Davidson quoted in *New York Times*, 9 August 1938. John N. Garner, from Texas, was prominent at the time because he was Vice President of the United States, 1933–41.

7 George C. Dix supplemental affidavit, 22 August 1938, NANY.

8 Dix, Order to Show Cause and Affidavits, 27 June 1938, and Dix, Supplementary Affidavits in Support of Motion for Commission, 2 July 1938, both in NANY; *New York Times*, 3 July 1938.

9 Order, *USA v. Karl Schluter et al.*, 29 July 1938, NANY.

10 *New York Times*, 8 September 1938.

11 Louis A. Langille report, 'Guenther Gustav Maria Rumrich', 5 April 1943, p. 41, FNAZ 38/1664.

12 E.A. Tamm memorandum for the files re Rumrich case, 6 October 1938, FBIT 1/3/1.

13 Griebl quoted in Strassman, *Strassmans*, p. 137.

14 Attorneys' report paraphrased by FBI special agent Brantley, in Tamm memo of 6 October 1938.

15 All quotations from Tamm memo of 6 October 1938.

16 Liddell, 'Liaison with the United States Government Intelligence organisations arising out of the German Espionage Case', March–April 1938, pp. 1–2, VNST; Liddell paraphrased in Turrou Rumrich/Espionage report, 2 April 1938, p. 41, FNAZ 5/213; Foxworth Memorandum for Mr Tamm, 26 May 1938, FNAZ 10/450; Curry, *Security Service*, p. 137.

17 *New York Times*, 17 May 1938.

18 *Daily Herald*, 22 June 1938.

19 *New York Times*, 29 June 1938; *Daily Mail*, 4 July 1938.

20 *Daily Express*, 26 July 1938.

21 P.J. Rose (assistant secretary of state, Scottish Office) to Vernon Kell (head of MI5), 26 July 1938, HH16/212, file 4139, SNA.

22 Lorenz biography in Pfeiffer's list of personnel associated with his Abwehr work, Appendix XX, p. 26, 020R.

23 020R, p. 32.

Chapter 15

1 Turrou, *Nazi*, p. 267.

2 *Daily Express*, 20 October 1938; Soviet reportage recorded in *New York Times*, 22 October 1938; *Washington Post*, 9 October 1938; *Völkischer Beobachter* and a sample of other German newspapers scanned by the author's research assistant, Leonie Werle.

3 Guy Liddell, 'German Espionage Case in the United States', March–April 1938, p. 14, VNST; Kimball, 'Dieckhoff' 218.

4 Rowan, *Secret Service*, p. 1.

5 *Los Angeles Times*, 18 October 1938; *New York Times*, 28 October 1938; *Washington Post*, 25 October 1938.

6 *Daily Mirror*, 19 October 1938.

7 Certificate of Dr T.J. Schück, Hoboken, NJ, 23 August 1938, and Lamar Hardy, Opinion, *US v. Udo Von Bonin, In the Matter of the Application of Maria Griebl*, #963, 16 September 1938, p. 3, both in NANY; Maria Griebl's 'Petition for Control and Appointment of Administrator by the American Property Control Office', Vienna Area Command, 14 September 1945, accessed online via Fold3; Collins quoted in Batvinis, *Origins*, p. 26; *New York Times*, 29 July and 23 September 1938.

8   Tamm, Memorandum for the File re Rumrich Case, 10 October 1938,
    FBIT 1/3/1.

9   Dix quoted in *New York Times*, 10 November 1938; Tamm, Memorandum
    for the Files re Rumrich Case, 6 October 1938, FBIT 1/3/1; Turrou,
    Nazi, p. 268.

10 *Washington Post*, 22, 25 October 1938; *Los Angeles Times*, 17, 22 October
    1938.

11 Defence attorneys' quotation in *Los Angeles Times*, 22 October 1938;
    Washington Post, 25 October 1938.

12 C.K. Lee, Parole report on Johanna Hofmann, 14 December 1938,
    FNAZ 27/1255.

13 Hofmann quoted in *Los Angeles Times*, 21 October 1938.

14 Hofmann–Dix petition, 16 September 1938, in NANY.

15 Digest of Dix's statement in P.E. Foxworth, Memorandum for
    Mr E.A. Tamm, 17 October 1938, FBIT 1/3/1.

16 Steuer statement, 14 March 1938, Turrou, Report, 13 March 1938, p. 33,
    FNAZ 4/141.

17 *New York Times*, 22 November 1938.

18 Dix quoted in *Washington Post*, 29 November 1938.

19 Dialogue and *Sun* quotation from Patenaude, *Big Show*, p. 689; dialogue
    also from *New York Times*, 22 November 1938.

20 Tamm, Memorandum for the File re Rumrich Case, 10 October 1938,
    FBIT 1/3/1.

21 Hoover, handwritten note on Foxworth, Memorandum for the Director
    re Rumrich Case, 19 November 1938, FBIT 1/3/1.

22 Hoover, Memorandum for Mr Tamm, 26 October 1938, FBIT 1/3/1.

23 P.E. Foxworth, memorandum for Mr E.A. Tamm, 17 October 1938,
    FBIT 1/3/1.

24 Tamm, Memorandum of the files in re Rumrich Case, 2 November
    1938, FBIT 1/3/1.

25 Tamm, Memorandum for the files re Former Agent Turrou,
    30 November 1938, FBIT 1/3/1.

26 Foxworth, Memorandum for the Director re Leon G. Turrou, 5
    December 1938, FBIT 1/3/1.

27 Foxworth, Memorandum for the Director re Rumrich Case, 7
    December 1938, FBIT 1/3/1; Hardy's fifteen-minute appointment
    recorded in SD and TAD, 8 December 1937.

28 *Los Angeles Times*, 1 December 1938.

29 Weeping Hofmann photograph in *Los Angeles Times*, 3 December 1938;
    Knox quotations in the same place and in Turrou, *Nazi*, p. 273.

Chapter 16

1   E.A.Tamm, Memorandum for the File, 1 December 1938, FBIT 1/3/1.
2   Quotations from Ludwig Lore, 'Spies, Plain and Fancy', *Nation*, 8 July
    1939; Rowan, *Secret Agents Against America*; Wittels, *Nazi Spies in America*,
    p. 114. At various times a socialist, communist and Trotskyist, Lore had
    in the early 1930s spied for the Soviet Union, but was respected for his
    independence of mind.
3   020R, p. 32; computer-aided survey by Leonie Werle of online 1930s
    German press, drawing on resources in the State Library Berlin, the
    Cooperative Library Network Berlin-Brandenburg and the libraries of
    the Free University of Berlin and Humboldt University.
4   *Indianapolis Times*, 3 February 1940.
5   *Washington News*, 28 April 1939.
6   *Pittsburgh Post*, 2 May 1939.
7   Hoover's annotation to a clipping from the *Boston Herald*, 17 November
    1939, in FBIT 1/3/1. On Hoover and the origins of the FBI's Crime
    Records Division, see Cecil, *Branding*, pp. 14–15.
8   Transcript of Turrou lecture enclosed with SAC B.R. Sacket to Director
    FBI, 5 February 1940, in FBIT 1/5/1.
9   Turrou quoted in *Kansas City Journal*, 6 April 1939.
10 Earl Richert writing in the *Indianapolis Times*, 3 February 1940; text of
    'Sylvan Seal' WCAU radio broadcast, 2 May 1939 in FBIT, 1/4/1.
11 Diggins, *Mussolini*, p. 113; WHUD, 8 July 1937; Donovan and Mowrer,
    Fifth Column Lessons. Hemingway's play *The Fifth Column* was not pro-
    duced until 1944: *Guardian*, 18 March 2016.
12 Doherty, *Hollywood and Hitler*, pp. 335–6.
13 Quotations from Gabler, *Empire of Their Own*, pp. 2, 6.
14 Rosenzweig, *Hollywood's Spies*, p. 93.
15 Doherty, *Hollywood and Hitler*, p. 12.
16 Jack Warner quoted in Herzstein, *Roosevelt and Hitler*, p. 280.
17 Vaughan, 'Spies', 366; Warner Bros. Studios press release, 30 January 1939,
    in FBIT 1/3/1; Lya Lys obituary, *Los Angeles Times*, 8 June 1986; Doherty,
    Hollywood and Hitler, p. 338; George S. Kullen, 'Little Caesar Joins the
    G-Men', *Screen Book* (June 1939), 97.
18 Quotations from Kullen, 'Little Caesar', 37, and see Moldovan,
    'Romanian Jew in Hollywood', 43–4, and *Washington Sunday Star*,
    15 January 1939.
19 The Warners arrived at 3.30 p.m., and the president had nothing further
    scheduled until 6.15 p.m.: SD and TAD, 17 March 1939.
20 *New York Daily News*, 5 May 1939.

21 *Daily Worker*, 23 June 1939; Greene reviews in *The Spectator*, 23 June and
   7 July, 1939.

22 Sandeen, 'Anti-Nazi Sentiment', 73; Franz Hoellering review of
   Confessions, *Nation* (20 May 1939), 595–6; *Los Angeles Examiner*, 28 April
   1939; Lorentz quoted in *Halliwell's Film Guide*, p. 149.

23 Pfeiffer paraphrased in 020R, p. 32.

24 William J. Donovan and Edgar Mowrer, article in the *New York Times*, 22
   August 1940. On the FBI's suspicions, see Bureau documents cited in
   Lownie, 'Tyler Kent', 67–8, 77nn92–106.

25 Vetterli to Director FBI, 28 June 1938, FBIT 1/2/1.

26 Louis Loebl to Director FBI, re Leon George Turrou, 24 August 1938,
   FBIT 1/3/1.

27 *Pittsburgh Press*, 26 July 1941. Dr Samuel Harding, President of the
   Carnegie Institute, had offered a one million dollar reward for the cap-
   ture of Hitler and his delivery to a court of justice.

28 Turrou to La Guardia, 23 July 1940, Hoover to La Guardia, 27 July 1940,
   Hoover comment on Ed Tamm to Director, 5 June 1942, Hoover com-
   ment on dinner conversation report by informant (name redacted), 3
   July 1942, all in FBIT 1/5/1; Batvinis, *Hoover's Secret War*, pp. 296–7n23.

29 Alston Purvis, *Vendetta*, p. 312.

30 Turrou, *Where My Shadow Falls*, pp. 199–212; Corson, *Armies of Ignorance*,
   p. 87.

31 'Fabrik der Gerechtigkeit: Mit Gott für J. Edgar Hoover', *Der Spiegel*
   (22 December 1949): 18–19.

32 Tamm to Hoover, 5 June 1942, FBIT 1/5/1.

33 Turrou quoted in Getty, *Autobiography*, p. 254; Corson, *Armies of Ignorance*,
   p. 88.

34 Turrou to Hoover, 13 April 1965, C.R. Davidson Memorandum,
   20 April 1965, Hoover airmail to Turrou, 1 June 1965, Turrou to Hoover,
   20 July 1965, FBI Notification, signed 21 June 1965, all in FBIT 1/6/1.

Chapter 17

1 Brantley memorandum, 15 December 1938, FNAZ 27/1251.

2 Hermann Wobrock interview with Theo Long, 1955, denying he had
  divorced Marga, cited in Jeffrey, *Dangerous Menace*, p. 24; prison invigila-
  tor's notes on conversation between Jessie Jordan and her daughter
  Marga, 25 October 1938, HH16/212, file 4139, SNA. It is unclear
  whether, at the time of the Gretna Green ceremony, Tom Reid was yet
  divorced from Jessie Horan, the woman he had married in 1930 in Ayr
  when he was 17 years old: Andrew Jeffrey comments sent to the author
  in November 2017.

3   Photograph of 4-year-old Jessie peeping from behind a cabin door on
     the SS *Gothland*, Glasgow *Bulletin*, 14 November 1938.
4   Cooke to Col Leith-Ross of the Prisons Department for Scotland,
     26 August 1938 and John Sturrock (Royal Infirmary, Edinburgh) to
     Mr Sloan, 23 September 1938, both in HH16/212, file 4139, SNA.
5   Transcript of conversation between Tom Reid and Jessie Jordan signed
     by the governor, Edinburgh Prison (Saughton), 30 January 1939, and
     sent to the Secretary of State, Scottish Office, London, HH16/212, file
     4139/2, SNA.
6   Hamburg death certificate kindly supplied to the author by Donald
     Haddow, dated 26 January 1939, and referring to the patient's perforated
     uterus; prison warder's transcript of conversation between Jessie Jordan
     and Tom Reid, who had just returned from a futile visit to Germany
     aimed at bringing the child Jessie to Scotland, 7 March 1939, HH16/212,
     file 4139/2, SNA; Andrew Jeffrey notes sent to the author, November
     2017, indicating Reid's marriage to Grace Nisbet in Hillhead, Glasgow,
     in 1940.
7   Report on Jordan by governor of Aberdeen Prison, 23 December 1939,
     enclosing Jordan handwritten note to governor, same date, HH16/212,
     file 4139/2, SNA; Crown (Rumrich) to anonymous Abwehr controller,
     17 January 1938, KV2/3421.
8   For a comparison of Mata Hari with Jessie Jordan, see Jeffreys-Jones,
     'Verraden', pp. 45–9.
9   Report to the secretary of state, governor of Aberdeen Prison, 23
     December 1939, and Rose letter to the governor, 9 January 1940, both
     in HH16/212, file 4139/3, SNA.
10 Particulars of Convict recommended for License, Jessie Wallace or
     Jordan, 30 November 1940, HH16/212, file 4139/4, SNA; Donald
     Haddow, 'Jessie Wallace – "The Platinum Blonde Spy"', an essay by the
     half grand nephew of Jessie Jordan, based on family interviews and other
     research. Completed in 2016, it was written for inclusion in a private
     family history book and was supplied to the author by kind courtesy of
     its author.
11 Haddow, 'Jessie Wallace'.
12 *New York Times*, 20 August 1945.
13 Flindt-Larsen summary, interrogation of Bonin at the British Military
     Mission Denmark, 31 August 1945, and accompanying correspondence,
     all in KV2/1973, TNA.
14 Batvinis, *Hoover's Secret War*, pp. 232–47; handwritten comment 'shown
     to FBI 4.12.45', on Flint-Larsen summary.
15 FBI report on Ritter, 2 September 1945, and accompanying British
     documents, in KV2/87, TNA.

16 Report re CELERY [double agent Walter Dicketts] and SNOW, 1 April
   1941, KV2/86, TNA; Andrew, *Secret Service*, pp. 440–1.

17 Preliminary Interrogation Report on Obstlt Nikolaus Fritz Adolf Ritter,
   alias Rantzau etc., 20 November 1945, KV2/88, TNA; Ritter, *Deckname
   Dr Rantzau*, pp. 9–10, 28–32, 51–2.

18 Langille report, 5 April 1943, FNAZ 38/1664.

19 Edward C. Kemper Jr report, 25 September 1943, FNAZ 39/1713.

20 Julius H. Rice report, 21 October 1943, FNAZ 42/1788.

21 J.T. McLaughlin, round-up report on the spy case fugitives, 25 February
   1939, FNAZ 39/1333.

22 C.K. Lee, report on Rumrich case, 28 December 1938, FNAZ 28/1279;
   quotation from Judge John C. Knox's memorandum in the case *USA v.
   Erich Glaser et al.*, 16 December 1938, NANY.

23 C.K. Lee, report of 21 June 1939 enclosed with Hoover to SAC NY, 12
   July 1939, FNAZ 30/1369; Louis A. Langille report on Rumrich case,
   5 April 1943, FNAZ 44/1847.

24 C.K. Lee, parole report on Johanna Hofmann, 14 December 1938,
   FNAZ 27/1255; Langille report, 5 April 1943, FNAZ 38/1664.

25 C.K. Lee, parole report on Otto Hermann Voss, 14 December 1938,
   FNAZ 27/1254; criminal case docket C102–462, NANY; Louis A.
   Langille, case report on Rumrich [and associates], 5 April 1943, FNAZ
   44/1847.

Chapter 18

1 Ronnie, *Counterfeit Hero*, pp. 6, 140.

2 Ritter, *Deckname*, pp. 45–58, 87–8; Ronnie, *Counterfeit Hero*, pp. 213–14;
   Breuer, *Spy in Bed*, pp. 17–18.

3 Counter-Intelligence War Room London, 'Liquidation Report No. 206:
   KDM Hamburg', 28 March 1946, with enclosures, KV3/204.

4 Memorandum for the file re Frederick Joubert Duquesne/Espionage,
   13 September 1941, enclosed with J. Edgar Hoover to SAC Cincinnati,
   5 November 1941, FNAZ 36/1527.

5 J.M. Gwyer letter to anonymous colleague in MI6, 26 March 1942,
   KV2/87.

6 Duffy, *Double Agent*, pp. 64–5.

7 Duffy, *Double Agent*, pp. 114, 124.

8 Ronnie, *Counterfeit Hero*, pp. 220–1.

9 Stafford, *Roosevelt and Churchill*, pp. 9, 29; Field, *All This*, p. 30.

10 Busch's criticism of his colleagues may have been coloured by the
   fact that he was an anti-Nazi. See J.C. Hales interrogation report

dated 13 August 1945 and Leroy Vogel US interrogation report dated
11 January 1946, both for US Army and located in KV2/529.

11 Miller, 'Spies in America', p. 44; list of the unindicted in Batvinis, *Origins*,
pp. 265–6; Hoover quoted in the *Scotsman*, 1 July 1941; *New York Times*,
9 September 1941.

12 Hoover quoted in Ronnie, *Counterfeit Hero*, p. 258.

13 Quotations from the DVD of the movie; Klemperer, *German Resistance*,
p. 154; Kollander, 'Boomerang Resistance,' p. 639.

14 Dulles cited in Adams, *Historical Dictionary*, p. 4.

15 Handlin, *The Uprooted*, pp. 272, 285.

16 'Spies, Guerrillas and Violent Fantasies' (1971, summary of collective
finding supplied to the author by psycho-analyst Lily Pincus of the
Tavistock Institute of Human Relations, London). The finding was
based on interviews with contemporary Palestinians, but Tavistock had
a link to the Second World War studies of spy personality through the
work of former SOE psychiatrist P.M. Turquet. See Bailey, 'Psychiatrists
and Secret Agents', 2864.

17 List of those indicted on 1 July 1941 in Batvinis, *Origins*, pp. 263–4;
Kater, *Nazi Party*, pp. 236, 238.

18 On Von Bonin's role, see J.A. Cimperman, from 1 Grosvener Square
(the American Embassy) to Winston M. Scott, War Department,
14 November 1945, KV2/1873. On the Meiler affair, see Batvinis,
Hoover's Secret War, pp. 232–47.

19 Liquidation Report No. 206, p. 16.

20 According to a later, more detailed report, by the time news of
Sebold's defection came through, the German authorities were already
through with Ritter and had moved him to new responsibilities. He
was in any case recovering from injuries sustained in an African air
crash. British Army on the Rhine, Preliminary Interrogation Report
on Obstlt Nikolaus Fritz Adolf Ritter, 14 December 1945, pp. 3–4,
KV2/88.

Chapter 19

1 020R, Appendix I, p. 89.

2 'Erich Pfeiffer, Details of Property', 9 October 1945, KV2/267. Pfeiffer
had much more luggage than his fellow voyagers.

3 'Agnostio' report on Eitel, 24 July 1944, KV2/383; Camp 202, 'Interim
Report in the Case of Karl Eitel', 28 October 1944, p. 1, KV2/384;
020R, p. 89.

4 House of Commons speech by Sir Ralph Glyn (Conservative,
Abingdon), 22 May 1940, *Hansard*, Vol. 361, column 197.

5 Hoare, *Camp 020*, pp. 20, 368; Fry, *London Cage*, pp. 18, 46; McKinstry, *Operation Sealion*, p. 40.

6 Captain Beith and Pfeiffer's own account in 020R, p. 90.

7 The quotation is an 020 heading for Turkish Abwehr desertion cases: Minute sheet, 6 September 1944, KV2/267.

8 Major C. O'Brien to A.J. Kellar, 1 September 1945, KV2/267.

9 Robin Stephens, 'A Digest of Ham', an account of Camp 020 printed in Hoare, *Camp 020*, p. 59.

10 A.J. Kellar to Aubrey Jones, 6 September 1945, and Jones to Kellar, 8 September 1945, both in KV2/267; Murphy, *Diplomat*, p. 240.

11 Fry, *London Cage*, p. 46.

12 Appendix III, p. 1, 8, 13, KV2/267; replica of Appendix III incorporated in R.G. Fletcher to D.M. Ladd, Memorandum re Rumrich/Espionage, 16 January 1946, FNAZ 45/1875. D. Milton Ladd was Director of the Domestic Intelligence Division of the FBI from 1942 until he was promoted to Assistant to the Director in 1949. He oversaw the Bureau's wartime counter-intelligence effort.

13 Author's extended conversations with Mulhouse's Striby family, of later political note, in the early 1960s.

14 Burgland report on 'Charles' Eitel, 25 September 1944, p. 39, KV2/382.

15 H.P. Milmo to C.P. Hill of the Aliens Department, Home Office, 5 October 1944, KV2/382; Eitel translated and paraphrased in Burgland report, p. 7.

16 Eitel translated and paraphrased in Interim report on Eitel, pp. 10, 11.

17 020R, pp. 1, 90.

18 Stephens, 'Digest of Ham', p. 326.

19 020R, p. 14.

20 020R, Appendix III, pp. 9, 11, 13.

21 020R, pp. 1, 90; Appendix XX, Near East Personalities; Abwehr Personnel: Agents Other Contacts, 020R.

22 020R, p. 59.

23 Quotations from 020R, pp. 17, 18; O'Halpin, *Spying on Ireland*, p. 38.

24 020R, p. 59; Robinson, *Invasion*, p. 204; McKinstry, *Operation Sealion*, p. 182.

25 Ronge, *Kriegs*, pp. 367–9; 020R, p. 67.

26 020R, p. 60.

27 Summary of Pfeiffer communications, 5 May 1940 to 11 March 1945, KV2/267; 020R, pp. 57, 59.

28 Memorandum, Lt Col A.H. Stimson to Major M.N. Forrest, 9 October 1945, KV2/267.

29 The post-war fate of Erich Pfeiffer is a mystery. There is a personnel file on him in the Deutsche Dienststelle (WASt) military records in Berlin,

but it is available only to family members, and mistakenly holds that he died in the war: Mietle for Deutsche Dienststelle email to Leonie Werle, 17 August 2018. In 1953, a US Central Intelligence Agency source noted that a certain Erich Pfeiffer, whom it identified as 'a former SS war correspondent', was the editor of the Austrian newspaper *Linzer Tagblatt* and that he was interested in and informed about the formation of a new German intelligence service: Exhibit 1, Dr Anton Boehm to Dr Anton Fellner, 15 May 1953: www.cia.gov/library/readingroom/docs/ HOETTL,%20WILHELM%20%20%20VOL.%206_0062.pdf (accessed 11 February 2019). The BND has not responded to the author's inquiries. Erich Pfeiffer is quite a common name.

30 Stephens, 'Digest of Ham', p. 361; 020R, p. 91.

Chapter 20

1 Adler, 'War-Guilt Question', pp. 16–18, 25, 27.

2 Smith, 'Foreign Organization', p. 179.

3 Welles, Memorandum of conversation, 1 November 1938, *FRUS* 1938, *The British Commonwealth, Europe, Near East, and Africa*, II: pp. 447–51.

4 Dieckhoff, Memorandum on the Political Consequences of a Possible Rupture of Diplomatic Relations with the United States, 20 November 1939, *DGFP*, Series D, IV, Document 504.

5 Thomsen, telegrams 'for the Personnel Department', 30 November and 1 December 1938, *DGFP*, Series D, IV, Document 505; Compton, *Swastika and Eagle*, pp. 52–3.

6 Thomsen memorandum for Reich Minister of Foreign Affairs Joachim von Ribbentrop, 22 May 1940, *DGFP*, Series D, IX, Document 299.

7 Weizsäcker telegram to Thomsen, 10 June 1940, *DGFP*, Series D, IX, Document 411; Thomsen memorandum above.

8 Ribbentrop–Canaris meeting reported by the new head of the American desk at the Abwehr's Berlin headquarters, Friedrich Busch, in 'History of the Special Intelligence Service Division' (1947), II, 435, FBI Vault.

9 McPherson, *Annotated Bibliography*, reveals a twenty-first-century dropoff in interest in the causes of America's entry into the Second World War. Dr Andrew Johnstone, an authority on US entry into the Second World War, emailed the author noting the paucity of literature on the spy scandal's political repercussions: 'I would have to say that the case has not really been integrated into the wider literature on "the road to war" at all', email, 15 January 2018. Johnstone mentioned the scholarship of Michaela Hönicke Moore. The latter historian notes President Roosevelt's anti-Nazi stance in the 1940 presidential election and offers

the view that the Bund's Nazi propaganda was counterproductive, a judgment that is consistent with the argument that German spies adversely affected American public opinion: Hönicke Moore, *Know Your Enemy*, pp. 93, 94. In an unpublished master's dissertation, Joan Irene Miller did address the political impact of the spies. She argues that it was considerable and out of proportion to the actual threat proposed, for the media concocted a national spy phobia: Miller, 'Spies in America: German Espionage in the United States, 1935–1945' (M.A. diss., Portland State University, 1984).

10 To the examples given at the start of the chapter may be added another, one that involved Germany and preceded the events of 1938 by little more than two decades. For varying views on how and to what extent the affair of the Zimmermann telegram contributed to US entry into the First World War, see Tuchman, *Zimmermann Telegram*, p. 199, Boghardt, *Zimmermann Telegram*, pp. 9–22, and the forthcoming book by Dan Larsen, *Plotting for Peace* (Cambridge University Press).

11 See, for example, Batvinis, *Origins*, p. 257, and Luff, 'Covert and Overt', p. 752.

12 Guy Liddell, 'German Espionage in the United States' (March–April 1938), VNST, p.6.

13 *Daily Express*, 20 October 1938.

14 *New York Times*, 25 June 1938; *Los Angeles Times*, 18 July 1939; Theodore Draper, 'Nazi Spies in France,' *New Republic* (23 August 1939): 72.

15 Daniel W. Bell, acting director of the budget, quoted in *Washington Post*, 11 May 1938; Table of FBI personnel 1908–97 in Theoharis, *FBI Guide*, p. 4.

16 Roosevelt press conference reported in *New York Times*, 25 June 1938; Historical branch, G-2, 'Materials on the History of Military Intelligence in the United States, 1885–1944' (1944), Part 1, Exhibit B: 'Headquarters Personnel and Funds Military Intelligence Activities', MHFB; F.H. Lincoln (assistant chief of staff, G-2), 'The Military Intelligence Division, War Department General Staff' (typescript of lecture delivered at Fort Humphreys, Washington, DC, 5 January 1937), p. 3, MID.

17 *Los Angeles Times*, 18 July 1939; Jeffreys-Jones, *In Spies We Trust*, pp. 72–3.

18 Schwartz testimony, 18 November 1975, *Hearings before the Select Committee to Study Governmental Operations with Respect to Intelligence Activities*, 94 Cong., 1 sess., Vol. 6, Federal Bureau of Investigation (1976), p. 24.

19 *New York Times*, 1 December 1938; *New Republic* (10 June 1940), p. 77.

20 Undated draft in Box 55, folder 'Justice: 1938–39', PSF/FDR; Jeffreys-Jones, *FBI*, p. 128; Charles, *Hoover and Anti-interventionists*, p. 42.

21 Walter Trohan, 'New Deal Plans to Spy on World and Home Folks; Super Gestapo Agency is Under Consideration', *Chicago Tribune*, 9 February 1945; President Truman agreed 'we have to guard against a Gestapo' in an off-the-record press conference, 18 April 1946, noted in general file, folder 'Intelligence Service', EAA.

22 Jeffreys-Jones, *We Know*, p. 91.

23 Leigh, *Mobilizing Consent*, p. 42; summary of Lindsay telegram of 12 September 1938 in Reynolds, *Creation*, p. 34.

24 Langer and Gleason, *Challenge to Isolation*, pp. 50–1; Berinsky, *In Time of War*, p. 46.

25 According to the *New York Times*, 22 October 1938.

26 Ambassador Hugh R. Wilson, Memorandum of the Conversation with Reich Minister of Propaganda Dr Goebbels, 22 March 1938, in Schewe, ed., *Franklin D. Roosevelt and Foreign Affairs*, IX, Document 1037a, pp. 458–9.

27 Lt Flint-Larsen, transcript of Von Bonin interrogation at the Civilian Interrogation Centre, British Military Mission Denmark, 31 August 1945, p. 7, KV2/1973. The author's research assistant Leonie Werle used a variety of German media search engines, but found no references to the New York spy trial.

28 See Friedländer, *Prelude to Downfall*, pp. 128–9, and Bernd Martin, 'German Perpective', 230.

29 Ed Tamm, Memorandum for the Director, 5 December 1938, FNAZ Section 3, Serial 1.

30 See, for example, Doenecke, *Storm on the Horizon*, p. 1.

31 Divine, *Foreign Policy 1940*, p. vii.

32 Stouffer, *Communism, Conformity*, pp. 59–66, 220.

33 For a summary of historians' assessments of Roosevelt's sensitivity to public opinion on foreign policy, see Kimball, *Juggler*, p. 204n13.

34 Author's frequency survey of the digitised *Congressional Record*.

35 Langer and Gleason, *Challenge to Isolation*, p. 50; October 1939 Gallup poll cited in Kennedy, *Freedom from Fear*, p. 427.

36 'Is America Infested with Spies?' *Christian Century*, 55 (2 November 1938), 1316.

List of Abbreviations

020R	Camp 020 Interim Report on the Case of Erich Pheiffer [Pfeiffer] (September 1945), KV2/267
BArch	Bundesarchiv, Freiberg, Germany
CAD	Alexander Cadogan Papers, Churchill College, Cambridge
DbD	Pare Lorenz online Day by Day project, FDR
DGFP	*Documents on German Foreign Policy, 1918–1945: From the Archives of the German Foreign Ministry* (London: HMSO, 1949–1983)
DSM	Deutsches Schiffahrtmuseum (German Maritime Museum), Bremerhaven, Germany
DV	digital version in NLS
EAA	Eben A. Ayers Papers, HST
FBIT	FBI file on Leon Turrou, obtained via FOIA, Request No. 1366027-000. The notes supply File, Section and Serial numbers.
FDR	Franklin D. Roosevelt Papers, Hyde Park, NY
FM	Fries Museum (Freisian Museum), Leeuwarden, The Netherlands.
FNAZ	FBI documents on the Nazi spy case sent to the author in response to his FOIA application. All these have the classification number 1206800-0-065-HQ-748. The notes supply Section and Serial numbers.
FOIA	Freedom of Information Act
FRUS	*Foreign Relations of the United States* (Washington, DC: Department of State, 1861–)
HILS	Hoover Institution Library, Stanford, CA
HST	Harry S. Truman Library, Independence, MO
KV	MI5 files in TNA
LC	Library of Congress

MHFB	USA Centre of Military History Library, Forrestal Building, Washington, DC.
MID	Records of the War Department General Staff Military Intelligence Division, 1917–1941, NA
NA	National Archives, Washington, DC.
NANY	Court records from criminal case C102-462 (the Nazi spy trial), Record Group 21, National Archives at New York City
NLS	National Library of Scotland, Edinburgh
PSF	President's Secretary's File
SB	Staatsarchiv Bremen, Bremen, Germany
SD	Stenographer's Diary, DbD
SNA	Scottish National Archives, Edinburgh
SSC	Scottish Supreme Court, Old Parliament Building, Edinburgh
TAD	Tully's Appointments Diary, DbD
TNA	The National Archives, Kew Gardens, London
VNST	Papers of Robert Vansittart, Churchill College, Cambridge
WHUD	White House Usher's Diary, DbD

Bibliography

Adams, Jefferson, *Historical Dictionary of German Intelligence* (Lanham, MD: Scarecrow, 2009).

Adler, Selig, 'The War-Guilt Question and American Disillusionment, 1918–1928', *Journal of Modern History*, 23 (March 1952): 1–28.

Ahlström, Göran, *Engineers and Industrial Growth* (London: Croom Helm, 1982).

Allen, Robert, *Voice of Britain: The Inside Story of the Daily Express* (Cambridge: Stephens, 1983).

Anderson, Robert D., *European Universities from the Enlightenment to 1914* (Oxford: Oxford University Press, 2004).

Andrew, Christopher, *The Defence of the Realm: The Authorized History of MI5* (London: Allen Lane, 2009).

Andrew, Christopher, *Secret Service: The Making of the British Intelligence Community* (London: Heinemann, 1985).

Asada, Sadao, ed., *Japan and the World, 1853–1952: A Bibliographical Guide to Japanese Scholarship in Foreign Relations* (New York: Columbia University Press, 1989).

Ashdown, Paddy, *Nein! Standing up to Hitler 1935–1944* (London: William Collins, 2018).

Bailey, Bill, *The Kid from Hoboken: An Autobiography* (San Francisco: Circus Lithographic Prepress, 1993).

Bailey, Roderick, 'Psychiatrists and Secret Agents', *Lancet*, 388 (December 2018): 2864–5.

Bajohr, Frank, *'Aryanisation' in Hamburg: The Economic Exclusion of Jews and the Confiscation of their Property in Nazi Germany* (New York: Bergahn Books, 2002).

Barnes, James J., *The Life of Hans Wasemann, 1895–1971* (Westport, CT: Praeger, 2001).

Batvinis, Raymond J., *Hoover's Secret War against Nazi Spies: FBI in World War II* (Lawrence: University of Kansas Press, 2014).

Batvinis, Raymond J., *The Origins of FBI Counterintelligence* (Lawrence: University of Kansas Press, 2007).

Bell, Leland V., 'The Failure of Nazism in America: The German-American Bund, 1936–1941', *Political Science Quarterly*, 85 (December 1970): 585–99.

Bellaby, Ross W., *The Ethics of Intelligence: A New Framework* (Abingdon: Routledge, 2014).

Berinsky, Adam J., *In Time of War: Understanding American Public Opinion from World War II to Iraq* (Chicago: University of Chicago Press, 2009).

Boghart, Thomas, *Spies of the Kaiser: German Covert Operations in Great Britain During the First World War* (Basingstoke: Palgrave Macmillan, 2004).

Boghart, Thomas, *The Zimmermann Telegram: Intelligence, Diplomacy, and America's Entry into World War I* (Annapolis, MD: Naval Institute Press, 2012).

Booth, Alan R., 'The Development of the Espionage Film', in Wesley K. Wark, ed., *Spy Fiction, Spy Films, and Real Intelligence* (London: Frank Cass, 1991).

Bowd, Gavin, *Fascist Scotland: Caledonia and the Far Right* (Edinburgh: Berlinn, 2013).

Breitman, Richard. *US Intelligence and the Nazis* (Cambridge: Cambridge University Press, 2005).

Breuer, William, *Nazi Spies in America* (New York: St Martin's Press, 1990).

Breuer, William, *The Spy Who Spent the War in Bed: And Other Bizarre Tales from World War II* (Hoboken, NJ: John Wiley, 2003).

Cadogan, Alexander, *The Diaries of Sir Alexander Cadogan, 1938–1945*, ed. David Dilks (London: Cassell, 1971).

Cantril, Hadley, ed., *Public Opinion, 1935–1946* (Princeton, NJ: Office of Public Opinion Research, 1951).

Cecil, Matthew, *Branding Hoover's America: How the Boss's PR Men Sold the Bureau to America* (Lawrence, KS: University Press, of Kansas, 2016).

Charles, Douglas M., *J. Edgar Hoover and the Anti-Interventionists: FBI Political Surveillance and the Rise of the Domestic Security State, 1939–1945* (Columbus, OH: Ohio State University Press, 2007).

Christgau, John, *Enemies: World War II Alien Internment* (Lincoln: University of Nebraska Press, 2009 [1985]).

Christiansen, Arthur, *Headlines All My Life* (London: Heinemann, 1961).

Church Hearings 6, *Federal Bureau of Investigation.* Volume 6, *Hearings before the Select Committee to Study Governmental Operations with respect*

　　　to Intelligence Activities of the United States Senate, 94 Cong., 1 sess., 18,
　　　19 November and 2, 3, 9, 10 and 11 December 1975.

Cobain, Ian, *Cruel Britannia: A Secret History of Torture* (London: Portobello, 2012).

Cole, Wayne S., *Roosevelt and the Isolationists 1932–45* (Lincoln: University of
　　　Nebraska Press, 1983).

Cole, Wayne S., *Senator Gerald P. Nye and American Foreign Relations*
　　　(Minneapolis: University of Minnesota Press, 1962).

Compton, James V., *The Swastika and the Eagle: Hitler, the United States and
　　　the Origins of the Second World War* (London: The Bodley Head, 1968).

Cook, Blanche W., *Eleanor Roosevelt* (New York: Penguin, 1993).

Corson, William R., *The Armies of Ignorance: The Rise of the American
　　　Intelligence Empire* (New York: Dial, 1977).

Craig, Mary W., *A Tangled Web: Mata Hari, Dancer, Courtesan, Spy* (Stroud:
　　　The History Press, 2018).

Cummings, Homer S., and Carl McFarland, *Federal Justice: Chapters in the
　　　History of Justice and the Federal Executive* (New York: Macmillan, 1937).

Curry, John Court, *The Security Service 1908–1945: The Official History*
　　　(London: Public Record Office, 1999).

Dallek, Robert, *Franklin D. Roosevelt and American Foreign Policy, 1932–1945*
　　　(New York: Oxford University Press, 1979).

Davies, Sarah, and James R. Harris, *Stalin's World: Dictating the Soviet Order*
　　　(New Haven: Yale University Press, 2014).

Denniston, Robin, 'Yardley's Diplomatic Secrets', *Cryptologia*, 18 (April
　　　1994): 48–70.

Diamond, Sander T. *The Nazi Movement in the United States, 1924–1941*
　　　(Ithaca, NY: Cornell University Press, 1974).

Diggins, John P., *Mussolini and Fascism: The View from America* (Princeton, NJ:
　　　Princeton University Press, 1972).

Divine, Robert A., *Foreign Policy and US Presidential Elections 1940–1948*
　　　(New York: New Viewpoints, 1974).

Doenecke, Justus D., *Debating Franklin D. Roosevelt's Foreign Policies, 1933–
　　　1945* (Lanham, MD: Rowman & Littlefield, 2005).

Doenecke, Justus D., *Storm on the Horizon: The Challenge to American
　　　Intervention, 1939–1941* (Lanham, MD: Rowman & Littlefield, 2000).

Doerries, Reinhard R., ed., *Hitler's Last Chief of Foreign Intelligence: Allied
　　　Interrogations of Walter Schellenberg* (London: Frank Cass, 2003).

Doherty, Thomas P., *Hollywood and Hitler, 1933–1939* (New York: Columbia
　　　University Press, 2013).

Donovan, William, and Edgar Mowrer, *Fifth Column Lessons for America*
　　　(Washington, DC: American Council on Public Affairs, n.d. [1940?]).

Duffy, Peter, *Double Agent: The First Hero of World War II and How the FBI
　　　Outwitted and Destroyed a Nazi Spy Ring* (New York: Scribner, 2014).

Erickson, John, 'Soviet War Losses: Calculations and Controversies', in John Erickson and David Dilks, eds., *Barbarossa: The Axis and the Allies* (Edinburgh: Edinburgh University Press, 1994): 255–77.

Farago, Ladislas, *The Game of the Foxes: British and German Intelligence Operations and Personalities which Changed the Course of the Second World War* (London: Hodder & Stoughton, 1971).

Ferguson, Niall, *Paper and Iron: Hamburg Business and German Politics in the Era of Inflation, 1897–1927* (Cambridge: Cambridge University Press, 1995).

Field, Rachel, *All This, And Heaven Too* (London: Collins, 1939).

Friedländer, Saul, *Prelude to Downfall: Hitler and the United States, 1939–1941*, transl. Aline B. and Alexander Werth (London: Chatto & Windus, 1967).

Fry, Helen P., *The London Cage: The Secret History of Britain's World War II Interrogation Centre* (London: Yale University Press, 2017).

Frye, Alton, *Nazi Germany and the American Hemisphere, 1933–1941* (New Haven, CT: Yale University Press, 1967).

Gabler, Neal, *An Empire of Their Own: How the Jews Invented Hollywood* (London: W.H. Allen, 1989).

Gentry, Curt, *J. Edgar Hoover: The Man and the Secrets* (New York: Norton, 1991).

'German Espionage and Sabotage Against the United States in World War II', *Office of Naval Intelligence Review*, 1 (January 1946): 33–8.

Getty, J. Paul, *As I See It: The Autobiography of J. Paul Getty* (Englewood Cliffs, NJ: Prentice-Hall, 1976).

Geyer, Michael. 'National Socialist Germany: The Politics of Information', in Ernest R. May, ed., *Knowing One's Enemies: Intelligence Assessment Between the Two World Wars* (Princeton, NJ: Princeton University Press, 1986): 310–46.

Goldstein, Robert Justin, *American Blacklist: The Attorney General's List of Subversive Organisations* (Lawrence, KS: University Press of Kansas, 2008).

Goodman, Walter, *The Committee: The Extraordinary Career of the House Committee on Un-American Activities*. New York: Farrar, Straus & Giroux, 1968.

Griffiths, Dennis, *The Encyclopedia of the British Press, 1422–1992* (London: Macmillan, 1992).

Halliwell, Leslie, *Halliwell's Film Guide* (London: Granada, 1979).

Handlin, Oscar, *The Uprooted: The Epic Story of the Great Migrations that Made the American People* (New York: Grosset & Dunlap, 1951).

Hart, Bradley W., *Hitler's American Friends: The Third Reich's Supporters in the United States* (New York: St Martin's Press, 2018).

Haynes, John E., and Harvey Klehr, *Venona: Decoding Soviet Espionage in America* (New Haven, CT: Yale University Press, 1999).

Heardon, Patrick J., *Roosevelt Confronts Hitler: America's Entry into World War II* (DeKalb: Northern Illinois Press, 1987).

Heinemann, Winfried, 'Abwehr', in I.C.B. Dear and M.R.D. Foot, eds., *Oxford Companion to the Second World War* (Oxford: Oxford University Press, 1995).

Hemingway, Ernest, *The Fifth Column and the First Forty-Nine Stories* (New York: Scribner, 1938).

Hemming, Henry, *M: Maxwell Knight, MI5's Greatest Spymaster* (London: Arrow, 2018).

Herzstein, Robert E., *Roosevelt and Hitler: Prelude to War* (New York: Paragon House, 1989).

Hinsley, Francis H., and Simkins, C.A.G., *British Intelligence in the Second World War*, Vol. 4: *Security and Counter-Intelligence* (London: HMSO, 1990).

Hoare, Oliver, ed., *Camp 020: MI5 and the Nazi Spies: The Official History of MI5's Wartime Interrogation Centre* (Richmond: Public Record Office, 2000).

Hogan, Michael J., *Paths to Power: The Historiography of American Foreign Relations to 1941* (Cambridge: Cambridge University Press, 2000).

Huchthausen, Peter A., *Shadow Voyage: The Extraordinary Wartime Escape of the Legendary SS Bremen* (Hoboken, NJ: Wiley, 2005).

Iriye, Akira, *Japan and the Wider World: From the Mid-nineteenth Century to the Present* (London: Longman, 1997).

Jeffrey, Andrew, *This Dangerous Menace: Dundee and the River Tay at War, 1939 to 1945* (Edinburgh: Mainstream, 1991).

Jeffrey, Keith, *MI6: The History of the Secret Intelligence Service* (London: Bloomsbury, 2010).

Jeffreys-Jones, Rhodri, *American Espionage: From Secret Service to CIA* (New York: Free Press, 1977).

Jeffreys-Jones, Rhodri, *The FBI: A History* (New Haven, CT: Yale University Press, 2007).

Jeffreys-Jones, Rhodri, *In Spies We Trust: The Story of Western Intelligence* (Oxford: Oxford University Press, 2013).

Jeffreys-Jones, Rhodri, 'Jessie Jordan: A Rejected Scot who Spied for Germany and Hastened America's Flight from Neutrality', *The Historian*, 76 (Winter 2014): 766–83.

Jeffreys-Jones, Rhodri, 'The Montreal Spy Ring of 1898 and the Origins of "Domestic" Surveillance in the United States', *The Canadian Review of American Studies*, 5 (Fall, 1974): 119–34.

Jeffreys-Jones, Rhodri, 'United States Secret Service', in Donald R. Whitnah, ed., *Government Agencies* (Westport, CT: Greenwood, 1983): 592–7.

Jeffreys-Jones, Rhodri, 'Verraden', *Geschiedenis Magazine*, 52/1 (January/February 2017): 45–9.

Jeffreys-Jones, Rhodri, *We Know All About You: The Story of Surveillance in Britain and America* (Oxford: Oxford University Press, 2017).

Johnstone, Andrew, *Against Immediate Evil: American Internationalists and the Four Freedoms on the Eve of World War II* (Ithaca: Cornell University Press, 2014).

Johnstone, Andrew, '"A Godsend to the Country?" Roosevelt, Willkie, and the Election of 1940', in Andrew Johnstone and Andrew Priest, eds., *US Presidential Elections and Foreign Policy: Candidates, Campaigns, and Global Politics from FDR to Bill Clinton* (Lexington: University Press of Kentucky, 2017): 19–39.

Johnstone, Andrew, 'To Mobilize a Nation: Citizens' Organisations and Intervention on the Eve of World War II', in Andrew Johnstone and Helen Laville, eds., *The US Public and American Foreign Policy* (London: Routledge, 2010): 26–40.

Jones, John P., *The German Spy in America: The Secret Plotting of German Spies in the United States and the Inside Story of the Sinking of the Lusitania* (London: Hutchinson, 1917).

Kahn, David, 'Intelligence Studies on the Continent,' *Intelligence and National Security*, 23 (April 2008): 249–75.

Kahn, David, *The Reader of Gentlemen's Mail: Herbert O. Yardley and the Birth of American Codebreaking* (New Haven, CT: Yale University Press, 2004).

Kater, Michael H., *The Nazi Party: A Social Profile of Members and Leaders, 1919–1945* (Oxford: Blackwell, 1983).

Kennedy, David M., *Freedom from Fear: The American People in Depression and War, 1929–1945* (New York: Oxford University Press, 2001).

Kessler, Ronald, *The Bureau: The Secret History of the FBI*. New York: St Martin's Press, 2002.

Kimball, Warren F., 'Dieckhoff and America: A German's View of German–American Relations, 1937–1941,' *The Historian*, 27 (February 1965): 218–43.

Kimball, Warren F., *The Juggler: Franklin Roosevelt as a Wartime Statesman* (Princeton, NJ: Princeton University Press, 1991).

Klemperer, Klemens von, *German Resistance Against Hitler: The Search for Allies Abroad, 1938–1945* (Oxford: Clarendon Press, 1992).

Klemperer, Klemens von, *Mandate for Resistance: The Case for German Opposition to Hitler* (Northampton, MA: Smith College, 1969).

Kluiters, Frans A.C., and Etienne Verhoeyen, 'An International Spymaster and Mystery Man: Abwehr Officer Hilmar G.J. Dierks (1889–1940) and his Agents', being an online summary of the authors' *Spionnen aan de achterdeur: de Duitse Abwehr in België, 1936–1945* (Antwerp: Maklu Uitgevers, 2015).

Kollander, Patricia, 'Boomerang Resistance: German Emigrés in the US Army during World War II', in Thomas W. Zeiler, ed., *A Companion to World War II* (Oxford: Blackwell, 2013): 638–51.

Kusielewicz, Eugene, 'Paderewski and Wilson's Speech to the Senate, January 22, 1917', *Polish American Studies*, 13 (July–December 1956): 65–71.

LaFeber, Walter, *The American Age: United States Foreign Policy at Home and Abroad since 1750* (New York: Norton, 1989).

Langer, William L., and S. Everett Gleason, *The Challenge to Isolation. Volume I: The World Crisis of 1937–1940 and American Foreign Policy* (New York: Harper, 1952).

Leigh, Michael, *Mobilizing Consent: Public Opinion and American Foreign Policy, 1937–1947* (Westport, CT: Greenwood Press, 1976).

Lokhova, Svetlana, *The Spy Who Changed History: The Untold Story of How the Soviet Union Won the Race for America's Top Secrets* (London: William Collins, 2018).

Lorenz, Marita, *The Spy Who Loved Castro* (London: Ebury, 2017).

Lownie, Andrew, 'Tyler Kent: Isolationist or Spy?' in Rhodri Jeffreys-Jones and Andrew Lownie, eds., *North American Spies: New Revisionist Essays* (London: Thistle Publishing, 2013 [1992]): 49–78.

Luff, Jennifer, 'Covert and Overt Operations: Interwar Political Policing in the United States and United Kingdom,' *American Historical Review*, 122 (June 2017): 727–57.

Macdonnel, Francis, *Insidious Foes: The Axis Fifth Column and the American Home Front* (Oxford: Oxford University Press, 1995).

McKercher, Brian, 'Reaching for the Brass Ring: The Recent Historiography of Interwar American Foreign Relations,' in Michael J. Hogan, ed., *Paths to Power: The Historiography of American Foreign Relations to 1941* (Cambridge: Cambridge University Press, 2000).

McKinstry, Leo, *Operation Sealion: How Britain Crushed the German War Machine's Dreams of Invasion in 1940* (London: John Murray, 2014).

McPherson, Alan, ed., *SHAFR Guide Online: An Annotated Bibliography of US Foreign Relations since 1600* (Leiden: Brill, 2017).

Mahoney, M.H., ed., *Women in Espionage: A Biographical Directory* (Santa Barbara, CA: ABC-Clio, 1993).

Martin, Bernd, 'The German Perpective', in Akira Iriye, ed., *Pearl Harbor and the Coming of the Pacific War* (Boston: Bedford/St Martin's, 1999).

Melanson, Philip H., *The Secret Service: The Hidden History of an Enigmatic Agency* (New York: Carroll & Graf, 2002).

Middendorf, Stefanie, "Verstoßenes Wissen': Emigranten als Deutschlandexperten im *Office of Strategic Services* und im

Amerikanischen Außenministerium 1943–1955', *Neue Politische Literatur*, 46/1 (2001): 23–52.

Miller, Joan Irene, 'Spies in America: German Espionage in the United States, 1935–1945.' M.A. diss., Portland State University, 1984.

Moldovan, Raluca, 'A Romanian Jew in Hollywood: Edward G. Robinson', *American, British and Canadian Studies*, 22 (2014): 43–62.

Moore, Hönicke Michaela, *Know Your Enemy: The American Debate on Nazism, 1933–1945* (Cambridge: Cambridge University Press, 2010).

Mueller, Michael, *Canaris: The Life and Death of Hitler's Spymaster*, transl. Geoffrey Brooks (London: Chatham, 2007).

Murphy, Robert, *Diplomat Among Warriors* (New York: Doubleday, 1964).

Naftali, Timothy, 'Reinhard Gehlen and the United States', in Richard Breitman and others, *US Intelligence and the Nazis* (Cambridge: Cambridge University Press, 2005).

O'Halpin, Eunan, *Spying on Ireland: British Intelligence and Irish Neutrality during the Second World War* (Oxford: Oxford University Press, 2008).

Olmstead, Kathryn S., *Real Enemies: Conspiracy Theories and American Democracy, World War I to 9/11* (New York: Oxford University Press, 2009).

Omand, David, and Mark Phythian, *Principled Spying: The Ethics of Secret Intelligence* (Oxford: Oxford University Press, 2018).

Oppenheim, E. Phillips, *The Evil Shepherd* (London: Hodder & Stoughton, 1922).

Paehler, Katrin, *The Third Reich's Intelligence Services: The Career of Walter Schellenberg* (Cambridge: Cambridge University Press, 2017).

Patenaude, Bertrand M., *The Big Show in Bololand: The American Relief Expedition to Soviet Russia in the Famine of 1921* (Stanford, CA: Stanford University Press, 2002).

Perlman, Selig, *A Theory of the Labor Movement* (New York: Augustus M. Kelley, 1949 [1928]).

Persico, Joseph E., *Roosevelt's Secret War: FDR and World War II Espionage* (New York: Random House, 2001).

Phillips, Timothy, *The Secret Twenties: British Intelligence, the Russians and the Jazz Age* (London: Granta, 2017).

Powers, Richard Gid, *Broken: The Troubled Past and Uncertain Future of the FBI* (New York: Free Press, 2004).

Powers, Richard Gid, 'J. Edgar Hoover and the Detective Hero', *Journal of Popular Culture*, 9 (1975).

Powers, Richard Gid, *Secrecy and Power: The Life of J. Edgar Hoover* (London: Hutchinson, 1987).

Purvis, Alston W., *The Vendetta: FBI Hero Melvin Purvis's War Against Crime, and J. Edgar Hoover's War Against Him* (New York: Public Affairs, 2005).

Quinlan, Kevin, *The Secret War Between the Wars: MI5 in the 1920s and 1930s* (Woodbridge: The Boydell Press, 2014).

Reile, Oscar, *Die Geheime Westfront: Die Abwehr 1935–1945* (Munich: Welsermühl, 1962).

Reile, Oscar, *Frauen im Geheimdienst* (Illertissen: Federmann, 1979).

Remak, Joachim, 'Friends of the New Germany: The Bund and German–American Relations', *Journal of Modern History*, 29 (March 1957): 33–41.

Reynolds, David, *The Creation of the Anglo-American Alliance 1937–41: A Study on Competitive Co-operation* (London: Europa, 1981).

Reynolds, Siân, 'Jordan, Jessie', in Elizabeth Ewan and others, eds., *The New Biographical Dictionary of Scottish Women* (Edinburgh: Edinburgh University Press, 2018): 223.

Richmond, Clint, *Fetch the Devil: The Sierra Diablo Murders and Nazi Espionage in America* (Lebanon, NH: ForeEdge, 2014).

Ritter, Nikolaus, *Deckname Dr Rantzau: Die Aufzeichnungen des Nikolaus Ritter, Offizier im Geheimen Nachrichtendienst* (Hamburg: Hoffmann & Campe, 1972).

Robinson, Derek, *Invasion, 1940: The Truth About the Battle of Britain and What Stopped Hitler* (London: Constable, 2005).

Ronge, Maximilian, *Kriegs- und Industrie-Spionage* (Leipzig: A.H. Payne, 1930).

Ronnie, Art, *Counterfeit Hero: Fritz Duquesne, Adventurer and Spy* (Annapolis, MD: Naval Institute Press, 1995).

Rose, Norman, *Vansittart: Study of a Diplomat* (London: Heinemann, 1978).

Rosendahl, Charles E., 'The Loss of the Akron,' *US Naval Institute Proceedings* (July 1934): 921–33.

Rosenzweig, Laura B., *Hollywood's Spies: The Undercover Surveillance of Nazis in Los Angeles* (New York: New York University Press, 2017).

Rout, Leslie B. Jr, and John B. Bratzell, *The Shadow War: German Espionage and United States Counterespionage in Latin America during World War II* (Frederick, MD: University Publications of America, 1986).

Rowan, Richard W., *Secret Agents Against America* (New York: Doubleday, Doran, 1939).

Rowan, Richard W., *Story of Secret Service* (Garden City, NY: Doubleday, Doran, 1937).

Rosenzweig, Laura B., *Hollywood's Spies: The Undercover Surveillance of Nazis in Los Angeles* (New York: New York University Press, 2017).

Sandeen, Eric J., 'Anti-Nazi Sentiment in Film: *Confessions of a Nazi Spy* and the German–American Bund', *American Studies*, 20 (Fall 1979): 69–81.

Schewe, Donald B., ed., *Franklin D. Roosevelt and Foreign Affairs* (New York: Clearwater Publishers, 1979–83).

Simms, Brendan, *Hitler: Only the World Was Enough* (London: Allen Lane, 2019).

Smith, Arthur L. Jr, 'The Foreign Organization of the Nazi Party and the United States, 1931–39', in Hans L. Trefousse, ed., *Germany and America: Essays on Problems of International Relations and Immigration* (New York: Brooklyn College Press, 1981): 173–82.

Smith, Geoffrey S., *To Save a Nation: American Countersubversives, the New Deal, and the Coming of World War II* (New York: Basic Books, 1973).

Sparrow, James T., *Warfare State: World War II Americans and the Age of Big Government* (Oxford: Oxford University Press, 2013 [2011]).

Spivak, John L., *Secret Armies: The New Technique of Nazi Warfare* (New York: Modern Age, 1939).

Stafford, David, *Roosevelt and Churchill: Men of Secrets* (London: Little, Brown, 1999).

Stephenson, Jill, *The Nazi Organisation of Women* (London: Croom Helm, 1981).

Stouffer, Samuel Andrew, *Communism, Conformity, and Civil Liberties: A Cross-Section of the Nation Speaks its Mind* (Gloucester, MA: Peter Smith, 1963 [1955]).

Strassman, W. Paul, *The Strassmans* (New York: Berghahn, 2008).

Summers, Anthony, *Official and Confidential: The Secret Life of J. Edgar Hoover* (New York: G. P. Putnam's Sons, 1993).

Swift, Will, *The Kennedys Amidst the Gathering Storm: A Thousand Days in London, 1938–1940* (New York: Collins, 2008).

Theoharis, Athan and John Stuart Cox, *The Boss: J. Edgar Hoover and the Great American Inquisition* (London: Harrap, 1989).

Theoharis, Athan, *Chasing Spies: How the FBI Failed in Counterintelligence but Promoted the Politics of McCarthyism in the Cold War Years* (Chicago: Ivan R. Dee, 2002).

Theoharis, Athan G., ed., *The FBI: A Comprehensive Reference Guide* (New York: Facts on File, 2000).

Theoharis, Athan G., *Spying on Americans: Political Surveillance from Hoover to the Huston Plan* (Philadelphia: Temple University Press, 1978).

Trefousse, Hans L., 'Failure of German Intelligence in the United States, 1935–1945', *Mississippi Valley Historical Review*, 42 (June 1955): 84–100.

Tuchman, Barbara W., *The Zimmermann Telegram* (New York: Macmillan, 1966 [1958]).

Turrou, Leon, *Le Bonheur en Sursis* (Paris: Del Duca, 1960).

Turrou, Leon, with Tom Tracy and George Daws, *How to Be a G-Man* (New York: R. M. McBride, 1939).

Turrou, Leon, with David G. Wittels. *The Nazi Spy Conspiracy in America* (London: George G. Harrap, 1939). Published in the United States as *Nazi Spies in America*.

Turrou, Leon, *Where My Shadow Falls: Two Decades of Crime Detection* (Garden City, NY: Doubleday, 1949).

Vasey, Christopher, *Nazi Intelligence Operations in Non-Occupied Territories: Espionage Efforts in the United States, Britain, South America and Southern Africa* (Jefferson, NC: McFarland, 2016).

Vaughan, Stephen, 'Spies, National Security, and the "Inertia Projector": The Secret Service Files of Ronald Reagan', *American Quarterly* 39 (Fall 1987): 355–80.

Waller, John H., 'The Double Life of Admiral Canaris', *International Journal of Intelligence and Counterintelligence*, 9 (Fall 1996): 271–89.

Wark, Wesley K., ed., *Spy Fiction, Spy Films and Real Intelligence* (London: Frank Cass, 1991).

Wark, Wesley K., *The Ultimate Enemy: British Intelligence and Nazi Germany 1933–1939* (Oxford: Oxford University Press, 1985).

Watt, Donald Cameron, 'The Relationship Between the Far Eastern and European Wars, 1922–1941', in Robert W. Love, ed., *Pear Harbor Revisited* (Basingstoke: Macmillan, 1995): 1–12.

Weinberg, Gerhard, 'Hitler's Image of the United States', *American Historical Review*, 69 (July 1964): 1006–21.

Weiner, Tim, *Enemies: A History of the FBI* (London: Penguin, 2012).

West, Nigel, *MI5: British Security Service Operations 1909–1945* (London: Triad, 1983).

Whalen, Richard J., *The Founding Father: The Story of Joseph P. Kennedy* (New York: New American Library, 1966).

White, Rosie, *Violent Femmes: Women as Spies in Popular Culture* (London: Routledge, 2007).

Whitman, James Q., *Hitler's American Model: The United States and the Making of Nazi Race Law* (Princeton, NJ: Princeton University Press, 2018).

Wighton, Charles, *The World's Greatest Spies* (London: Odhams, 1962).

Williams, David, '"Without Understanding": The FBI and Political Surveillance, 1908–1941', Ph.D. diss., University of New Hampshire, 1981.

Index